FROM
COLONIALS TO
PROVINCIALS

FROM COLONIALS TO PROVINCIALS

American Thought and Culture, 1680–1760

NED C. LANDSMAN

Cornell University Press

ITHACA AND LONDON

First published 1997 by Twayne Publishers
First printing, Cornell Paperbacks, 2000

Printed in the United States of America

Library of Congress Cataloging-in-Publication Data
Landsman, Ned C., 1951–
    From colonials to provincials : American thought and culture, 1680–1760 / Ned C.
Landsman.
        p. cm.—(Cornell paperbacks)
    Originally published: New York : Twayne Publishers, c1997.
    Includes bibliographical references and index.
    ISBN 0-8014-8701-3 (acid-free paper)
    1. United States—Civilization—To 1783.   2. United States—Intellectual life.   3. United
States—Religious life and customs.   4. Colonists—United States—Attitudes—History—17th
century.   5. Colonists—United States—Attitudes—History—18th century.   I. Title.
E162.L36 2000
973.2—dc21   00-060150

Cornell University Press strives to use environmentally responsible
suppliers and materials to the fullest extent possible in the publishing
of it books. Such materials include vegetable-based, low-VOC inks
and acid-free papers that are recycled, totally chlorine-free, or partly
composed of nonwood fibers. Books that bear the logo of the FSC
(Forest Stewardship Council) use paper taken from forests that have
been inspected and certified as meeting the highest standards for
environmental and social responsibility. For further information, visit
our website at www.cornellpress.cornell.edu.

Paperback printing   10 9 8 7 6 5 4 3 2 1

For Allie and Em

Contents

Contents

Illustrations

Preface

More than a decade has passed since I first agreed to write this book. Not long after, I happened upon a book review, the subject of which is long since forgotten, that referred to the period I was to cover as the "Death Valley" of surveys. The reviewer's meaning was clear: the decades after 1680 were sorely lacking in the sort of dramatic and well-remembered historical events on which surveys usually depend. Certainly that was true of this period in comparison to the earlier era of colony founding or of the succeeding years, as America's membership in the British empire rapidly waned. It was doubtful, for example, whether even well-read undergraduates could cite more than a handful of happenings from our period. The average layperson might well recall none at all.

Such an apparent lack of activity may be less of a disadvantage than it appears. If the eight decades after 1680 were lacking in dramatic occurrences, much was happening below the surface. Whereas the broadest patterns in thought and culture are occasionally disrupted by traumatic happenings in social life, cultural adaptations more often are gradual and slow. Such was the case in the early part of the eighteenth century, as the citizens of Britain's American colonies, who previously had viewed themselves as remote and isolated outposts of European culture, came to view themselves as integral parts of a British and European cultural world, participants in the dramatic cultural advances of the age, and meriting on their own all of the rights and privileges of members of a European culture and of a British empire. When we consider the varied forces that led to such an adaptation—the forging of a provincial identity; the extension of the press, and the world of books, pamphlets, and reading; the advent of evangelical religion; the dissemination of the culture of the Enlightenment; the adoption of the rhetoric of British liberty and the extension of the claims of rights and liberties—such a period hardly seems lacking in human drama. That the extension of such privileges to some provincials may have led inexorably to some diminishing of opportunities among other inhabitants of the Americas of different national and racial backgrounds is a further element of our story.

Acknowledgments

A project such as this inevitably incurs many debts. Lewis Perry of Twayne's American Thought and Culture Series, in which this book originally appeared, originally asked me to contribute the volume and has helped at numerous points along the way. So have the librarians at the New York Public Library, the Presbyterian Historical Society, Princeton University Library, the National Library of Scotland, and New College Library. The American Council of Learned Societies and the New Jersey Historical Commission provided research support. John Murrin has been a continual source of inspiration, and his peerless knowledge of colonial America saved me from many errors. Various portions of the manuscript were delivered before meetings of the Columbia Seminar on Early American History, the Philadelphia Center for Early American History and Culture, the Folger Institute, the East Coast Branch of the American Society for Eighteenth-Century Studies, and the Eighteenth-Century Scottish Studies Society. I would like to thank the members of all of those organizations, especially Richard Dunn, Herb Sloan, Dick Bushman, Elaine Crane, John Robertson, and Richard Sher, for helpful advice and support.

From Colonials to Provincials

Introduction

Just two weeks after the end of the year 1760, at the very end of the period we are considering, the Reverend Samuel Davies, the youthful, scholarly, and charismatic president of what was then the College of New Jersey, mounted the pulpit in Nassau Hall at Princeton to deliver a funeral address for an important public figure recently deceased. The setting was in many ways a familiar one in early America. Davies was a Protestant minister; for anyone else to have served as a college president would have been almost unthinkable in what was then an overwhelmingly Protestant society. Ministers everywhere were expected to address the public on all important public occasions.

If the setting was traditional, certain other aspects of the occasion differed markedly from what one would have encountered in the American colonies just 60 or 80 years before. For one thing, the College of New Jersey was an institution of only 15 years' standing; it had been settled at Princeton for only 5 of those years. Eight decades earlier, there had been only one college in English-speaking America: Harvard, which had been founded by Massachusetts Puritans in 1636 principally for the training of Puritan ministers. William and Mary had been added before 1700 and Yale a year after that date, but there was still no institution of higher learning between New England and Virginia until the founding of the Jersey college in 1746; by 1760 there were three. That was partly because the mid-Atlantic region, comprising the colonies of New York, New Jersey, and Pennsylvania, had barely been open to English settlement 80 years before.

Several aspects of Davies's performance would not have appeared at the beginning of the period. Unlike the presidents of the earlier colonial colleges, Davies did not speak for an established church; New Jersey had no religious establishment in the eighteenth century. Davies was a Presbyterian, a dissent-

1

Samuel Davies, president of the College of New Jersey (Princeton University). *University Archives, Department of Rare Books and Special Collections, Princeton University Library.*

ing denomination in England that had barely established its presence in seventeenth-century America but was now emerging as one of the leading provincial denominations, especially in the mid-Atlantic. Much of its growth, and that of the Middle Colonies generally, resulted from the immigration of settlers from Scotland, Ireland, and Germany; in 1680, the settler population of England's American colonies had been overwhelmingly English in origin. That change was partly the product of events at home; the Union of England and Scotland in 1707 created a larger and more diverse nation-state from which the colonies could draw. After 1714 it was ruled by the House of Hanover, composed of German-speaking kings. It was the death of the second of those Hanoverian kings, George II, that Davies was now commemorating, in a performance that ministers and other public figures repeated throughout the British colonies and the British world.[1]

The celebration of kingship, including public displays of mourning for the monarch's passing, was a regular feature of early American society, just as it had been for most Europeans. Even a monarch as unpopular in much of English America as Charles II of the autocratic Stuart line had received the usual commemorations upon his death in 1685. The only real exception was Charles's father, Charles I, whose execution by Puritan revolutionaries had provoked celebration in Puritan New England and lamentation among Virginian and West Indian cavaliers. Still, the striking fact about American eulogizing of George II was its unanimity. At a time when Britons at home remained significantly divided between supporters of the Protestant Hanoverians and their Catholic Stuart rivals, 16 years after the last rebellion by supporters of the Stuarts, known as Jacobites, and just 15 years before American independence, American colonists were probably more united in their attachment to the reigning family than was any other segment of the British world. Moreover, as Davies's sermon illustrates, that attachment was due to their reputation as defenders of Protestantism and liberty, allowing Britons to remain, as Davies described, "free in a world of slaves." Indeed, it was British liberty that gave provincials their claim to citizenship within the empire.[2]

How the colonists arrived at such a position, how they came to identify so firmly with those symbols of British culture, is a large part of the story of this volume. The suggestion that, during the eighteenth century, Americans came to view themselves as more fully British in important respects than they had before cuts against the grain of common understanding, especially when viewed against the end-product of the American Revolution that was shortly to follow, but it is accurate nonetheless. Whereas colonials before 1680 had largely defined themselves with reference to their particular colonial experiments, as New Englanders or Virginians or Barbadians, for example, living on the margins of civilized settlement, during the eighteenth century provincial Americans increasingly came to view themselves as Britons and as Protestants, whose positions were secured by a system of British liberty.[3]

It must be emphasized, however, that American colonists did not identify with everything British. Instead, over the course of the eighteenth century, they would identify themselves increasingly as provincial Britons, citizens of the British provinces, with a particular provincial point of view. That identification increasingly linked colonial citizens to one another and to the other citizens of the expanding provincial sectors of the empire: Lowland Scots, Protestant Irish, and even the inhabitants of England's growing provincial towns and outports, such as Whitehaven, Manchester, and Newcastle, with whom they were increasingly connected through patterns of trade, in their common support for dissenting religious denominations, for a broadly provincial variety of Enlightenment culture, for a "country" politics against the interests of the "court," and in their shared attachment to the liberties of Britons secured by the "Glorious Revolution" of 1688 against the allied forces of Popery and tyranny.

There were many factors in that alteration in American identities. In part it resulted from increased contact between the colonies and such provincial outports as Glasgow, Londonderry, and Whitehaven. In part it was due to the altered political situation in the homeland. England in 1680 was under the rule of Charles II, third of the Stuart line, who had been restored to the throne two decades before, following the collapse of the Cromwellian Protectorate and the end of the English Revolution. He was succeeded five years later by his brother James II of England and VII of Scotland, the last British king to assert the independence of the monarch from the rule of Parliament and an advocate as well of more centralized and autocratic colonial rule. By the end of that decade, James had been deposed and a new succession established in a "Glorious Revolution," to which most colonials happily acceded. Two decades after that, England and Scotland were linked together in a United Kingdom that was firmly Protestant and Parliamentarian.

The suggestion that American colonials evolved into British provincials recalls Perry Miller's magisterial *New England Mind: From Colony to Province*, written more than 40 years ago and still the best account we have of the transformation of colonial intellectual life in response to the American environment. Still, Davies's sermon suggests several ways we need to modify Miller's understanding of provinciality. For one, as Miller's title indicates, his was a study of the *New England* mind only. In the decades since Miller wrote, a multitude of successors have continued to develop and sharpen his insights; yet what they have produced remains, ultimately, a portrait of a single American region. Davies's sermon offers a window into different strands of American culture, whose origins lay not in the unique history of the Puritan experiment but in a much broader mix of British and European traditions of Reformed religion that came together in the polyglot that America became in the eighteenth century almost everywhere except in New England. Davies himself was the grandson of a Welsh farmer and was trained by Irish Presbyterians in the denomination that became, outside of New England, the principal voice of Reformed religion in America.[4]

Part of the discrepancy arises because the "New England Mind" that Miller examined was a public mind based on published sources. Thus Miller necessarily focused principally on the writings of the clergy, who dominated publication in that region throughout the colonial period. Only recently have historians begun to give due weight to other kinds of materials, such as unpublished sources, or the vast quantity of works written outside of the colonies but imported into America, or the various materials produced by nonelite groups. Moreover, they have developed new ways of looking at published sources, in order to tease from them important information not only about how they were written but about how they were read or heard. The growth in both the printing and the importing of books and other printed materials during the eighteenth century was great enough to suggest new meanings for those materials not only for the small group of American writers but for the much larger number of colonial readers, common people as well as elites, women as well as men, even (occasionally) persons not of European origin.[5]

The engagement of provincials with British works linked them ever closer to some of the principal trends in eighteenth-century culture, such as the scientific revolution, evangelical religion, and the world of the Enlightenment. The publication of Isaac Newton's *Principia Mathematica* and the work of his many disciples and popularizers for the first time persuaded substantial segments of the reading public that the natural world operated on the basis of a system of fixed, uniform, and comprehensible laws. That idea would have far-reaching implications, extending well beyond the fields we would normally think of as science. To a greater extent than Newton himself realized or even wished to concede, natural events in the post-Newtonian world came to seem less the product of divine whim and more the result of natural forces.[6]

To be sure, Newton and most of his interpreters saw no contradiction to orthodox Christianity in any of this; the laws they uncovered were simply lucid expressions of the ultimate perfection of the divine plan. Nonetheless, Newtonianism certainly went a long way toward changing the focus of intellectual inquiry from divine intention to the laws by which it was manifest in the natural world. For at least a century thereafter, among the most prominent goals in intellectual inquiry was to extend the Newtonian achievement beyond the realm of natural science to religion, philosophy, and morals and to create what eighteenth-century intellectuals called, without stopping to ponder possible implications for gender relations, a science of man.

The name for that inquiry, which extended beyond Britain to encompass much of western Europe and its American colonies, was the Enlightenment. The Enlightenment took many forms in many countries, from the philosophical, often anticlerical French Enlightenment of Voltaire or D'Holbach to the generally Christian, moralistic Enlightenments of Scotland and America. But everywhere, the Enlightenment was characterized by the widespread belief among the educated classes that western civilization had crossed a threshold from superstition to science, from the chains of ancient belief to a new era of worldly improvement founded on intellectual discoveries patterned on the scientific method. Theirs was a cosmopolitan movement that reached beyond the confines of particular countries or particular locales. Its influence was pervasive, affecting not only philosophical reasoning but public and private conversation and literary styles. In those respects, Americans was as Enlightened as any other place.[7]

Still another innovation in British culture that had important ramifications for Americans was the rise of evangelical religion, or religion based on the personal, felt experience of communion with God, both within and outside of established churches (where they existed). The idea of a felt, personal experience, an old one, had particular resonance for Protestants from the Reformation. It had been characteristic of early Puritan experiences in America. But evangelicalism in the eighteenth century was different, in part because it was not confined to local preachers or to particular denominations and locales but involved the work of intercolonial and even transatlantic revivalists; further, evangelicals for a time were far more willing than most older varieties of Protestants to segregate the experience of conversion from the life of faith.

In some respects, evangelism and the Enlightenment were rival movements. Evangelicals everywhere questioned the Enlightenment's exaltation of religion of the head over religion of the heart and its effort to explain the divine plan according to natural laws. Conversely, the literati and advocates of natural religion scoffed at evangelical visions and emotional displays, which they labeled "enthusiasm" and superstition.

For all of that antagonism, evangelicalism and the Enlightenment had a good deal more in common than many in either group recognized. Such similarity might best be illustrated by considering how both movements differed from more traditional religious groups. Fundamental to both was the rejection of scholasticism, or inherited wisdom, as the basis for knowledge. Evangelicals and the Enlightened also shared a surprisingly cosmopolitan view of the world. The revivals that eighteenth-century preachers promoted were not confined to regions, nations, or denominations but were viewed as the products of an omniscient God.

The conjunction of religion, science, literature, and Enlightenment is well illustrated in the career of Samuel Davies. Davies was deeply committed to evangelical religion; he had grown up in the world of the Great Awakening, a massive religious revival that swept through much of the colonies during the second quarter of the eighteenth century, and he himself had preached revivalism throughout Virginia, where he was installed as pastor of that colony's first Presbyterian Church from 1746 until his removal to Princeton in 1757. But Davies was also, in many ways, a literary figure and a man of the Enlightenment. He penned poems and hymns, some of which were published in colonial newspapers and magazines. He was also an active enquirer into politics, natural phenomena, and all of the interests that fall under the category of the Enlightenment, although he always sought to reconcile such knowledge with religion rather than to oppose them. In that respect he was wholly in keeping with most of the leading figures of the American Enlightenment. His career represents some of the ways in which the cultures of Americans of learning were coming to share elements of a common provincial culture.

For all of those increasing interconnections, Americans did not become culturally English so much as British. The distinction is an important one: for colonials to claim Britishness in the eighteenth century was to advance a particular set of statements about their place within the empire. In England, *Briton* was most often used as a synonym for English, and *North Briton* was a notorious term of abuse. By identifying themselves as Britons, Americans, in common with Scots and Irish Protestants, were asserting the claim of those on the periphery, of varied backgrounds and faiths, to the same rights and privileges as those held by the inhabitants of the metropolis.[8]

In our day, we have come to think of that claim of rights as a natural phenomenon, characteristic of all peoples in all times and places, whenever they are provided with the opportunity to voice it. That assumption may be deceptively simple. Colonial culture in the seventeenth century was built on markedly different ideas, as we shall see, that reflected a much more limited set of possibilities deriving from an undeveloped economy, a pervasive clash of cultures, and the acute sense of strangeness perceived by people living at a great physical and psychological distance from their cultural foundations. In the heterogeneous human environment that existed on the colonial peripheries for much of the seventeenth century, it was far from clear how a unified culture could be formed, or even exactly who the American citizenry would come to be. The creation and delineation of such a citizenry from among those diverse populations, and their claim to possess the rights of imperial citizens, comprises a large part of the story of provinciality and provincial identity.

The eighteenth century was the age of the province in the British world, as the provinces gained prosperity, self-confidence, and assertiveness. Provincials increasingly came to participate in transatlantic discussions of all sorts, not only as spectators but, increasingly, as contributors. That was one of the reasons the College of New Jersey was founded, along with other American colleges in the middle years of the eighteenth century, to create, in Davies's words, "a seminary of loyalty, as well as learning and piety; a nursery for the state, as well as the church."[9] In their most optimistic moments, provincials viewed themselves as embodying both the moral center and the most dynamic sector of the British world.

There was paradox in all of this. By Davies's day, the very confidence that provincials exuded began to worry imperial authorities, who were increasingly conscious of the importance of the American provinces in the empire. At the same time, that confidence served to encourage provincials to insist on their rights and privileges as British citizens. The resulting confrontation would tear the empire of liberty apart.

one

From New English to New Britons

Around the year 1680, about the time that Samuel Davies's paternal grand-father left Wales for the "Welsh Tract" lands in the new colony of Pennsylvania, the cultural landscape of early America looked quite different from the way it would appear in Davies's day. To most American settlers during the last quarter of the seventeenth century, the colonies' most significant characteristic was their remoteness. They were distant from the European centers of learning and culture. They were far removed from civilization as the colonists understood it. They were remote even from each other.

The sense of remoteness colonials felt had a factual basis; for most of the seventeenth century, England's colonial settlements were quite isolated from their cultural moorings. Before 1680, the mainland colonies were divided into two principal groupings. In the north, a cluster of settlements inhabited by the descendants of the many Puritans who had migrated to Massachusetts Bay during the 1630s would grow to house almost 100,000 people by the end of the century, but in 1680 these societies remained huddled along the north-eastern coastline from Maine to New Haven and inland through the Connecticut River Valley. There they had formed a "New England" dedicated to establishing a purified, or Puritanized, form of English religion and English society on the frontiers of the New World. New England was hemmed in on all sides, with French colonies and their native allies to the north; New York, taken from the Netherlands only a decade and a half earlier and still largely Dutch in culture and loyalty, to the south; ocean to the east; and powerful Native American tribes to the west. The fragile nature of England's colonial settlements had been exposed in the 1670s, during which the Dutch briefly retook New York during the Anglo-Dutch War and King Philip's War in New England wiped out the populations of many towns there. It was little wonder that for many years one of the most popular forms of literature produced in New England was the Indian captivity narrative, including one work entitled *The Sovereignty & Goodness of God, Together, with the Faithfulness of His Promises Displayed; Being a Narrative of the Captivity and Restauration of Mrs. Mary Rowlandson,*[1] which was reprinted many times. For years, the fear of captivity would haunt even settlers living far from the colonial frontiers.

The other main cluster of English settlement before 1680 was in the twin Chesapeake colonies of Virginia and Maryland, separated from the English colonies to the north by several hundred miles of coast. There some 60,000 plantation dwellers raised tobacco largely by the labor of white indentured servants and a small but increasing force of African slaves. The most striking feature of Chesapeake society was the rampant mortality due to a variety of diseases, especially malaria, which during the early years killed as much as 40 percent of the new arrivals to the region. As late as the end of the century the average life expectancy still did not exceed 50, even for men and women who had survived the dangerous childhood years. Widows, widowers, and orphans were everywhere, and so few lived long enough to raise families that new immigrants continued to dominate the population for most of the century.

The continuing influx of English settlers constituted a kind of contact for the colonists with their homeland, to be sure, but it resulted in a very unstable society that was predominantly young and single and in which males far outnumbered females. Communities there were conspicuously rude and impermanent; ramshackle dwellings were scattered seemingly at random throughout the countryside. There was little evidence of planning for the future. Virginians were intensely aware of their distance from the centers of culture and civilization; letters from England addressed to the colonies had to await the next unscheduled sailing of the trade ships and could take many months to arrive. "Wee are here att the end of the World," wrote the prominent planter William Byrd to an English correspondent in 1690, "and Europe may bee turned topsy turvy ere wee can hear, a Word of itt."[2]

Beyond the bounds of the regional societies in New England and the Chesapeake one found hostile neighbors: French, Spanish, and Dutch colonies, along with numerous Indian nations—some friendly, some not. In between were scattered a few fledgling settlements, such as New York and New Jersey, English colonies only since the 1660s and 1670s, and Pennsylvania, a colony only since 1682. Those settlements contained varied populations of religious refugees from New England, including such radical sectarian groups as Quakers and Baptists along with the diverse peoples left over from the colonies of New Netherland and New Sweden.

At the peripheries, some frontier settlements lived in what the historian Richard White has called a "middle ground," where European colonists of whatever nationality were forced into an accommodation with Native Americans. What they achieved was by no means a common way of life or a common understanding; Indian ways and European ways still diverged too dramatically. As long as no one group was powerful enough to dictate all of the terms of their cohabitation, they were forced to coexist, and each, of necessity, had to respect the customs of the other. Yet the invariable goal of most English colonists was to move beyond such frontier circumstances, away from the mutual accommodation of the middle ground and toward a more distant and domineering relationship with their Indian neighbors.[3]

By far the largest English plantations in the colonial world were in the West Indian "sugar" islands of Barbados and Jamaica, to which England sent many thousands more settlers before 1680 than went to the mainland colonies, and thousands of African slaves. There settlers created societies far wealthier than those on the mainland, so much so that by 1670 West Indian planters had established a mainland colony of their own in Carolina.[4] Their wealth and power only intensified the sense of remoteness experienced by English inhabitants of mainland North America, whose importance to the authorities at home ranked distinctly below that of their island neighbors.

The New England Way

Not all of the isolation the settlers felt was attributable to causes beyond their control. Among New Englanders the isolation occurred partly by design. Half a century earlier, when thousands of Puritans had embarked for the new colony at Massachusetts Bay, the avowed intention of many had been to remove themselves from what they perceived as the corruptions of England and the English church. In much of New England they established a new and quite distinctive religious order, based on village-centered Congregationalist churches and on the strict enforcement of Puritan orthodoxy and a rigid moral code. At the outset, some had hoped that England itself might follow their example, but those hopes had been dashed in England's Civil War, when Oliver Cromwell's Puritan Commonwealth turned abruptly toward toleration, and in the Restoration of Charles II, which brought with it an Episcopal establishment hostile to Puritan views. Still, American Puritans continued to follow their "New England way" with zeal, rejecting any compromise in the Congregational order they had established or in the religious doctrines they espoused. Massachusetts was a Bible commonwealth, and whatever was not in accord with their understanding of Scripture—that is to say, "innovation" of any sort—was resisted, persecuted, or warned away.

Puritans manifest what in the largest sense might be called the paradox of Protestantism. Fundamental to Protestants was the belief that Scripture represented the definitive word of God and that it was the duty of each and every believer to read and comprehend the Bible for himself or herself. Yet at the outset Protestants were anything but tolerant of differing ideas. On the contrary, the requirement that believers interpret the word of God was coupled with the assumption that if they did so sincerely, each would understand it in essentially the same way.

The belief in the authority of Scripture gave Puritans and other like-minded Protestants a particular angle of vision. At the heart of Puritan worship was the belief in the sovereignty of God, who determined the fates of nations and individuals according to his will, subject only to the limitations granted by specific scriptural promises. In that conviction, the Puritans were Calvinists, adherents to the general religious teachings of the Genevan Reformer John Calvin (1509–1564), which had been disseminated throughout the Reformed churches of western Europe. Other important features of Calvinist theology that the Puritans adopted were the belief in justification by faith in God rather than by the performing of good works, and predestination, by which some are irrevocably elected for salvation and others for damnation.

Freed in the New World from the constraints imposed by kings and worldly magistrates, New England's Puritans implemented their religious policies with rigor. The faith that alone could save sinners was manifest, according to their ideas, in a felt experience of conversion, and New Englanders developed a practice, apparently unknown elsewhere, of requiring aspiring church members to recount the stories of their conversions before the whole of the congregation.[5]

How those experiences were judged apparently varied considerably from community to community. Many were willing to apply what was called a judgment of charity, which allowed members to be accepted more easily than the strict Puritan rhetoric suggested. Yet Puritans took the Protestant paradox a step further than most, organizing Congregationalist churches ostensibly independent of one another even as they insisted on general agreement. The result was probably a greater commitment to the language of agreement than to conformity in fact, so long as overt public disputes could be avoided. Non-members were still permitted to attend church services and were required to do so by law, but not as full or voting members of the congregations. There they would hear sermons, the centerpiece of the Puritan service, that lasted as long as three hours and were delivered twice every Sabbath. Churchgoing Puritans might hear 3 sermons per week, 150 or more per year.[6]

In some respects, cultural expression in New England may have been more limited in 1680 than it had been half a century before. In the early days, New England had attracted to the region a host of Puritans whose beliefs and practices were not so easily confined within the parameters of the New England way. A variety of radical sectarians, from Roger Williams and Anne Hutchinson to Samuel Gorton, arrived in the region and preached separatism, Anabaptism, or the voice of the Holy Spirit, in tones that put them well beyond the pale of Puritan orthodoxy everywhere but in Rhode Island, to which most of those individuals were eventually banished.[7] By mid-century, most of the region's clergy had closed ranks against such unbridled expression and against the occasions that afforded it. In some congregations even the use of personal spiritual testimonies declined in significance and were replaced by ritualized performances, such as the congregational rite of owning the covenant. Women were often excused from public testimony entirely.

The belief in the sovereignty of God led to considerable introspection among Puritans about their own fates and that of their colony. Puritans searched their lives and their feelings for signs of grace, or the lack thereof. Puritan leaders scrutinized the course of events in their region, recording their histories when settlement began and using them to persuade themselves of divine favor on their mission. It was, of course, a New English rather than an American story they set out to tell. They found the signs of that approbation chiefly in "remarkable providences"—unusual happenings, strange coincidences, or wondrous events suggesting a supernatural intervention in the ordinary course of affairs. Puritan historian Edward Johnson recounted such practices in *The Wonder-Working Providence of Sions Saviour in New England*.[8] As late as 1702, Cotton Mather related "the Wonders of the Christian Religion" in his providential epic *Magnalia Christi Americana*, which in spite of its title was set exclusively in the region north and east of the Hudson River.[9]

If the purpose of those histories was to persuade New Englanders of their role as a special people, the historian offered a warning as well: whatever calamities befell them signified God's displeasure. Thus the bloody ordeal of King Philip's War in 1675 was recognized as a token of divine anger against a people increasingly taken up with worldliness and irreligion. By the latter part of the seventeenth century, Puritan ministers had adopted the style of sermon known as the jeremiad, named after the Biblical prophet, warning New Englanders of the punishment to follow if they failed to uphold their covenant with God. Yet such warnings also constituted an affirmation of their mission as well. Whether thanking God for unexpected deliverance or forecasting doom, such historical preaching was intended to underscore the distinctiveness of the Puritan errand.[10]

The Puritans' reliance on such signs in their providential histories reflected deeper concerns as well. New Englanders, and almost all seventeenth-century Americans, lived in what they perceived as a world of magic, or what David Hall has called a "world of wonders," where supernatural forces impinged constantly on everyday life.[11] Before the ascendancy of the scientific viewpoint associated with the work of Isaac Newton, the appearance of a comet or a war or a plague was sure to be a sign of powerful forces at work on the lives of individuals and nations. Puritans as well as other Protestants opposed attributing such events to the spells of magicians and sorcerers or to the influence of the stars but not to supernatural powers in general. All were signs of the providential will, carried out by angels and spirits under God's command. Smaller signs—a dream, a chance encounter with an unexpected piece of good or bad luck, or the arrival of a stranger of uncommon appearance—were indicative of individual fates.

Locating the Chesapeake

Devotion to their religion served to separate New Englanders from other English colonists. In the Chesapeake and in the West Indies, the majority of settlers appear to have been a good deal less preoccupied with religious matters than were their Puritan counterparts. Their belief and manner of worship were also rather different. We know much less about the religious lives of early Virginians, other than that most were formally identified with the Church of England. We know also that there was considerable diversity of belief within that church, as was the case with most religious establishments. Some of the Anglican clergymen in early Virginia had strong Puritan leanings, including three who were exiled from the colony by the governor, Sir William Berkeley, in 1648 for their refusal to follow Anglican forms and who ended up among a community of Puritan emigrants to Maryland.[12] Others favored a different strand of Anglican religiosity, one that became increasingly prominent in Anglican circles after 1660: an emphasis on ritual and the liturgy, with close attention to such devotional works as those of the English divine Jeremy Taylor, including *Holy Living and Dying* and such other standards as the aptly named *Whole Duty of Man*. Together those works emphasized piety, the moral life, and religious duties over the enforcement of orthodoxy or the testing of personal conversions. They advocated just the sort of devotional piety that Puritans scorned because it was not derived from a felt experience of conversion.

For most of the seventeenth century, life in the Chesapeake prompted much less pondering of the meaning of the American settlement than was the case in New England. There is little evidence of a sense of history in early Virginia. Most of what was written about the colony was promotional, designed to describe in highly flattering and often unrealistic terms the state of the colony and the land. Promotional writers, attempting to draw settlers and investors to Virginia, were more likely to distinguish their colony from others rather than emphasize any common bond between them.[13]

By the end of the century, some Virginians had begun to pay more attention to their history. Between 1697 and 1724 several histories appeared, including the collaborative *Present State of Virginia, and the College* (1697) and Hugh Jones's *Present State of Virginia* (1724). The titles of those works suggest the perspective they employed as a rule; Robert Beverley's *History and Present State of Virginia* (1705) constitutes only a partial exception. In moving a bit beyond mere description of the present, Virginians were attempting to locate themselves, both for their own audience and for a metropolitan one. That they still addressed the latter audience as remote outsiders is suggested by Beverley's introductory apology: "I am an Indian, and don't pretend to be exact in my Language."[14]

English colonials nonetheless shared more with each other than they recognized. Although the inhabitants of New England and of the Chesapeake stood on opposing sides in politics and religion, in both places most formal intellectual endeavor was the product of social elites: the clergy and a few allied landed or merchant families in the North, the landed gentry and a handful of Anglican clergymen in the South. In both societies, intellectual aspiration beyond theology was still shaped by the tradition of the virtuoso, a term whose meaning has long since disappeared: the Renaissance man of science followed the world of learning almost as a hobby, collecting specimens and dipping into as many fields of knowledge as possible without necessarily aspiring to unusual achievement in any one. A virtuoso was of necessity a gentleman—a man of wealth, leisure, and social position adequate to gain access to intellectual conversation. His knowledge was measured more by its breadth than by its depth. The virtuoso's persona kept colonials in the position of intellectual consumers who looked to England and Europe to advance the world of knowledge as far as possible.

Few colonials fit the model of virtuoso precisely. Although a Virginia gentleman such as William Byrd II (1679–1744) read and conversed about a wide range of subjects, from natural history and letters to politics and law, his endeavors also had an important practical side. He wrote witty descriptive narratives of *The History of the Dividing Line betwixt Virginia and North Carolina Run in the Year of Our Lord 1728*, *A Progress to the Mines in the Year 1732*, and *A Journey to the Land of Eden Anno 1733*, each designed to inform as well as entertain with its descriptions of the land, the plants, and the people. Byrd was also an improver and a promoter; everything he wrote was intended to persuade investors and settlers to aid in the development of his manorial empire in the west.[15]

New Englanders were even further from classic virtuosos. To orthodox Puritans, the pursuit of knowledge for mere personal pleasure was sinful indulgence, and the acquisition of such learning surely ranked far below such useful intellectual pursuits as theology or scriptural history. Nonetheless, by the second half of the seventeenth century, some ministers, especially those who had spent time among the learned community in mid- or late-seventeenth-century England, sought to extend their intellectual horizons. Uriah Oakes, returning to Massachusetts from England in 1671 to take up the presidency of Harvard College, lamented the lack of learning he found there, even among the ministry. Cotton Mather engaged in a vast variety of intellectual pursuits, including writing a work entitled *The Christian Philosopher*, in which he intended to reconcile Puritanism with intellectual pursuit; the work's original title, "The Christian Virtuoso," was borrowed from Robert Boyle, the great English man of science and promoter of Christian causes.[16]

Still another cause of the colonists' sense of isolation came from their increasing reluctance to recognize any commonalities with the land's other inhabitants. To be sure, the Indians' ways were among the strangest aspects of the New World to the settlers, but the colonists' failure to comprehend that strangeness only exaggerated the gap. However rudely English men and women lived on the colonial frontiers, they continued to define themselves as "civil" and the Indians as "savage." It is difficult to develop precise definitions of those terms. Historically, civility was connected to government, to civil administration, and to urban places. More than anything else, civility suggested societies organized according to the rule of law, although it often carried other connotations, including refined manners and Christianity.[17]

Actually, most colonial societies in the seventeenth century could not boast all that much civility of the sort just described, but that did not stop English settlers from considering it a mark of their differentiation from the natives. The Puritans' belief in their civility was one reason that, despite their announced intentions at the start of settlement, not even they devoted much effort to converting Native Americans to Christianity (although there were a few notable exceptions, such as the Roxbury minister John Eliot, who translated the Bible into Algonquian). Most English colonists assumed that there could be no true Christianizing without prior civilizing. The result was that the efforts of English Protestants' to convert Indians were notably less successful than those of their French or Spanish Catholic neighbors.

Native Americans were not, in fact, lacking all attributes of civility. Many were certainly adept at diplomacy. The Iroquois, for example, repeatedly played one European power against another to maximize their gains, siding with Dutch against the Hurons in order to establish control over the lucrative fur trade, joining New England against the Narragansett Indians in 1675, and later serving as the balance of power between New England and New France. The English, Dutch, and Iroquois set up a regular consultation at Albany and a flexible mechanism for frontier relations known as the "Covenant Chain," and the Iroquois gained the respect of those colonial leaders who dealt with them. A few, such as William Byrd II and Robert Beverley, viewed intermarriage with the Indians as the most likely means to bridge the gap, but nearly all of their countrymen disagreed.[18]

Some colonials knew better. Those who were captured during Indian wars often came to believe that they were better treated by their captors than by the colonists. They were commonly adopted into their new tribes and sometimes obtained respected places; consequently, many chose to remain voluntarily with their captors as "white Indians," much to the horror of their fellow colonials. Native Americans, by contrast, were rarely welcomed among Europeans. Even those who were Christianized were segregated into separate "praying" villages. Native captives much less frequently chose to remain among the English when they had the chance to return to their own people.[19]

English colonists in 1680 perceived no greater link with the African laborers they increasingly employed. The slave population of most of the mainland colonies was still small in 1680, constituting less than 20 percent of Virginia's population even at the end of the century, for example, but it was growing and would soon begin to grow much faster. Moreover, although slavery as an institution no longer existed in much of Europe, slaves were found in every colony and formed one of the colonial world's distinguishing features. In part the trend was a simple spillover from the South American and Caribbean plantations, which were worked predominantly by slaves: English Barbados had a black majority during the last four decades of the seventeenth century. But such concentrations were rare on the mainland, where slaves, still referred to as servants, worked side by side with masters or fellow servants. Increasingly, however, Africans were treated differently from other servants, in ways that were never beneficial to them.[20]

Even working together did not necessarily create a bond between black and white workers. The issue was not so much race, which was not yet an overwhelming concern. Rather, it was the still-present gulf in language and culture. Many slaves could not communicate even with one another in the early years, having been brought from widely scattered parts of Africa, where they had spoken a great many different languages. Paradoxically, it was not until the mainland colonies built up a native-born slave population that slaves and masters came to speak much the same language; by then, much of the close working contact present in the earliest years had given way to separation.

Restoration and Reorganization

During the half-century after 1680, many of the conditions that had led to a sense of remoteness in the colonies changed dramatically. For example, whereas in 1680 a colonist awaiting news from the metropolis in England had to wait for the next chance sailing to the vicinity of the person he was addressing, by 1730 sailings were sufficiently frequent and American posts had expanded enough to allow something much more like a regular correspondence. American trade increased, not only with London but with British outports in England, Scotland, and Ireland and among the colonial cities as well. The changes were mental as well as physical; new links between Britain and the colonies and even new forms of communication encouraged colonials, who previously had been passive recipients of English culture, to become increasingly active participants as provincial citizens of an empire in which provincials would play an increasingly large role. If Americans still retained a sense of living on the periphery, it was a periphery with much closer connections to the center and, increasingly, to the various centers of British culture.

The impetus to change was already present in 1680 in several respects. It was once common for historians to slight the significance of the Restoration years (1660–1688), during which the restored Stuart monarchs Charles II and his brother the Duke of York, who succeeded him as James II, attempted to impose a measure of order on a country and an empire recovering from the instability of two decades of civil war. Historians often assumed that the Restoration represented only a temporary interlude in the larger story of the growth of English and colonial liberty, and that whatever changes the Stuarts

16

succeeded in implementing were easily and speedily reversed after the Revolution of 1688. In fact those years were critical on several counts. During that period, English proprietary groups connected to the Restoration government organized the settlement of the missing links along the Atlantic coast—New York, East and West New Jersey, Pennsylvania, and the Carolinas—forming a continuous chain of English colonies from the Maine settlements to South Carolina.

The Restoration governments in America all originated as proprietary colonies, the possessions of one or a group of individuals or families who received grants of land, often in exchange for favors at court. The proprietorships introduced into the colonial enterprise individuals of a status previously almost unknown in the colonies, such as the Duke of York, the Earls of Shaftesbury and Perth, and the prominent Quaker gentlemen Robert Barclay and William Penn. Those men in turn brought a whole class of merchants, gentlemen, and sons of gentlemen into the colonies. Similar persons came into the older colonies after the Restoration also; thus the colonies had a whole new class of leaders.[21]

From the beginning, Restoration politicians led by the Duke of York embarked on an aggressive program to shore up the empire in America. In 1664, the duke sent a fleet commanded by Richard Nicolls to seize New Netherland from the Dutch. The duke's charter gave him as proprietor vast power over a large domain extending from the Connecticut River to the Delaware and encompassing what would become New York, the Jerseys, and much of western New England. New Englanders, who had been sympathetic to the king's Puritan opponents during the English Civil War, found themselves tightly hemmed in on the west. In 1684, Charles revoked the Massachusetts charter and merged that colony first with its New England neighbors and then with New York and the Jerseys in an enlarged "Dominion of New England," ruled by a hostile governor, Edmund Andros. Although the Dominion lasted for only a few years, New Englanders never again attained the level of independence they had enjoyed earlier.

The Dominion's failure resulted not from events in America but from developments at home, such as the growing opposition to the authoritarian and largely ineffectual rule of the Catholic James II (1685–1688). English Protestants tolerated James as long as it seemed that his Protestant daughter, Mary, wife of the Protestant William of Orange, would succeed him. But James's ill-conceived attacks on the powers of Parliament and on the local corporations, coupled with the birth of a son in 1688, led Protestants, including most of the political establishment, to rebel. They invited William and Mary to take the throne in his stead. William landed at the head of an army, James fled, and the Protestant succession was secured in a bloodless "Glorious Revolution."*

---

*It was bloodless in England only. Supporters of the rival claimants to the throne fought a bloody civil war in Ireland, and bloodshed followed in Scotland as well.

As soon as word of William's landing reached America, colonists in Massachusetts, New York, and Maryland in turn overthrew James's unpopular governments and replaced them with regimes loyal to the Protestant succession—albeit with considerable bloodshed and enduring factionalism in New York. The Glorious Revolution would long form a common point of reference across the colonies and across the Atlantic. Thereafter all of the colonies, including those of New England, were more concerned with defining their places within the empire than in working outside of it.

Even Massachusetts was drawn into the imperial orbit. In the wake of the Glorious Revolution, the colony's agent in London, the Puritan minister Increase Mather, sought a renewal of its original charter. After arduous negotiations, Mather returned with a new charter that reestablished Massachusetts as a distinct colony but that would now be ruled by a governor appointed by the crown rather than chosen by the colony. Some traditionalists advocated holding out for fuller autonomy, but most recognized that henceforth the Bible commonwealth could be Puritan in religion but not in government.

Paradoxically, Restoration proprietors and settlers brought to the colonial system an emerging concern for constitutionalism and an emphasis on liberties. In drafting plans for his colony, William Penn began with the idea that a society required a fixed and well-ordered constitution, and he and his associates drafted more than a dozen plans for the colony, drawing ideas as well as criticisms from a number of the most influential political thinkers of the day. East and West Jersey and the Carolinas also began with fundamental constitutions. Even New York, captured from the Dutch and granted to the arch-imperialist Duke of York, eventually received a "Charter of Liberties," albeit a somewhat restricted one by the standards of the other Restoration colonies.

Pennsylvania and the Middle Colonies

At the center of the new colonial world was Pennsylvania, the last and largest of the Restoration settlements, granted to William Penn in 1681 and intended to be an international Quaker homeland. Penn belonged to the Society of Friends, a small, radical outgrowth of English Protestantism that drew much of its strength from the lower and middle classes in London, northern England, and such provincial outports as Bristol, Dublin, and Aberdeen. Friends also looked abroad, to Holland, Ireland, and America, and between 1676 and 1682 they established three American colonies adjoining one another in the Delaware Valley: a largely Scottish Quaker enterprise in East Jersey and two dominated by English Friends in West Jersey and Pennsylvania. During the 1680s, Pennsylvania received the greatest influx of settlers since the great Puritan migration of a half century before. Unlike the New England settlements, the Quaker colonies continued to attract immigrants steadily throughout their existence.

The Society of Friends took Puritan ideas a good deal further than their predecessors had. Whereas Puritans attacked Catholics and Anglicans for emphasizing ritual and hierarchy within the church, Quakers rejected not only such rituals as reading from the Prayer Book and wearing vestments but even the church as an official body and the ministry itself. They insisted instead on a "Priesthood of all believers." And unlike the Puritans, Quakers believed that the religious experience they valued was not restricted to an "elect" few through predestination; the "inner light" was present in everyone. Quakers' emphasis on the indwelling spirit led them to value individual experience in ways that others did not, a value that was reflected even in their child rearing, which de-emphasized the strict authority of elders in favor of a nurturing principle designed to develop individual character. One historian has even described Quakers as the originators of the modern American family.[22]

Much of the radicalism of the Quakers is difficult to recognize in the twentieth century, in which our images of them are dominated by the pictures of Quakers in old-fashioned gray clothes and hats that adorn our cereal boxes and by recollections of speech laced with such archaic terms as *thee* and *thou*. In the seventeenth century those features had rather different connotations. Wearing clothes appropriate to one's station and doffing one's hat to one's superiors were important marks of social distinction. The use of the familiar *thee* and *thou*—rather than *you*, which was still a term of respect in the seventeenth century—and the refusal to remove one's hat were not individual quirks but deliberate displays of disdain for the symbols of worldly rank.

Penn was a devoted Quaker, but he was also a prominent gentleman with connections at court. His father, Admiral Penn, was an important political figure in Restoration England. William Penn recruited a number of important Quaker merchants and gentlemen for his colony who helped transform it into a focal point of transatlantic culture. Quakers traded regularly all over the Atlantic world.[23]

The first principle in Penn's plan was religious toleration, part of the Quaker belief in the unfettered conscience of the individual and a cause to which Penn had long devoted himself. Such toleration certainly distinguished Pennsylvania from England's earlier colonies, most of which had assumed the necessity of an established church, whether Anglican or Puritan. In fact, all of the Restoration colonies allowed at least limited toleration to attract settlers to the New World, but Pennsylvania went far beyond mere toleration of religious dissenters to something approaching true religious liberty.[24]

What made Pennsylvania significant among the Restoration colonies was its size and reach. Quaker merchants were among the most active transatlantic traders, relying on extensive networks of Friends merchants in Europe and America. William Penn actively recruited settlers among not only English Quakers but also Welsh, Scottish, Irish and Dutch Friends, along with other sectarian groups of German origin. Seeking economic opportunity and toleration, all of those groups, as well as Anglicans, Presbyterians, German Lutherans, and German Reformed worshipers, flocked to the Friends' colonies in Pennsylvania and West Jersey, which became the most diverse colonies. Within two decades, Quakers were already a minority in Pennsylvania; by 1720 they no longer represented the bulk of the population even in Philadelphia, their capital city.

The advent of all those newcomers provided another link among the colonies. Philadelphia quickly became the center of immigration into British America, attracting settlers from Britain and across the European Continent. From Pennsylvania the colonists fanned out in all directions, eastward to New Jersey or westward as far as Lancaster and then south along the "Great Wagon Road" into the backcountry of Maryland, Virginia, and the Carolinas. The latter areas, which were as diverse as Pennsylvania, came to resemble that colony more than they did the plantation south. Philadelphia became the center of important communications networks extending both to the North and to the South.

Pennsylvania formed an important contrast as well to New York, the other important Restoration colony of the mid-Atlantic, which had been seized from the Dutch by the authority of James, Duke of York, in 1664. Whereas William Penn sought to establish a colony where proprietors and settlers would work together within a mutually agreed-on constitutional framework, James advocated uncompromising imperial and proprietary authority. Whereas the Quaker colony maintained a considerable degree of religious and ethnic tolerance, conflict between Dutch and English—and occasionally between Protestants and Catholics—formed an important focal point of New York affairs, in spite of the duke's consistent support for a policy of toleration. Many Protestants, however, in the wake of Louis XIV's revocation of the Edict of Nantes and expulsion of the Huguenots from France, refused to believe that James truly supported toleration. When a largely Dutch group of Protestant New Yorkers rebelled against what they viewed as James's popish government in 1689 and proclaimed the accession of William and Mary, English elites rallied against the rebels and had their leader, Jacob Leisler, and an associate executed for treason. New York's power structure survived the Glorious Revolution relatively intact.[25]

British Union and the New Provincial Elite

In certain respects, the diversity that characterized the mid-Atlantic region represented an extension of trends in the home country. In 1707, the parliaments of England and Scotland united, leaving only their churches and legal systems intact. For England, the principal motive for union was to secure the Protestant succession and preclude the possible development of a hostile power on their northern border. For Scots, the main benefit was the opportunity to trade freely with England and its overseas empire. After the Union, Scots flocked to their new capital in London and spread themselves throughout the new British empire with unprecedented rapidity.

Most colonials paid little attention to the Union at the outset. England, however laxly, still ruled the colonies, and the Union secured rather than altered the Protestant succession, therefore requiring no change in allegiance. But the context of colonial authority was irreversibly changed. Henceforth, colonies that had been isolated English dependents became provinces of a United Kingdom that were entitled to claim the same rights and privileges as other British provinces.

It did not take long for the consequences of that change to emerge. Early in 1707, an Irish-born Presbyterian minister named Francis Makemie was arrested in New York by that colony's Anglican governor on the charge of preaching without a license. Makemie initially claimed the protection of the English Toleration Act of 1689, which granted toleration to dissenters. But Lord Cornbury, the governor, denied the act's jurisdiction beyond the borders of England proper.

Makemie was still awaiting trial on May 1 of that year when the Union took effect. Soon thereafter, the clergyman changed his defense. He now agreed that the Toleration Act did not extend beyond England's borders. In securing the legal rights of dissenters, the act implied the existence of an established church; without such an establishment there would be no need for the legal relief the act granted. Makemie denied that New York had such an establishment. There, all were "upon an equal level and bottom of liberty."[26]

He subsequently explained the rationale behind his new claim. In the new United Kingdom, there was no state establishment. The Anglican Church was established in England only; in Scotland, the Presbyterian Church had an equal national establishment, "as highly related and annexed unto the Crown as the Church of England." The colonies, as dominions of the crown, were not subordinate to the English establishment at all. Makemie was acquitted by a jury—although the court imposed full court costs on him—and he published a narrative of his trial. Cotton Mather in Boston called him "that brave man, Mr. Makemie," who "without permitting the Matter to come so far as to Pleading the Act of Toleration" had proved that England's Act of Uniformity was but a local law and had "nothing to do with the Plantation."[27] Thereafter Makemie's case was cited and celebrated by non-Anglicans throughout the colonies for affirming their independence from Anglican control.

The Union had other effects as well. Among the most important was the arrival in the colonies of a new group of educated provincials. Some were merchants: Scottish and Irish Protestant merchants quickly appeared in every colonial city. Young Scots, most from in or around Glasgow, began to move to the Chesapeake region in considerable numbers to work in the tobacco trade. Closely connected to those were Scots and Scots-Irish officials, a disproportionate number of whom came to fill posts in the imperial service as governors, councillors, military officers, and revenue officials. Still others came as clergymen and educators, tutors and teachers in colonial academies.

There were several reasons for the unusual participation of those provincials in colonial affairs. One was the relatively backward state of the economies in Scotland and Ireland, impoverished nations on Europe's fringes. Educated elites from those places had long sought their fortunes abroad. Scotland in particular had a large population of skilled and educated young men who lacked positions at home. In addition, educated provincials were beginning to develop an enlightened interest in America. One of the motives for union among the Scots had been their widespread belief that their nation suffered in its relationship with England because of Scotland's lack of wealth and power, which could be remedied by colonial trade. Those Scottish administrators who came to America developed a distinct posture in colonial affairs, as defenders of a decidedly commercial vision of empire. Almost all of those officials were educated men with broad interests characteristic of the provincial Enlightenment.[28]

A good example of those elite groups were the Scots who settled in New York and New Jersey during the tenure of Governor Robert Hunter (1710–1719), a Scots native with an extensive military background. Hunter was also a man of letters and a friend and correspondent of such British literary figures as Joseph Addison and Richard Steele, editors of such popular journals of polite letters as the *Spectator* (1711–1714) and the *Tatler* (1709–1711), and the satirist Jonathan Swift. Hunter himself wrote what may have been the first play composed in America, the political satire *Androboros*. During his years in New York Hunter used his powers to bring to the colony a number of talented young Scotsmen, including James Alexander, who would become a prominent attorney with interests in science, politics, and law; the customs official and imperial writer Archibald Kennedy; and most noteworthy of all, Cadwallader Colden, a physician, politician, and one of the leading men of science in America. Hunter drew around him a larger circle of prominent families from provincial backgrounds, including the Livingstons, who were also Scots, and the Morrisses, one of whom married a Scot. When Hunter returned to Britain, he selected as his successor William Burnet, son of the prominent Scottish bishop Gilbert Burnet. Together Hunter and Burnet set the tone for intellectual life in colonial New York for most of the century.[29]

Another significant group of educated provincials was attracted to Pennsylvania. The most important among them was the Scottish Quaker James Logan, who arrived in the colony in 1699 to serve as William Penn's personal secretary and remained for more than half a century. Logan's interests extended to politics, science, philosophy, and literature; he wrote and published in all of those fields and developed one of the largest libraries in the American colonies. Other important provincials who settled in Pennsylvania early in the eighteenth century included the lawyer Andrew Hamilton, known for his defense of John Peter Zenger in that printer's famous libel trial;

the Revolutionary pamphleteers Joseph Galloway and John Dickinson; and the Irish-born ministers and educators William Tennent and Francis Alison. Most of those men arrived while the colony was administered by a succession of Scottish governors.

Scottish and Irish elites played important roles of a different sort in the intellectual life of the southern colonies. After 1710, Virginia was administered by such Scottish governors as Alexander Spotswood and Robert Dinwiddie. Another important circle of Scots, who entered North Carolina during the tenure of Governor Gabriel Johnstone, included Henry McCulloh, an important writer on imperial matters; the prominent imperial agent James Abercromby; and the revenue officer and pamphleteer John Rutherfurd, all of whom contributed extensively to the discussion of imperial affairs. So did another group of southern colonial officials, including James Glen in South Carolina and a group of Ulster Scots connected to Georgia that included the explorer Henry Ellis and his protégé William Knox.

Perhaps the most important group of provincial immigrants were the Scottish doctors, more than 150 of whom settled in the colonies. They included such prominent individuals as Colden of New York, William Douglass of Massachusetts, John Mitchell of Virginia, and Alexander Garden and John Lining of South Carolina, along with a host of others. Those men formed almost the entire elite of the colonial medical profession, owing partly to the rise of Edinburgh University as a center of medical education. Most were men of wide learning: Colden, Douglass, Mitchell, and Garden all were involved in imperial politics; Mitchell also wrote on agriculture, Lining and Garden on botany, Colden on almost everything. Together they formed the core of the colonial scientific community and corresponded with virtually every man of science in the colonies and with important British scientific networks as well.[30]

Collectively, those elites did much to unify the colonies, partly because few of them arrived with strong ties to any one colonial venture and because almost all of them had a more than purely local perspective on the colonial world. Colonial governors frequently moved from one post to another: Robert Hunter, for example, served as governor of Virginia, New York and New Jersey, and Jamaica. Alexander Spotswood of Virginia was among the principal advocates of an intercolonial postal service. The doctors were instrumental in establishing intercolonial networks of correspondence. And nearly all of the administrators worked actively and persistently to promote the cause of intercolonial union throughout the century, which frequently put them in conflict with often recalcitrant local legislatures.

Those provincial elites in turn influenced other leading residents in the colonies. Benjamin Franklin, for example, was a close political ally of Andrew Hamilton in Pennsylvania and a regular correspondent of Colden, Alexander, Kennedy, and many others, with whom he discussed science, politics, and imperial affairs. We will see in a later chapter how much Franklin's ideas were affected by his Scottish contacts. Such Virginia gentlemen as Robert Carter intermixed with Scottish governors and often employed Scottish tutors on their estates. In the eighteenth century young gentlemen at William and Mary studied under a growing number of Scottish teachers. The Ulster-born clergymen Francis Alison and William Tennent, both educated in Scotland, became among the most important educators in the Middle Colonies.

The "Reinvention of New England"

The only part of early America that was not inundated with newcomers from Scotland or Ireland was coastal New England, which remained predominantly English and Puritan. That region also experienced changes resulting both from an altered relationship with the mother country and from the arrival of new elites. During the Restoration years, those colonies received an influx of English merchants, some of whom were Anglicans and shared little with the older residents of the region. Others, Dissenters who left the Restoration troubles behind to join their coreligionists in the New World, included such clergymen and educators as Harvard's Uriah Oakes and the schoolmaster Charles Morton, and such tradesmen as Josiah Franklin, whose son Benjamin would play so important a role in early American history. With the granting of a new charter to Massachusetts in the aftermath of the Glorious Revolution, New Englanders were committed to a policy of tolerating their fellow Protestants. The newcomers brought with them some of the most important cultural influences emanating from late-seventeenth-century England.[31]

Among the most important of the newcomers was Benjamin Colman, whose parents had left England for Massachusetts in 1671, just two years before the birth of their son. Colman entered Harvard in 1688, when the college's president, Increase Mather, was busy in London seeking the renewal of the charter and the bulk of the teaching devolved to the tutors, John Leverett and William Brattle. Both Leverett and Brattle had been influenced by the newcomer Charles Morton, and they were actively engaged in bringing the new learning of Restoration England to Harvard. After completing his master's degree in 1695, Colman left for England, where he became associated with several of the leading Dissenters, including Isaac Watts, who was famous for his psalms and hymns. Colman also became acquainted with the work of a more tolerant group of Anglicans known as "Latitudinarians," especially Archbishop John Tillotson.[32] Colman also witnessed the results of the "Heads of Agreement" that was negotiated between England's Congregationalists and Presbyterians in an effort to establish a "United Brethren" among those previously divided dissenting groups.

In 1699, while preaching in England, Colman received an invitation to minister to a new and innovative congregation in Boston. The Brattle Street Church, as it came to be called, was organized by a group of merchants and liberal ministers, including Thomas and William Brattle and John Leverett. It was intended to move New England worship away from strict conformity to local tradition in the ecumenical directions plotted by English Dissenters and Latitudinarians. The Brattle Street organizers renounced some of the most particular manifestations of the New England way. They dispensed with requiring personal relations of religious experience as a term of communion; the power of admission devolved from the congregation to the minister. The Brattle Street service included both devotional prayer and reading from Scripture without subsequent interpretation—what the Puritans had called "dumb reading" and had likened to a Catholic mass. Expecting opposition from the Massachusetts clerical establishment, Colman received a Presbyterian ordination in England before assuming his post. So much for the strict Congregationalism of the New England way.[33]

Not all New Englanders were pleased by the Brattle Street innovations. To Cotton Mather, they represented an attempt by "Head-strong" men to "utterly subvert our churches." For others, the solution was to found the new college of Yale in Connecticut in 1701 to combat the growing "liberal" tendencies at Harvard as well as to supply the pulpits of that colony with an educated ministry.[34]

The most spectacular attempt to limit the penetration of outside forces into New England was the outbreak of witch accusations at Salem Village, Massachusetts (now Danvers), in 1692, which Cotton Mather helped instigate by publishing his *Memorable Providences, Relating to Witchcraft and Possessions* (1689). There was nothing new about such accusations, which had been a regular feature of New England communities from the beginning. But until the 1690s, most of the cases had been almost solitary affairs, affecting no more than a few people at a time. In 1692, a group of young girls influenced partly by tales told by a West Indian slave woman fell into hysterical fits. When questioned, they blamed the fits on neighboring women, whose images or specters, they said, were torturing them. The authorities took the women into custody, but the fits continued and the girls cited other specters. At the urging of Samuel Parris, the local minister, and with the support of Cotton Mather, the colony convened a special court to try the witches. In all, almost 200 people, most of them women, were charged as witches, and 19 were hanged for their participation in the assault that Satan had launched against Massachusetts.[35]

The belief in witches was well rooted in contemporary theology. Of more immediate concern was how those beliefs were directed. Rarely did the girls accuse their own families or their friends or close neighbors. Salem Village was a conservative, close-knit agricultural village. But others in the village had principal ties outside, with the neighboring commercial port of Salem town. Such people seemed to be outsiders in the community or, worse, locals who abetted the penetration of outside influences on village life.

A larger point is that most of those accused at Salem were women, as were most accused witches throughout the western world. Moreover, they tended to be women who did not play their usual community roles. Some were widows or spinsters, often women who had inherited property and administered it outside of the normal channels of male authority; their very presence, in a sense, threatened the customary lines of social authority in the village. Others were linked to local groups of Quakers and other sectarians, who also stood outside of New England's traditional community structure; in those sectarian groups, women played particularly strong and untraditional roles. They were often involved in disputes with their neighbors over property and other matters. Such women seemed to embody all that was threatening to community order.[36]

The trials soon got out of hand. The girls, whose accusations initially served to illuminate the fault lines in the community that separated the traditional village from its untraditional elements, did not target only those that town leaders feared. The accusations now seemed to threaten the very order they had previously seemed to uphold—especially when they included the governor's wife and other respected women of the community. At that point Increase Mather, who had watched the proceedings without comment, published his *Cases of Conscience Concerning Evil Spirits Personating Men* (1693), which questioned the validity of the "spectral evidence" on which the court had relied and helped to undermine the proceedings. Mather did not question the validity of witch trials, nor did he doubt that real witches had been hanged at Salem. Rather, he contended that the mere fact that Satan attacked the girls in the shape of a particular woman—the principal evidence the court was using—did not necessarily prove that the person whose shape he used had consented. The devil's powers were greater than that. Indeed, some began to suspect that the town's confusion suggested that Satan had impersonated innocent persons for the very purpose of wreaking havoc in staid New England. Cotton Mather, with some support from his father, continued to defend at least the initial actions of the court.

Perhaps the most surprising aspect of the witch trials at Salem was that they occurred as late as they did. England had experienced witch frenzies of its own during the seventeenth century but none after 1660. In the British world, only remote New England and, in 1695, the equally remote and equally devout region of western Scotland tried witches in the last decade of the seventeenth century. Thereafter, witch trials were confined to still more-remote areas, such as the Scottish Highlands. A significant portion of the population still believed in witches, but some educated persons began to doubt their existence, and most came to doubt the courts' ability to detect them. Without the support of such elite persons, belief in witches could persist; witch trials could not.[37]

The witch trials at Salem, and the diverse responses to them, help illuminate the uncertainties that accompanied the intellectual crosscurrents to which professing Puritans were subjected. That uncertainty is well illustrated in the case of Increase and Cotton Mather, the father and son who served for nearly 40 years as copastors of Boston's North Church. Both men denounced the innovations at Brattle Street and continued to defend the concept of New England's special mission. Both endorsed the doctrine of special providences and rejected purely natural or materialist explanations of worldly affairs. Yet neither altogether opposed the new learning or the new ways. If they tried to forestall the appearance of Episcopacy in New England and the trend toward Presbyterianism in the region's churches, they strongly supported the Heads of Agreement that produced a union of Congregationalists and Presbyterians in England. They even relaxed some of their opposition to Episcopacy per se. Thus when Increase Mather met the Anglican archbishop Tillotson in England when Mather was seeking a renewal of the Massachusetts charter, he wrote respectfully that "had the Sees in England, fourscore years ago been filled with such Arch-bishops and Bishops . . . there had never been a New-England."[38]

Both Mathers closely followed advances in science. In 1683, Increase organized a short-lived Boston Philosophical Society that was modeled on the Royal Society of London, to which he sent some of the Boston society's papers. Cotton sent papers repeatedly to London, some of which were published in the prestigious *Transactions*, especially those on his favorite subject of medicine. The Mathers were of that generation at the end of the seventeenth century for whom the Newtonian doctrine of a universe of predictable laws had not yet come to preclude an intervening or overruling providence, as it apparently did not for Newton himself, who continued to believe in a God who exerted his powers continuously to sustain the physical laws that Newton discovered.

The Mathers were certainly not the only New Englanders to preach and write about witchcraft, in which there was still a commonplace belief. Suspicions of witchcraft continued well into the eighteenth century, before the Newtonian ideal of a universe governed by regular laws began to be interpreted in a manner that excluded all opportunities for individual providences and a rejection of the supernatural. At the end of the seventeenth century, many, in both England and New England, looked for ways to join the idea of a predictable natural world with the traditional doctrine of providence.

Indeed, when the Salem trials were finally halted, it was partly through the efforts of Puritan ministers, including Increase Mather, whose arguments against spectral evidence were as fully rooted in the Puritan worldview as those that his son Cotton used to support the same evidence. In his *Cases of Conscience*, the elder Mather fully accepted the presence of specters. His only caution concerned their reliability as evidence: Satan could impersonate innocent persons as well as witches. Spectral evidence was still useful, but only as corroboration of guilt, not as certain proof.

Increase Mather's writings on the spiritual world present an illuminating picture of a loyal Puritan attempting to come to terms with the advances of science—without, insofar as possible, breaking with New England tradition.

Following the appearance of two comets in 1682 and 1683, Mather read every-thing he could find on comets and produced his *Kometographia, Or a Discourse Concerning Comets* (1683). The work began by recounting the latest scientific explanations of comets, but for Mather, science was only part of the story. He went on to survey the history of comets, restating their traditional meaning as portents or warnings and arguing that every appearance in history of a comet had been followed by war or plague or famine. Mather was able to "improve" the occasion by turning his study of comets into a jeremiad against the sins of the people and the dangers that would befall them if they did not return to the godly path that their ancestors had tread.[39]

In *The Doctrine of Divine Providences* (1684), Mather offered his own explana-tion of the role of scientific observation within a religious worldview. Accord-ing to Mather, God had indeed established a regular order of nature, which followed laws fully observable by scientific methods. In that sense, his under-taking represented an application of scientific methods to the realm of special providences. But the purpose of uncovering those laws was not to allow for scientific prediction or technological improvement. Not all events followed those laws, and the principal benefit of scientific reasoning was to highlight those occasions when they did *not*, providing a "clear demonstration that they were over ruled by a divine hand"—in short, special providences. In that sense, Mather's agenda was quite the opposite of Newton's. Thus although the Bostonian could capably summarize the natural causes of comets, he unequivocally disavowed the ability to predict when they would recur.

Others had fewer reservations than Increase Mather. In 1727, when a seri-ous earthquake struck New England, ministers throughout the region lec-tured their congregations on the latest natural explanations for the appearance of such quakes. None believed that such explanations posed a serious chal-lenge to the doctrine of God's providence, however. Although the earthquake might have followed a series of wholly natural happenings underneath the surface of the earth, it was divine providence that had allowed those things to happen. Thus the discovery by modern science of the event's immediate cause did not necessarily challenge either Puritan theories of original causation or the belief that earthquakes were divine warnings to an unrepentant people. The proper response to earthquakes remained reformation and prayer.[40]

Perhaps the most important result of the new intellectual influences on the region was what Bruce Tucker has called the reinvention of New England at the end of the seventeenth century. In the wake of the Glorious Revolution and the granting of a new charter to Massachusetts in 1691, the colony became, in form, like other colonies, a royal province, Puritan in worship but not in government. Under such circumstances, it became increasingly diffi-cult to conceive of the history of the region as a special mission on behalf of true religion, and New Englanders began to refine their view of the original Puritan errand. In the newly tolerant atmosphere of the late seventeenth and early eighteenth centuries, it was no longer politic for the descendants of the

Puritans to claim religious purity as the principal virtue of their colonizing efforts. Now, with their coreligionists in England joining with other Reformed denominations under the banner of Protestant unity, New Englanders proclaimed that religious liberty rather than ecclesiastical purity had been the founders' motive. New England's participation in the Glorious Revolution had been motivated by the same cause as England's: the defense of liberty and property. In the process, the static, circular, or apocalyptic model of history on which the founders relied was gradually replaced by a newer progressive model; the creation of New England constituted a significant point in the progressive development of liberty.[41]

New Influences in the Chesapeake

The Chesapeake also was considerably affected by the advent of new ideas derived from such groups as the Latitudinarians. The sermons of Archbishop Tillotson were possibly the most popular religious works throughout the colonies in the early years of the eighteenth century. They were certainly important in Virginia, where they appeared in almost every significant library. William Byrd II's diary mentions frequent readings of his sermons, as on February 13, 1709, when he recorded that he had "said my prayers devoutly, having read a sermon in Dr. Tillotson."[42]

Among the most important conduits for those ideas was James Blair, an Episcopal clergyman from Scotland who arrived in Virginia in 1685 and served for half a century as the representative, or commissary, of the Bishop of London and leading clergyman in the colony. Blair came from the Scottish city of Aberdeen, which had a long history of moderate Episcopalianism and a long association with higher learning. He was a protégé of the famous Aberdonian bishop Gilbert Burnet. In Virginia, Blair helped found the College of William and Mary, the region's first institution of higher learning, and presided over it for 50 years.

During his years in Virginia, Blair published a four-volume series of sermons on *Our Savior's Divine Sermon on the Mount*, which illustrates his moderate temper. In those sermons, the Virginian preacher dissociated himself from religions based on a strict adherence to particular creeds. It was a "pernicious error," he wrote, to judge religion by mere "soundness of opinion." He was equally opposed to those who relied upon personal impressions of faith. Instead he preached a life of faith and works, a constant attention to "the narrow way of duty" fostered by devotion and piety. Blair identified with Anglican devotional writers, but he did not restrict his religion to their example. He was receptive as well to pietistic and evangelical influences and in 1739 was among the few Anglican clergymen in America to open his pulpit to the itinerant evangelist George Whitefield.[43]

Another important Episcopal official was the Maryland commissary Thomas Bray, like Blair a man of ecumenical spirit with an attachment to learning. Among the many projects that active churchman advocated was a proposal for the creation of circulating libraries in all Episcopal parishes in England and its colonies. Bray also founded two organizations that would play important roles in the colonies: the Society for the Promotion of Christian Knowledge, or S.P.C.K. (1699), and the Society for the Propagation of the Gospel in Foreign Parts, or S.P.G. (1701). The former was dedicated to disseminating Protestant literature; the latter funded missionary work in the colonies. A third organization, the Associates of the Late Rev. Dr. Bray (1724), concerned itself with the education and conversion of African-Americans.[44]

One of the first missionaries the S.P.G. sent was George Keith, like Blair a graduate of Marischal College in Aberdeen. Keith was a former Quaker who had come to the colonies originally as part of the Quaker migration to the Delaware Valley. In a schism that bore his name, he separated from the Society of Friends in 1692, charging Friends with insufficient attention to gospel order and Christian doctrine. He then traversed the colonies, visiting especially with former Quakers, many of whom he persuaded to leave the Society of Friends for the orderly worship of the Episcopal Church.[45]

The S.P.G. would have a long history of employing Scottish Episcopalians with ties to Aberdeen, partly because Episcopacy was disestablished in Scotland after the Glorious Revolution and Presbyterianism restored, and those who stood firm on Episcopal principles lost their places. But Scottish Episcopalians also shared with their countrymen the growing interest in the prospects for advancement in the American colonies. They would be especially active in promoting colonial education, in efforts undertaken not only by James Blair at William and Mary but by such others as Jefferson's teacher William Small, and William Smith, another Aberdonian, whom Benjamin Franklin recruited to head the important College of Philadelphia in 1753.[46]

Thus in the last quarter of the seventeenth century and in the first quarter of the eighteenth, colonial Americans were affected by a great many British influences, including the changing structure of British politics and British nationality, the changing conception of the prospects for advancement in the colonies, and the many new groups traveling to the colonial world. If the colonists were as yet hardly unified as Americans, they at least inhabited a continuous and connected series of British provinces. One result was that those societies were rendered less remote from the centers of intellectual life in Britain and less removed from each other. At the same time, their emerging identities as Britons probably served to harden the cultural and psychological distinction provincials felt between themselves and their native neighbors on the periphery.

two

A Transatlantic "Republic of Letters"

The elder William Byrd's lament in 1690 that "We are here att the end of the World, and Europe may bee turned topsy turvy ere wee can hear, a Word of itt" suggests another dimension of the isolation of seventeenth-century colonists: the absence of a rapid or regular communications network with the acknowledged center of their cultural world. It was not that the really important news failed to arrive in the colonies but that its arrival, dependent on whatever ships happened to turn up in American ports, was slow and uncertain. Dissemination of the news could be even more haphazard. It traveled first to those in authority, to merchants, gentlemen, and government officials, and from them to their regular correspondents on something of a "need-to-know" basis. News spread much more slowly beyond the port towns and below the level of colonial elite groups.[1]

Most of the organs for disseminating news and information that are familiar nowadays were conspicuously absent then. Electronic communications of any sort, of course, were wholly absent, but the differences extend far beyond technology. Printers in the American colonies had existed since the establishment of a press in Cambridge, Massachusetts, in 1638. Yet there were no newspapers or magazines printed in English America in 1680; the only periodical the colonials saw was the occasional outdated issue of an English paper that made its way aboard ship to America.

Printing itself remained a limited endeavor in the seventeenth-century colonies. By 1680, the first Cambridge press had been supplemented by another in that town and one in Boston, but the press's function, to serve the needs of the ministry, the government, and the college, was little different than it had been almost half a century earlier. Presses published the colony's laws and religious codes, along with psalm books, catechisms, and other reli-

31

gious works, whose orthodoxy was guaranteed by a clerical board of censors. After 1680, they also published the numerous works of the Mathers, father and son, the leading ministers in Boston; their clerical adversaries often had to send their responses to London for publication. Thus the early presses were certainly not intended to promote the free dissemination of knowledge.

By seventeenth-century standards, however, the colonies were not as badly served as it might seem. England itself had only one printed newspaper, the *London Gazette*, and competition was precluded by strict licensing laws. There were no papers printed in England's provincial cities, nor in Ireland or Scotland. Several of those places did have printers, and during the height of political agitation in the 1640s and 1680s both political and religious rebels managed to publish highly controversial handbills, pamphlets, and tracts, but in calmer days most of what saw the light of day was still tightly restricted by the dependence of printers on the authorities' license and patronage. That dependence was part of the reason that printing was still largely confined to the metropolis, or rather to the respective capitals of England, Scotland, and Ireland, with just a few other presses servicing the needs of the universities at Oxford, Cambridge, and Glasgow and of the diocese at York.[2]

Over the next half century, the availability of information underwent a dramatic series of changes in the colonies. Boston had five or more printers by 1730; three newspapers were printed in that city, and others appeared soon thereafter. Other papers were issued in Philadelphia, New York, Annapolis, and Kingston, Jamaica. A decade later, 13 newspapers printed in British North America served seven colonial cities. The total colonial output of printed works had increased four- or fivefold, to more than 100 publications annually.[3]

Equally dramatic was the increased availability of other kinds of printed materials. Throughout the eighteenth century, as during the century before, most of what Americans read was imported from abroad. During the first six decades of the century, colonial merchants and booksellers began to participate in a thriving transatlantic book trade, bringing to colonial readers a vastly expanded array of books in such diverse fields as religion, history, literature, science, and philosophy, and a growing number of literary journals from the European presses. Colonists developed an expanding and interlocking network of merchants, printers, booksellers, and even libraries to disseminate those works to provincial readers. By the middle of the eighteenth century, provincials were able to keep abreast of European news and culture to an extent that would have been impossible for their predecessors.

The first two William Byrds of Virginia help illustrate the effects of such changes on the reading habits of a wealthy planter. Whereas at the end of the seventeenth century the elder William Byrd lamented his lack of contact with the metropolis, his son was able to follow the news with considerable regularity in papers and literary journals that he acquired from London. He also managed to acquire one of the largest libraries in early America, comprising some 3,600 volumes in a wide array of fields.[4] William Byrd II was far from a typical provincial citizen. He was a book collector rather than just a reader and was one of the few Americans with sufficient wealth to fully indulge such a habit. But if few colonials followed the world of letters as actively as Byrd, the most striking development in intellectual life during those decades was the much greater range of colonists who were able to partake of an increasingly varied transatlantic world of learning. Some became active contributors to that world, including Byrd, who wrote three literary descriptions of his expeditions to the Virginia frontier, adapting the literary style of Augustan England—the England of Jonathan Swift, Alexander Pope, Joseph Addison, and Richard Steele—to his provincial surroundings. As we shall see, he was not alone.

The term for the literary world of the eighteenth century in which Byrd participated was the "republic of letters." That was also the name of an important literary journal that circulated in the eighteenth century and kept its European and American readers up to date on the latest productions in the world of knowledge. To that journal and many similar periodicals such provincials as James Logan and Jonathan Edwards owed much of their familiarity with developments in European scholarship, such as the works of the philosopher John Locke or the scientific theories of Isaac Newton.[5] That the republic was one of letters suggested the broad interest in a varied array of literary styles that developed among enthusiasts of knowledge. These were not narrow specialists in particular disciplines but followers of a wide spectrum of knowledge. That the literary community was called a republic suggested that participation was not confined to those of aristocratic birth or privileged place but was open to those who could contribute, including country gentleman and artisans, and, significantly, not only metropolitans but provincials.

The Press and the Provincial Public

So rapid was the growth in printing and the press that scholars examining the history of western Europe in this period have suggested that in those years a fundamental change in the nature of public expression took place. The combination of growth in the vehicles for public expression and the increasing ability to surmount the legacy of censorship led to the development of what Jürgen Habermas has termed an autonomous "public sphere," an arena in which an enlarged portion of the citizenry was able to register its opinions about civic affairs, and public opinion itself came to play a dramatically increased role in public life.[6]

The idea of the public sphere is provocative and useful if applied with restraint. It helps us to understand the significance of important facets of eighteenth-century American culture, including the prominent contributions made by printers, presses, and booksellers—most notably Benjamin Franklin, but several others as well—in diverse areas of public life. It also suggests the importance of the growing use of oppositionist political rhetoric by provincial legislative assemblies throughout the colonies, who identified themselves as the spokesmen for the public against the interests of governors and the empire.[7]

As is the case with most provocative ideas, there is much about provincial culture that the concept of the public sphere does not explain. Vehicles other than the newspaper may convey information sufficient for the creation of public space, as we shall see later in this chapter. Surely the type of combative public voice that began to appear in the press during the eighteenth century was not without precedents during earlier periods of public unrest, nor do assertions about the development of a public sphere explain all of what was happening in the world of transatlantic communications.

More important, perhaps, few papers actually served that role in eighteenth-century America, and such an interpretation takes inadequate account of the actual contents of the colonial press, very little of which was devoted to the kind of domestic political issues that would call for that sort of public stance. Most news in colonial papers was actually foreign news, lifted verbatim from London and other overseas papers, rather than commentary on domestic affairs. The rest was largely advertisements, mostly relating to commercial matters—ships arriving in port, imported commodities for sale—hardly sources of public contention. Indeed, the provincial press on the whole remained a good deal less autonomous than that of the metropolis for much of the eighteenth century. Even without formal licensing, colonial governments were still able to wield considerable influence over printers whose livelihoods depended, to a considerable degree, on the patronage of those in power.

More than just contributing to the development of a public consciousness, the provincial·press certainly helped foster a consciousness of the status of colonials as provincial citizens in an extended empire. During the first decade of the eighteenth century, Americans acquired a far greater knowledge both of the affairs of the farthest reaches of the empire and of their own place within it. In the process they became increasingly conscious of ties to other British and provincial citizens, such as a shared language and traditions, common loyalties to the nation and its political system, and a common participation in an extended commercial community, whose products formed the constant staple of advertisements and trade news in newspapers across the empire. In short, they increasingly came to belong to what the anthropologist Benedict Anderson, referring to the development of Third World nationalism, has termed an "imagined community" with other citizens of the empire, and especially with other provincial citizens.[8]

In fact, the growth of printing and the press in the colonies was one manifestation of a larger process in the British world generally, the spread of the press from the metropolis into the provinces. Before the licensing laws expired in 1695, no British newspapers were printed outside of London, but shortly thereafter they appeared in a variety of provincial towns: the port of Bristol in 1702, Exeter, Yarmouth, and Nottingham by 1710. Ireland and Scotland were not subject to English licensing, but neither had a newspaper before 1695, although both did by 1700. By 1725, there were 24 provincial papers in England alone; by 1745 the number exceeded 40.[9]

The spread of the press to the provinces had important results both within and outside of them. The provincial presses served not only to offer provincial readers greater access to news and information but also to put into print a far greater quantity of provincial news generally. Since much of what was published in the eighteenth-century newspaper was borrowed directly from other papers, the result was a larger amount of provincial coverage everywhere, which increased interest in provincial affairs in the metropolis. It also increased provincial awareness among other provincials. That increased awareness was exemplified in 1741 when two Philadelphia printers began rival journals— Bradford's *American Magazine* and Franklin's *General Magazine*—designed to cover, as the latter's subtitle proclaimed, "All the British Plantations in America." In the process, those provincial presses helped bolster the confidence and self-awareness of provincial communities.

The Emergence of the Provincial Public

The first newspaper published in the American colonies was the weekly *Boston News-Letter*, founded in 1704 by the Scottish-born bookseller John Campbell. Campbell had recently been appointed postmaster, and he used that position to advantage for his paper, obtaining early access to the news both from personal correspondence and by borrowing extensively from incoming English papers. His goal was to offer colonial readers a continuous narrative of foreign and imperial news, with a somewhat larger focus on Scottish affairs than was found in metropolitan papers. Campbell was replaced as postmaster by William Brooker in 1719, who began a competing paper, the *Boston Gazette*, the third in British America and the second in the mainland colonies. (Another paper had appeared in the British West Indies the year before.) Also in 1719, Andrew Bradford, postmaster in Philadelphia, began printing the *American Weekly Mercury*.

The association of those early papers with postmasters suggests something of their character. The *News-Letter* carried the heading "Published by Authority," and Campbell remained dependent on colonial authorities to keep his position as postmaster. Thus he intended not a controversial production but simply a running chronicle of foreign affairs as he received it; he fell well behind when he could not manage to fit all he received into his weekly half sheet, especially when he had military reports or other dramatic affairs to report. In fact, it was the news-hungry colonists' desire for reports of the war with Spain in 1719 that created the demand for two additional papers that year. Thus the market for news was driven by imperial and not domestic affairs.

The exception among those early papers was Boston's third weekly, the *New England Courant*, founded by James Franklin, an ambitious young printer who employed his even more ambitious younger brother Benjamin as apprentice. James Franklin had trained in London, where he had observed the growth of a flourishing newspaper industry that had specialized papers devoted to entertainment and to political controversy, and he incorporated both of those styles in his paper. Unlike its two rivals, the *Courant* was concerned less with transmitting news from abroad than with commenting on affairs at home. In particular, both Franklins opposed the Puritan clergy's claims to intellectual authority in the city and the colony, and they used satire to attack the ministers' pretensions. The paper's contributors, in addition to the two Franklins, included several of the town's prominent Episcopalians and others who scoffed at all religious authority; for that they were dubbed the "Hell-Fire club."

If the *New England Courant* marked an important stylistic departure from earlier papers, it was unable to sustain its approach for long. In 1722, local authorities, annoyed by Franklin's tactics, insisted that he clear his publications with them in advance. The printer ignored the requirement, pleaded the cause of press freedom, and attacked the civil authorities as well. That would prove to be his undoing. When the General Court forbade James Franklin to continue the paper, he tore up his brother's contract of indenture (while holding another in secret) and printed the *Courant* in Benjamin's name. That provided the younger Franklin with the opportunity to leave his apprenticeship and escape the confined environs of Boston for the freer air of Philadelphia, a story recounted in his famous *Autobiography*.[10] A few years later, James would leave Boston for Newport, Rhode Island, where he was able to publish his paper with less interference from civil authorities.

If the emphasis in the *Courant* on secularization and freedom of the press seems natural and modern to most of us, it is worth remembering that the world in which it existed was vastly different from our own. Such issues hardly had the same meaning in the eighteenth century as they do in the twentieth. When the *Courant* first appeared in 1721, Boston was in the midst of an outbreak of smallpox. The city was racked with controversy over a plan, proposed by Cotton Mather and supported by most of the city's clergy, to inoculate residents against the disease. Inoculation was still an untested idea in 1721, and the *Courant* entered the fray in opposition to the clergy and its plan. Adopting a satirical tone, the paper recalled Mather's earlier support for the witchcraft trials at Salem and the great good his meddling had done for that community.

In fact the *Courant*'s position was not without scientific basis. It was supported by most of Boston's medical community, including the Scottish-born doctor William Douglass, the only doctor with an actual medical degree, from the world-renowned medical school at Leyden. Douglass did not dispute the possibility that inoculation might work in individual cases. His concern was for the public health, and he questioned whether the application of such an untested procedure by untrained hands in the midst of an epidemic would not introduce more disease into the already stricken city than it would prevent. As it turned out, inoculation was successful, and the Boston experiment was cited thereafter on both sides of the Atlantic—even by Douglass—to justify the further use of inoculation during smallpox epidemics.[11]

Not until after 1730 did a dedicated oppositionist newspaper appear in the colonies: the *New York Weekly Journal*, founded by a faction of New York politicians opposed to the administration of the royal governor, William Cosby, and printed by John Peter Zenger. The *Journal*, written largely by the Scottish lawyer James Alexander, attacked Cosby for self-serving and tyrannical actions. Cosby then had the printer arrested on a libel charge, resulting in the trial for which Zenger became famous.

In American lore, the Zenger trial was a milestone in securing the freedom of the press. In fact it was a good deal less than that. In order to weaken Zenger's defense, the court had his principal lawyers, James Alexander and William Smith, disbarred. In their place they brought in Benjamin Franklin's friend Andrew Hamilton from Philadelphia, but the task Hamilton faced was considerable. According to legal precedent, the truth of the libel was no defense; in fact it was an aggravation, rendering the libel more likely to be believed. Hamilton had to persuade jury members to go beyond deciding the facts of the case—Zenger clearly had printed the attacks on the governor—which the court contended were the only issues they were to consider. He defended instead the right and even the duty of the public to maintain a watchful eye over the actions of its governors and of the jury as its representatives to judge their actions.

The Zenger case did less to establish the rights of the press than popular tradition suggests. In fact, colonial governments continued to try cases of seditious libel throughout the century, often with more success than Cosby had. The case may have been more significant as a political precedent than as a legal one. What Alexander's faction claimed was not press freedom per se but rather the people's right to challenge their governors; that, according to Alexander, marked the difference between political liberty and enslavement. Alexander's theme was popularized in such English oppositional writings as John Trenchard and Thomas Gordon's political essays, *Cato's Letters* (1720–1723), to which Alexander was certainly indebted. Zenger's defenders did not necessarily grant the governors a reciprocal right to free expression. James Alexander published a *Brief Narrative* of the trial, which achieved great popularity and was cited whenever conflict brewed between the public and its officials. It was twice reprinted in London in the midst of controversies there over citizens' rights to criticize the authorities, an example of the influence of provincial developments on metropolitan consciousness.[12]

Cato's Letters, and especially that series's letters on press freedom, were highly popular in the colonial press. When James Franklin was imprisoned in Boston, his brother Benjamin opened the next issue of the *Courant* with one of those essays on liberty of the press, and similar essays were republished repeatedly thereafter. Printers throughout the colonies regularly defended the *concept* of press freedom; in Philadelphia, for example, during the Zenger prosecution the city's rival newspapers, with opposing positions on the *politics* of the case, endorsed the case for press freedom.

Paradoxically, the very popularity of the Cato essays suggests some of the limits on free expression that remained in provincial America. One reason they were published frequently was that they were safe; they implied, but of course never expressed, any criticism of provincial authorities. Even without formal licensing, colonial printers who published attacks on local authority were still subject to prosecution and were subject even more to the threat of the removal of patronage; most colonial printers depended for their livelihoods on significant public business and could not afford the antagonism that a truly unrestricted stance would cause.

Thus even in its discussions of purely political matters, the colonial press often did as much to connect provincial readers to conversations in the larger imperial world as it did to link them to political conflicts at home. On imperial matters, the colonial press had considerable freedom to choose its position, and colonial papers overwhelmingly identified with English opposition spokesmen, such as Trenchard and Gordon, and with political and religious dissenters. The colonial press was at least as important in encouraging provincials to think of themselves as members of a commonwealth of liberty and trade as it was in promoting the exercise of that liberty at home.

The Provincial Spectator

After the collapse of the *New England Courant,* a new paper appeared in Boston, the *New England Weekly Journal.* Like the *Courant,* it employed an entertaining style with the goal of amusing its readers, but it did not have the earlier paper's overtly political stance. Both were modeled on the London *Spectator,* the spectacularly successful daily journal issued by Joseph Addison and Richard Steele from 1711 through 1714. Both its influence and its audience were immense; within a fortnight of its inception, Addison was estimating that the 3,000 daily papers printed reached some 60,000 readers in the city. Its long-term influence was even greater. The *Spectator* was reprinted in book form repeatedly over the next century and beyond, on both sides of the Atlantic, and was among the most frequently read works of that century. It spawned numerous imitators, including the *Gentleman's Magazine* of London, the Edinburgh-based *Scots Magazine,* and Eliza Haywood's *Female Spectator.*

The *Spectator* was as influential in America as it was abroad. In his *Autobiography*, Benjamin Franklin recounted how, as an apprentice, he had first taught himself to write effective prose by studying and then imitating the *Spectator*'s style and method of argument. In the colonial South, according to the intellectual historian Richard Beale Davis, the *Spectator* was easily the most popular literary journal in the eighteenth century, along with Addison and Steele's earlier compilation, the *Tatler*. William Byrd was receiving and reading the *Tatler* in Virginia as early as 1710. More than half a century later, on the Virginia estate of Robert Carter, the new tutor, Philip Fithian, commenced the eldest daughter's education with readings from the *Spectator*.[13]

The *Spectator* was renowned for its graceful, "polite" style, which was affable in tone, hostile to bigotry in religion or politics, and spread a moderate but uplifting influence both in manners and in taste. It was meant to persuade, rather than to argue or command, as much on the basis of style and sentiment as on the specifics of the case; its authority was that of reason and reflection rather than of ancient authority or social position. Its characteristic form was the essay, shorter and less definitive than the treatise but more substantial than mere assertion—the perfect form to achieve its goal of persuasion.

To modern sensibilities, the concept of politeness suggests affectation and a concern with superficials, but its implications were rather different in the eighteenth century, when the subject of manners seemed a good deal more important, and considerably more substantive, than it does today. Politeness was most often contrasted with the opposing attributes of rudeness or "barbarity," a state of society, characterized by violence and the rule of the sword, from which most of Europe was thought only recently to have emerged. Using polite manners was one of the principal means of elevating society; one spoke of "polishing" rudeness to achieve civility.

The persona of Mr. Spectator was vital to the paper's purpose: he was the citizen-observer, a nameless Everyman whose specific identity mattered less than the soundness of his argument. Although it certainly was assumed that his rank was considerably above the ordinary, his influence owed less to the splendor of his rank than to the justice of his sentiments, and those were deeply embedded in observation and reflection. Mr. Spectator observed and recounted the foibles of everyday life, in effect elevating the reader to the position of judge of both public and private manners, led only by the arts of persuasion.

The *Spectator* had a number of recurrent subjects, including love and courtship, the amusements of the town, and the simple pleasures of country life. It castigated bigotry, foppery, and deceit. It was particularly scornful of those popular fashions that seemed to partake of luxury, vice, or excessive foreign influence, such as masquerades or Italian opera. It frequently addressed women. Mr. Spectator described himself as a frequenter of coffeehouses and the merchant exchange—he was often mistaken for a trader, he wrote—and he expressed the values more of the man of commerce than of the man of power or leisure.

Although the *Spectator* was written and published in the metropolis, from its very beginning it had a particular resonance in provincial cities and towns in Britain and in America. That resonance was due largely to the spectatorial perspective—the citizen who observes, recounts, and comments on the lifestyles and behavior of all classes of persons, especially those given to idleness and extravagance. The *Spectator* appealed to the conscience of the citizenry in lieu of invoking the commands of established authorities of any sort, whether of church, state, or Scripture. It implicitly empowered the private judgment of reasonable citizens such as one might find in the upper or middling ranks of a provincial town. Within such settings, the manners of the opera and the masquerade did indeed represent foreign intrusions.

The *Spectator* offered those provincial citizens an early expression of a form of British nationalist sentiment that was at odds with some of the more extreme upper-class manners of the metropolis. Both Addison and Steele had been dramatists before turning their pens to essay writing, and both had established identities as true Britons, opposing the influence of foreign drama and opera. For example, Steele's 1705 play *The Tender Husband*, dedicated to Addison, boasted both of British justice and of the virtues of British theater—some two years before England and Scotland joined together to form the United Kingdom. The Britishness of their sentiments—both Addison and Steele were born and educated in Irish Protestant households—certainly contributed to their provincial appeal.[14]

The *Spectator*'s influence on colonial expression was immense. Benjamin Franklin is a case in point. We have already noted that the young Franklin taught himself to write by copying the *Spectator*'s style, a style that was evident in his first published works, his Silence Dogood papers, which appeared in the *New England Courant*. The first number of that series opened with a virtual paraphrase of the first *Spectator*, the remark that "the Generality of People, now a days are unwilling either to commend or dispraise what they read, until they are in some measure informed who or what the Author of it is," a lead-in to the invention of a fictional persona.[15] Even Franklin's *Autobiography* has a marked Spectatorial character; Franklin is ever the observer, ever the commentator, recounting the foibles of his own life as well as the lives of others, winning sympathy through a disarming and witty style coupled with sound reason and reflection.

After 1730, the *Spectator*'s influence began to appear in the several literary journals that sprang up in the colonies, including Franklin's *General Magazine*, its Philadelphia rival, the *American Magazine*, a series of "Monitor" essays in the *Virginia Gazette*, and especially William Smith's literary *American Magazine* of 1757–1758, among many others. Indeed, the subjects Mr. Spectator took up, from the manners of popular amusements to the morals of courtship, were frequent subjects of provincial magazines and newspapers.

Another colonial writer evidently influenced by the style of the *Spectator* was William Byrd II, whose writings circulated in manuscript in England and in Virginia during his lifetime. Byrd composed a trilogy, the *History of the Dividing Line Run in the Year 1728*, *Journey to the Land of Eden*, and *Progress to the Mines*, which described his visits to western properties in Virginia and Carolina. One of his purposes certainly was to amuse—the purpose for which he circulated the manuscripts. They did so by poking fun at both his and his fellows' foibles. In the *History of the Dividing Line*, Byrd described the joint expedition by Virginians and North Carolinians to survey the boundary line between the provinces. When the Carolinians, along with one of Byrd's fellow Virginians, elected to leave the expedition before the line was finished, Byrd wrote sarcastically, "This looked a little odd in our brother commissioner; though in justice to him, as well as to our Carolina friends, they stuck by us so long as our good liquor lasted, and were so kind to us as to drink our good journey to the mountains in the last bottle we had left." He continued, "This gentleman had still a stronger reason for hurrying him back to Williamsburg, which was, that neither the general court might lose an able judge, nor himself a double salary."[16]

Byrd's intentions went beyond mere entertainment, however. His works were also an acid commentary on the barbarity that lurked on the colonial frontiers, which he referred to as "Lubberland." There colonists lived with only the barest traces of civility. As Byrd described it, "One thing may be said for the inhabitants of that province, that they are not troubled with any religious fumes, and have the least superstition of any people living. They do not know Sunday from any other day, any more than Robinson Crusoe did, which would give them a great advantage were they given to be industrious. But they keep so many Sabbaths every week, that their disregard of the seventh day has no manner of cruelty in it."[17]

That concern with the barbarity around them constituted another reason for the interest of provincials in polite letters. The citizens of provincial towns and cities lived in conditions of civility surrounded by barbarity as they understood the term—Highlanders just outside the bounds of the commercial city of Glasgow, the "Wild Irish," the Indians of North America, and perhaps most important, colonials who seemed to regress to a state of barbarity on the colonial frontiers, as did Byrd's Lubberlanders. Polite letters were a means to polish, soften, and civilize, to advance society's progress and separate provincials from the wildness around them. The *Spectator* encouraged what one author has called a culture of refinement, the polishing of the rough edges of whatever incivilities one found either in manners or in sentiment. The culture of refinement even came to affect manners of decoration, pronunciation, and dress.[18]

The Spectatorial perspective had still other important ramifications in the provincial world, some of which we will discuss in succeeding sections of this and other chapters. The figure of the "impartial spectator," who judged his or her own moral behavior from a disinterested perspective, constituted the conceptual foundation of much of eighteenth-century moral philosophy. The figure was explicitly used in Adam Smith's 1759 treatise on *The Theory of Moral Sentiments,* and the term appeared in the dedication to volume 1 of the *Spectator,* from which Smith may have borrowed it.[19] The idea of the reader as spectator would play an important role in the development of a popular new form of literature, the novel. The *Spectator* would be read over and over by colonials familiarizing themselves with the world of polite letters and with the concept of civility itself. The perspective of the citizen-observer did much to enhance the confidence and enlarge the competence of a reflective citizenry living far from the centers of wealth and power. The persuasion to reflection found in the *Spectator* encouraged provincial readers to pronounce upon the manners and methods of the figures of authority at the center of the empire.

The Provincial Book Trade

Newspapers and literary journals were not the only kind of reading material that became increasingly available during the first half of the eighteenth century. Provincial readers also obtained access to printed books much greater in number, and of considerably greater variety, than they had had before. Local printers printed only a few of those varieties, chiefly almanacs, sermons, schoolbooks, and other short works that required a minimal investment from the printer. Longer works of every sort were almost always brought to the colonies through a rapidly developing and thriving transatlantic book trade, which continued to supply the bulk of American books to the end of the colonial period.

In 1680, that trade was far more limited. The only regular avenue for book imports, into New England, was led by a few Puritan booksellers, such as the Ushers, father and son. Their principal merchandise was religious works, principally those that the historian David Hall has referred to as "steady sellers," such as Joseph Alleine's *Alarm to Unconverted Sinners,* Lewis Bayley's *Practice of Piety,* John Bunyan's *Pilgrim's Progress,* and Richard Baxter's *Call to the Unconverted.* In fact, those were probably the principal religious books sold throughout the colonies. Other books were available, to be sure, but the only ones that arrived in large numbers were the ubiquitous chapbooks, or "penny histories," cheap, fragile, and abbreviated softcover works on almost any topic—from religion, mythology, and history to pornography—which appeared, and after several readings deteriorated and disappeared. That such works played a large role in shaping both popular and learned culture is beyond question. Precisely how those transient works affected those who read them or heard them read is a good deal more difficult to say.[20]

Half a century later, much had changed in the book trade. Religious works were still imported in great numbers; in fact, several new kinds of religious works were emerging as steady sellers in the colonies in the eighteenth century, including the hymns of Isaac Watts and the devotional works of Philip Doddridge and Eliza Rowe. More striking was the increasing number of other kinds of works that began appearing in America, such as philosophical works, histories, improvement manuals, secular poetry, and novels. Several of those kinds of works, and even a few of the genres, were almost never found in America at the beginning of the period.

Not only did the number and variety of books increase; so also did the methods for their dissemination in the American provinces. Before 1680, Boston's few booksellers engaged in the book trade as part of a general commerce; only near the end of the century did separate bookshops begin to emerge in that city. During the first half of the eighteenth century, booksellers and bookstores sprang up in many other provincial towns, including New York, Philadelphia, Charleston, and Williamsburg, while Boston's trade expanded apace. Equally important, book merchants and booksellers developed much more elaborate networks for selling their books outside the leading cities; Benjamin Franklin, for example, together with his Philadelphia partner David Hall, established additional partnerships with beginning printers and booksellers in South Carolina and elsewhere. Franklin and Hall continued to supply them with books, increasing the influence of that printing establishment, and of Philadelphia, in the colonial book trade generally.

As the center of the colonial book trade shifted gradually from Boston southward toward Philadelphia, the sources for the supply of books began to shift as well. Before 1680, of course, colonial book buyers had been supplied almost exclusively from metropolitan presses. Over the next 80 years those metropolitan sources were increasingly supplemented by contacts with the growing provincial presses. Even in Boston, Irish and Scots booksellers began to appear as early as the last two decades of the seventeenth century. South of New England—in New York, Philadelphia, and in the South—their presence was much greater. Those provincial traders certainly continued to buy from London suppliers, who remained the most powerful in the trade, but some new patterns even among the metropolitan sources suggest the growing influence of provincial Britons in British, and consequently American, cultural life.

The best example is probably David Hall, the young Scotsman whom Franklin took into his shop in 1744 and promoted to the role of active partner four years later. Before moving to Philadelphia, Hall had been employed by William Strahan, also a Scotsman and the head of one of London's most powerful book publishers. Strahan in fact was one of a small group of Scottish printers and booksellers who elbowed their way into the inner circle of the metropolitan book trade. At the same time they maintained their provincial contacts. Among the many works that group printed and sold were most of the principal works of Scotland's famed literati, such as David Hume, Adam Smith, and William Robertson. In part through Hall's influence, Strahan was

Charleston in South Carolina, by William Henry Toms, 1737–1739. I. N. Phelps Stokes Collection, Miriam and Ira D. Wallach Division of Art, Prints, and Photographs, The New York Public Library, Astor, Lenox, and Tilden Foundations.

able to extend his position as principal supplier of a large portion of the colonial book trade from Philadelphia south.[21]

Strahan was Hall's regular book supplier, but he was not the only one. By mid-century, the principal metropolitan houses were often undersold by cheaper provincial suppliers, who frequently printed without honoring copyrights, and Hall turned to several of those less expensive establishments for specialized purchases. Possibly at Strahan's suggestion, Hall began to buy Scottish Bibles and prayer books from several Edinburgh firms, and those sold well in the substantial Presbyterian market in the Middle Colonies. Hall also relied occasionally on book suppliers in Belfast and Liverpool. At the same time, a substantial group of printers and booksellers from those cities was congregating in Philadelphia.[22]

Books remained an expensive commodity for eighteenth-century Americans. One way that provincial readers increased their access to books was through borrowing, from the first American libraries. At the end of the seventeenth century, the Anglican missionary Thomas Bray began a campaign to develop parish libraries in Britain and America to give readers and rectors greater access to religious literature. Early in the century secular reading libraries began to appear, such as the Library Company of Philadelphia (1731), organized by Franklin, and the Corporation Library of New York, later part of the New York Society Library (1754). The latter was important as a circulating library, from which subscribers could borrow books, an idea suggested to New England clergymen at about the same time by the popular English Dissenting minister Isaac Watts. By mid-century, circulating libraries were appearing in numerous colonial villages and towns.[23]

One of the most interesting and revealing of those libraries was the one founded in Hatboro, Pennsylvania, to the northeast of Philadelphia, in 1755. It was organized by some of Hatboro's leading citizens, including Charles Beatty, the Presbyterian minister. The library contained its share of traditional books. Included in its early lists were such classic "steady sellers" as Bunyan's *Pilgrim's Progress*, Sir Matthew Hale's *Contemplations Moral and Divine*, and Baxter's *Call to the Unconverted*. There were numerous other religious works as well, including such newer devotional works as Philip Doddridge's *Rise and Progress of Religion in the Soul*, Elizabeth Rowe's *Friendship in Death; in Twenty Letters from the Dead to the Living*, and many works by Isaac Watts.[24]

The most interesting thing about the Hatboro library's list is that it contained so many newer works of a sort one would not have encountered at the beginning of the century. The list points out the importance of several whole categories of works, including literary journals, such as the *Spectator* and the *Tatler*; practical works and works on self-improvement, several kinds of histories, and novels. The rise of the last of those genres—the novel—was particularly closely related to the rise of the circulating libraries.

The Provincial Spectator and the Novel

Of all the types of works that became available during the eighteenth century, none had larger implications than the novel. Although literary scholars by no means agree on the exact definition of the genre or on what constituted the "first" novel, there is a general consensus that novels emerged as an important literary form during the first half of the eighteenth century, and especially in Britain. The novel's pioneers include such famous authors as Daniel Defoe, Henry Fielding, and Samuel Richardson, along with a host of other less well-remembered but once equally popular men and women, such as John Hill, Sarah Fielding, and Eliza Haywood. Novels were slow to take hold in America during the first several decades of the century, but after 1740, and in particular with the appearance of Richardson's novels, the works became increasingly popular and important.

In *The Rise of the Novel*, the literary scholar Ian Watt rooted the advent of the novel as a literary form in the particular social and cultural circumstances of the eighteenth century. Several points Watt noted are important for our purposes. Britain and its colonies in the eighteenth century were commercializing societies, ones in which working citizens were increasingly removed from the denser social web that one found in traditional economies. The novel both reflected and accentuated that individualism; indeed, the sense of individuality was essential to the emergence of the novel and distinguished it from more traditional allegorical forms. One of the earliest and most popular novels, *Robinson Crusoe*, examined man in isolation par excellence.[25]

The rise of the novel coincided as well with an increase in the reading public and especially with the development of an increasingly literate sector of urban women. Among the important themes that appeared in early novels—indeed, probably the predominant subject—was men's and especially women's career and marriage choices in the emerging commercial society of the eighteenth century, choices unguided by the hands of family authority in a world of ambition and deceit. That was the theme of *Pamela, Clarissa, Moll Flanders*, and many other early novels. It was no coincidence that Defoe published *Moll Flanders* and his advice manual on the subject of *Religious Courtship* in the same year.

The novel as a form was regularly condemned by leaders in church and society. Much of the negativity was due to the novel's subject matter, which often concerned seduction and romance; at best such novels were considered more entertaining than instructive. To combat that image, such moralists as Richardson—of a Dissenting background—attempted to make novels morally instructive, as in the tremendously popular *Pamela*, whose subtitle was *Virtue Rewarded*. Richardson's quest for the virtuous novel was ridiculed by Fielding, who maintained that the popularity of Richardson's novels resulted not from the virtuous sentiments they expressed but from the titillation they provided.

A number of recent interpreters have suggested that it was not only the novel's content but the form itself that caused opposition. By asking the reader to assume the place of the protagonists and imagine the appropriate thoughts and sentiments, novels transferred from writer to reader the final voice of authority, much in the manner of the *Spectator*, and thus allowed readers to reflect on and make moral choices for themselves. Although the narrator might seek to provide moral lessons, in the experience of reading and imagining it was the readers and not the writers who determined the work's meaning. In that sense novel reading also contributed to the self-awareness of a provincial audience.[26]

One can glimpse some of the implications of novel reading in the journal of Esther Edwards Burr of New Jersey, daughter of the famous theologian Jonathan Edwards, wife of Aaron Burr Sr., minister at Newark, and mother of the future vice president of the same name. After marrying Burr and moving to New Jersey in 1754, she kept a journal, addressed to her close friend Sally Prince in Boston, that recounted her activities, including her reading. During that time, Esther Burr, at her friend's suggestion, began reading Richardson's *Pamela*, the story of a poor but pious and virtuous servant girl who steadfastly resists the offers and advances of her less than virtuous employer. In the end, her would-be seducer is so charmed by her virtue that he becomes first her suitor and then her husband; hence virtue's reward. Esther Burr continued to write to her friend as she read the book, leaving us with striking information about its effects on such a reader.[27]

When Esther Burr began reading *Pamela*, she was prepared not to like it, having been told by Sally Prince that it was not the equal of Richardson's other novel, *Clarissa*, which they both had read. As Burr wrote to her friend, "Your judgment my dear has a very great influence on mine. Nay I would venture to report that such a Book surpast such an one, if you said so, if I had never laid my Eyes on 'em." She was far less willing to defer to the judgment of her author, despite her admiration for his other novel. After she had read the beginning, she asked, "[H]ow could Pamela forgive Mr. B. all his Devilish conduct so as to consent to marry him? Sertainly this does not well agree with so much virtue and piety. Nay I think it a very great defect in the performance." She even mistook the name of her author, calling him Fielding. "I am quite angry with Mr Fielding. He has degraded our sex most horridly. . . . I could never pardon him if he had not made it up in Clarissia." She conceded that the book contained "some exelent observations on the duties of the Married state" and apparently read those sections with great attention and care. By the book's end she was nearly satisfied, although she confessed, "I want to find a little fault for-all." She had no such reservations about her friend's judgment, remarking that "I have a poor judgment of my own. I wish you would be so good as to let me have your thoughts on this affair."[28]

Esther Burr was not alone in her willingness to criticize her author. In South Carolina, the genteel Eliza Lucas, soon to be Eliza Lucas Pinckney, recorded her reactions to the same novel in a letter to a friend in 1742, just two years after the book's first appearance. This young woman was far less enamored of Pamela herself than was Esther Burr. For all of Pamela's piety and virtue, Eliza Lucas considered her something of a braggart for allowing herself "that disgusting liberty of praising her self, or what is very like it, repeating all the fine speeches made to her by others when a person distinguished for modesty in every other respect should have chosen rather to conceal them or at least let them come from some other hand." She then proceeded to describe the changes in the text that would be required to accomplish that aim. Apparently she took the question of modesty, or at least the appearance of modesty, very seriously, which may have been an important value in the upbringing of a genteel southern lady, for she then interjected into the letter, "Here you smile at my presumption for instructing one so farr above my own level as the Authour of Pamella." Lucas concluded that Richardson's goal was simply to portray human imperfection, since "he designed to paint no more than a woman, and he certainly designed it as a reflection upon the vanity of our sex."[29]

By themselves, the lessons *Pamela* offered were hardly radical. Pamela was the model of the virtuous servant girl: she was pious and respectful toward her parents and her betters, except where their conduct precluded it. She valued her virtue above all things. It was precisely because her behavior was so unexceptionable that *Pamela* was able to induce its readers to engage with the novel, identify with its character, and apply their judgment to the situations at hand. *Pamela* was the first novel published in America—Franklin put out an edition in 1742—and quite possibly the most popular in its day, although there are some indications that Richardson's strident moralism was less popular in the southern colonies than was the detached wit of the more genteel Fielding.[30]

The rise of the novel has often been credited with an increase in literacy in eighteenth-century America, especially female literacy. Proving such an assertion is a task fraught with difficulties. For one thing, the attempt to measure literacy in the past, or even the present, is never a simple matter: reading leaves no marks. Thus historians attempting such a measure have generally had to infer reading from the ability to write, the latter often judged by the proportion of people who signed their names to their wills, compared to those who signed with a mark. Neither of those procedures is without flaws. For example, some individuals inscribed their names on one document and signed with a mark on another. Perhaps more important, historians have recently come to question just how close the correlation was between the ability to write and the ability to read. Writing and reading have different functions. Although in contemporary society those skills are normally taught together, in past times that was not always the case.[31]

All of which brings us to the far more difficult question of the meaning of literacy—why people learned to read or write, and how well. In provincial America, there were good reasons why more people could read than could

PAMELA:

OR,

VIRTUE Rewarded.

IN A SERIES OF

FAMILIAR LETTERS

FROM A

Beautiful Young DAMSEL,
To her PARENTS.

Now firſt Publiſhed

In order to cultivate the Principles of
VIRTUE and RELIGION in the Minds of
the YOUTH of BOTH SEXES.

A Narrative which has its Foundation in TRUTH
and NATURE; and at the ſame time that it agreeably
entertains, by a Variety of *curious* and *affecting* INCIDENTS,
is intirely diveſted of all thoſe Images, which in too many
Pieces, calculated for Amuſement only, tend to *inflame* the Minds
they ſhould *inſtruct*.

The FIFTH EDITION.

LONDON, Printed:

PHILADELPHIA; Reprinted, and Sold by B. FRANKLIN.

M.DCC.XLII.

Title page of Benjamin Franklin's edition of *Pamela* (1742), the first novel published in America. *Courtesy American Antiquarian Society.*

write. In most Protestant societies, the ability to read the Bible and the catechism in rudimentary fashion were considered essential components of religious education. One did not have to be able to read deeply, but one was expected to decipher passages for oneself. In colonial America as in such other intensely Protestant societies as Scotland and Sweden, reading was taught assiduously, and rudimentary literacy was high; in eighteenth-century New England, it was nearly universal.[32]

The purpose of writing was different. Writing was a craft, useful in keeping accounts in various professions and in the world of business. Only certain people were expected to know how to write. In general, women had much less need to write and much less opportunity. For most of the eighteenth century, reading was part of the standard education for males and females; writing was standard for males only. Thus the deliberately constructed writings of Esther Burr and Eliza Lucas take on added significance.

Despite the difficulties of measuring literacy in early America, certain aspects of it seem clear. Nearly everywhere, more men could read than women, and probably many more could write. Literacy was related to social position: the higher one's wealth and rank, the more likely that he or she could read and/or write. Literacy was more prevalent in the North, especially in New England, than in the South, which had a high proportion of young indentured servants, poor tenants, and slaves. Perhaps most important, literacy of all kinds apparently increased during the eighteenth century. The appearance of new kinds of reading materials apparently increased the importance of reading and writing and did much to alter the meaning of literacy for men and especially for women.[33]

Esther Burr's reading of *Pamela* illustrates some possible effects of the advent of novels on an educated female reader. Unlike the reading of the catechism or the psalmbook, for which the purpose was to imbibe the works' message and learn to recite it, Burr's reading of the novel was far more participatory. She and Eliza Lucas both reflected on the novel as they read it. If they absorbed its message of marital virtue and measured themselves against it, they also measured both Pamela's conduct and the author's artistry and intentions against their own standards. Neither woman developed those standards in isolation. Rather, Esther Burr worked hers out in her correspondence with Sally Prince, who in turn was part of a larger Boston circle of reading women, and probably in discussions with her husband as well; Eliza Lucas developed her standards while writing to a friend.

Richardson's novels thus encouraged readers not only to read and reflect but to discuss and write. The very form of his novels encouraged such communication; they were epistolary novels—works narrated in the form of letters. There is much reason to think that Esther Burr and Sally Prince were inspired to keep up a correspondence in the manner they did by the example of Richardson's other major novel, *Clarissa*, which both had already read. *Clarissa* is narrated largely through a series of letters between two intimate friends, who discuss their lives and thoughts with one another and reflect and comment on each other's behavior in an effort not only to maintain their intimacy but to improve their characters by reinforcing principles of piety and virtue. Burr and Prince had something similar in mind. As Burr wrote, "[Y]ou say ... that I must tell you all and every thing that is amiss in your private papers, and you seem to conclude before hand that if I dont find fault, it will be because I make *unreasonable allowances* for you." Sally Prince even referred to her friend, affectionately, as "Burrissa," a name obviously drawn from that of Richardson's heroine.[34]

For women to write in such a fashion, without the intervention of a male editor, was by no means traditional. Burr and Prince kept their correspondence private from all except Burr's husband, for fear that "all will be opened and exposed. . . . What in the World does any Villins want to see our Letterrs for?" When one Mrs. Browne, wife of the Episcopal minister Isaac Brown, asked Esther Burr to send her regards to Sally Prince, Burr did not tell her of their method of correspondence, for fear that "she would tell her MAN of it, and *he* knows so much better about matters than *she* that he would certainly make some Ill-natured remarks or other." She continued, "[E]verybody hant [haven't] such a Man as I have about those things."[35] Indeed they did not. On another occasion, Esther found herself in a lengthy argument with the college tutor John Ewing, later a Presbyterian minister, who told her, as she recollected, that "he never in all his life knew or heard of a woman that had a little more lerning then common but it made her proud to such a degree that she was disgusfull." Esther Burr let loose her tongue at him, as she described it, and after an hour had "talked him quite silent."[36]

Aaron Burr was a man of different sentiments. He was the only man to whom Esther Burr showed her friend's letters—she did show some of them to a few, carefully selected women—and Sally Prince requested his comments on several of her writings. When Aaron Burr was away from home, he evidently followed his wife's example; as she described it, "I am very proud I assure you for the good Man has followed our example and has wrote journalwise from day to day just as we do to each other."[37]

Thus Richardson's influence penetrated far. In Boston, Sally Prince helped organize a "female Freemason Club," undoubtedly because of the secret ritual in which they were all engaged—writing. Ellen Moers has remarked that for female readers, the principal lesson of Pamela may not have been so much *Virtue Rewarded*—the book's subtitle—as writing rewarded, since Pamela owed her victory not simply to her steadfast defense or her virtue but to her willingness to express her thoughts in writing.[38] To Eliza Lucas Pinckney, letter writing was part of the process of polishing the sentiments of a young woman of gentility and fashion. For Esther Burr and Sally Prince, there can be little doubt that both lessons were of vital importance. Reading as well as writing were important contributors to the establishment of their female identities.

If reading novels contributed to an expansion of literacy in America, especially among the female population, there is also reason to think that the novels' messages contributed to a broadened conception of the religious life. Esther Burr was the daughter of one of the most influential Calvinist clergymen in America, Jonathan Edwards, and the wife of another. Her journal reveals throughout a strong sense of religious duty. It also seems that she came to define those duties, including such activities as reading and writing and reflecting thereon, much more broadly than had her Puritan predecessors.

Libraries and Self-improvement

The most unusual of the Hatboro Circulating Library's records are the loan records, which contain the borrowing records for the library's early subscribers. An analysis of the borrowers list illuminates a number of the themes we have considered and also confirms the popularity and importance of such novels as *Pamela*, which was among the most popular borrowings. Of the 20 subscribers entered on the list between 1755 and 1762, the library's first 8 years, 9 borrowed *Pamela*, 6 of them during the first 2 years. For 2 of the subscribers it was the first book borrowed. Other novels were also popular, including *Tom Jones* (9 borrowers), Eliza Haywood's *History of Miss Betsy-Thoughtless* (8), and John Hill's *History of Charlotte Seymour* (6).[39]

There is no way to know for certain who actually read those books. All but one of the subscribers were male, but they seem to have been borrowing not only for themselves but for other family members also; some of the most popular books on the list were clearly intended for female readers, such as Eliza Haywood's *Female Spectator*, borrowed by 11 subscribers, James Fordyce's *Sermons to Young Women*, and William Biggs's *Biographium Foenineum: The Female Worthies*. Eliza Haywood was the most popular author on the list; her works were borrowed by 16 of the 20 members.

Another category that pervades the Hatboro list is works devoted to self-improvement, whether in learning, commercial skills, or manners. Such works could be found on almost any topic; at Hatboro we find such varied works as *The Art of Memory. A Treatise Useful for Such as are to Speak in Public; The Preceptor: Containing a General Course of Education; The Method of Teaching and Studying the Belles Lettres;* and a variety of more practical works on subjects ranging from farming and metallurgy to matrimony. Daniel Defoe was one of the most important writers of this kind of work, producing such varied works as *The Complete English Tradesman, Religious Courtship,* and *The Family Instructor*.

The eighteenth century has frequently been called the "age of improvement" in Great Britain. Nowhere was improvement more apparent than in the provinces, as provincial citizens, attending to their place in an expansive but increasingly interconnected empire, looked for ways to catch up to, or at least narrow the gap between themselves and, their metropolitan neighbors.

Thus in Scotland, one found countless projects devoted to improving the nation's agriculture, industry, commerce, manners, learning, and almost anything else one could think of.[40]

So it was in the American colonies. No work provides a better illustration of the projector's mentality than the *Autobiography* of Benjamin Franklin. Franklin was full of projects in almost every sphere: science, technology, politics, libraries, hospitals, and many more. Although his efforts in those areas exceeded those of nearly all his countrymen, they were far from unique: Americans sponsored institutions and inventions everywhere as part of a general effort to improve their society and refine their culture.

The quest for improvement was part of the novel's appeal. The works of Richardson and Eliza Haywood in particular were intended in large part as moral instruction with the goal of self-improvement. Certainly Esther Burr read *Pamela* that way, measuring herself against the character's virtuous pronouncements. After complaining repeatedly to Sally Prince that the author of *Pamela* seemed to be setting up riches and honor as life's only rewards, she finally observed, "I think there is some excelent observations on the duties of the Married state in *Pamela*. I shant repent my pains I guss."[41]

The standard Esther Burr used for measuring what she read was intensely Protestant: she read books as Protestants read the Bible, for their literal and moral meanings. She approved of those portions of *Pamela* that provided lessons in piety and virtue; she objected where she thought that the lesson offered was less beneficial, as when she thought that Richardson was "seting up Riches and honnour as the great essentials of happyness in a married state." She did not believe in multiple interpretations of what she read. Thus Esther asked Sarah to give her all of her thoughts about *Pamela*, for, as she wrote, "I know you have made every usefull remark that could be made." Throughout, Esther Burr was pleased with Pamela's display of virtue and especially pleased with the abundant moral lessons the book provided. In the end, despite her evident distaste for much that happened in the work, she concluded that it really was "a very good thing for all my ill nature about it."[42]

Because the benefits of novel reading were moral ones, Esther Burr made little distinction between the manner of reading a novel and that of reading any other kind of pious work. In fact, she barely distinguished between a moral character such as Pamela and any other devotional writer. Thus she used almost the same language to describe Pamela that she used for the English author Elizabeth Rowe. Rowe was "hardly mortal," according to Burr, and lived among "Angels and departed spirits." Pamela was "more than Woman—An *Angel imbodied*."[43]

That some of the Hatboro readers apparently shared Burr's sense of those novels is suggested by the pattern of book borrowing there. Of the nine members who borrowed *Pamela* during the first eight years of the minute book, three took it out at the same time that they took out Defoe's *Religious Courtship*, a book that advocated both affectionate marriage of the sort Richardson implied and proper attention to religious motives, including the idea that husbands and wives should hold compatible religious beliefs. Two other readers borrowed *Religious Courtship* or Defoe's similarly conceived *Family Instructor* together with Eliza Haywood's moral novel of courtship, *The History of Miss Betsy Thoughtless*. Such patterns suggest that those Hatboro readers, like Esther Burr, were reading *Pamela* as more than a simple romance. Perhaps those families had daughters of marriageable age. Perhaps the daughters themselves borrowed the books. It certainly seems that novels, beyond allowing readers unprecedented opportunities for reflection and self-assertion, were helping as well to inculcate moral principles in a spirit of self-improvement.[44]

The spirit of self-improvement was evident even in some of the religious literature that attracted provincial readers. An example was the volume of letters by the English poetess Elizabeth Singer Rowe entitled *Friendship in Death*, one of the most popular works at Hatboro. Rowe, an intimate of Benjamin Colman during his days in England, wrote her fictional letters with what might be called a practical spiritual goal: to impress upon her readers the reality of the state of immortality and to use that state to promote a life of piety and virtue. Esther Burr described her as "hardly a mortal altho she did die." Similarly popular were Philip Doddridge's *Rise and Progress of Religion in the Soul* and *Family Expositor,* both practical works intended to inspire and guide individuals to a religious life.[45]

The practical bent manifest by those provincials extended into the realm of science and technology, one of the principal areas in which Americans were able to contribute actively, as we shall see. Franklin's *Autobiography* illustrates how important the opening world of science was for young urban tradesmen in the early eighteenth century, how they eagerly sought to follow the latest experiments and learn of recent inventions. The same was true of artisans and provincial townsmen elsewhere in the provincial world, from Glasgow and Newcastle to Philadelphia.[46]

Much access to the latest scientific achievements came not from original works but from their reviews, including those in the *Philosophical Transactions* of the Royal Society and also in the journals devoted to summarizing the latest productions of the "republic of letters." Hatboro received the *Monthly Review (or Literary Journal)* along with the *Philosophical Transactions of the Royal Society;* other nearby libraries held much larger collections of that type of journal.[47]

Novels occasionally served a similar function. They were often the primary purveyors of information about places, ideas, and events in the literary world. *Pamela* is a good example; the long second part in particular contains lengthy discussions on such topics as the masquerade, the theater, and the world of ideas, including an exceedingly long discussion of John Locke's *Some Thoughts Concerning Education* (1693), perhaps the era's most influential work on education. It was probably in *Pamela* that Esther Burr first read about Locke. Novels therefore helped to draw a much larger circle of readers into the transatlantic republic of letters.

Provincial and Universal History

Perhaps the largest category of books at Hatboro, and probably at libraries throughout the mid-Atlantic and southern colonies, were works devoted to history and description. Nearly anything might be called a history in the eighteenth century, including such novels as *Tom Jones*, properly titled *The History of Tom Jones, a Foundling*, *The History of Charlotte Seymour*, and *The History of Miss Betsy Thoughtless*, among many others; calling novels "histories" provided an air of authenticity that blurred the line between fact and fiction in that still-controversial genre. A book on witchcraft at Hatboro was titled *Historical Essay on Witchcraft*, and James Mackenzie's medical manual was called *The History of Health and the Art of Preserving It*. Books on nature were called natural histories; there was also a *History of Oracles*. There were, in addition, histories of England, Scotland, China, Pennsylvania, and the Iroquois, along with histories of the popes, the Puritans, the Council of Trent, the British navy, and many others. If that were not enough, Hatboro also had general histories of Europe and the colonies, a general ecclesiastical history, Sir Walter Raleigh's *History of the World*, and a collaborative *Universal History*. And that was all in a small lending library![48]

There are many dimensions to the proliferation of histories in the eighteenth century. In part it reflected the decline of a wholly providential worldview and an attempt to relocate knowledge within a more tangible framework, in world history. In part it was a product of Europeans' growing concern with the concept of civility and what separated themselves from a rude, barbarous, and often violent past. Enlightenment thinkers, as we shall see, would develop an elaborate historical scheme for analyzing the stages of civilization from savagery to civility, a way of comprehending human societies that was referred to as "conjectural history" and that was considered no less valid than recorded history. Thus the historical came to be associated with the analytical, with realistic depictions of human society, as distinguished from legend and superstition—even if some of those depictions contained substantial legendary qualities themselves.[49]

Another significant dimension to the proliferation of histories was their great variety; provincials read not only their own histories but those of far-distant places, especially those to which they were connected by empire and trade. Histories thus had much in common with travel literature, such as Defoe's *Tour through the Whole Island of Great Britain*. Those tours, like newspaper coverage of distant parts of the empire and like the histories, helped to convey a sense of community within the empire and to allow provincials to view themselves as members of an imagined community of imperial and provincial citizens.[50]

Such histories differed greatly from the earlier histories New Englanders produced. To the Puritans, the purpose of histories was to record the fulfillment of the divine plan in their region. Their providential histories were simi-

lar to those produced throughout Protestant Europe and recorded in such earlier works as John Foxe's sixteenth century *Book of Martyrs* and the Scotsman
Robert Fleming's seventeenth-century *Fulfilling of the Scripture*, both of which
continued to be read in the eighteenth century. The newer histories differed
not only in their secularity but in their goal of empirical description, as well as
in their attention to matters of climate, custom, and lifestyle.

During the first half of the eighteenth century, as a mark of their new
provincial consciousness, provincials everywhere began to record their histories. They produced some outstanding works, such as those of William Smith
Jr. on New York and those of Cadwallader Colden on the Iroquois. The cul-
mination of such efforts was William Douglass's *Summary, Historical and Political, of the First Planting, Progressive Improvements and Present State of the British
Settlements in North America*. Douglass's work was, in effect, a universal history
of all the colonies that linked together into one grand summary the many
pieces his fellow provincials had provided.[51]

Provincial histories differed from earlier historical works in several
respects. Unlike the histories of New England, the provincial histories were
intended for an audience that was not a self-contained constituency identified
with the project at hand but a broadly informed citizenry both inside and outside of the province, capable of comparing the subject with similarly produced
works from other places and provinces. They assumed a set of common historical standards. Unlike the first Virginia histories, the reference point of the
provincial histories was not just the metropolis but the empire as a whole, of
which the provinces now seemed to compose a significant part. The later histories provided a sense of both tradition and location: in short, of provincial
identities.

Douglass, Colden, and Smith were all provincials by birth; the first two
were from Scotland, and Smith was born in New York and married to a Scot.
They came of age in the early part of the eighteenth century, in the aftermath
of the Union. They represented probably the first generation to identify itself
as both imperial and provincial citizens. In a number of areas, that generation
was the first to think collectively about the provinces' place within the
empire; thus it is appropriate that they were also among the first to write
provincial histories that moved beyond the particular to assume a larger
provincial and imperial story. Their histories were read by both metropolitans
and provincials. In that sense, the histories constituted a significant provincial
contribution to the world of information in the emerging transatlantic republic of letters.

three

Provincial Enlightenments

In the year 1752, a trio of young and well-bred lawyers in New York City set out to establish the first literary magazine published there. The *Independent Reflector* was the work of William Livingston, John Morin Scott, and William Smith Jr., all graduates of Yale, along with several other equally well bred associates. It appeared weekly for exactly 52 issues, until the journal's opponents, angered by its increasingly combative stance on matters of church and state, persuaded the printer to withdraw his press from the project. The *Reflector* was modeled on several British periodicals: one was the *Spectator*, represented in the new journal's production of polite essays, called "speculations"; two others were political publications by the Whig pamphleteers John Trenchard and Thomas Gordon, *Cato's Letters* and *The Independent Whig*. The three gentlemen's goal was to provide the citizens of their city with a journal of polite letters dedicated to civic improvement, to the advancement of the arts and sciences, and to resistance to civil and religious tyranny. In short, the *Independent Reflector* was designed to promote the principal values of the provincial Enlightenment.[1]

Three decades earlier, even before he began to work for his brother on the *New England Courant*, the young printer's apprentice Benjamin Franklin already was a great lover of books. Through the kind offices of a friend who was apprenticed to a bookseller, Franklin was able to borrow and read the latest works in a variety of fields: religion, science, philosophy, and literature. By 1725, at the age of 19, Franklin had composed a philosophical work that he called a *Dissertation on Liberty and Necessity, Pleasure and Pain*, which marked an early tendency toward religious and philosophical skepticism. Franklin was not alone among his artisan friends in having such interests: even as a teenager, both in Boston and in Philadelphia, he shared his reading and his ideas with a circle of eager young tradesmen; with those individuals he debated grand questions of religion, philosophy, and human nature, experimenting, in the process, in the various styles and methods of disputation and persuasion. Those young urban artisans already were absorbed in the world of the provincial Enlightenment.[2]

So, in her own way, was Esther Burr. The correspondence that the minister's daughter commenced with her friend Sally Prince, the daughter of another clergyman, was intended as much more than the expression of the feelings of friendship. It was also a forum in which to apply moral lessons. When Burr read poems, novels, or spiritual writings and discussed them with her friend, her purpose was to apply their lessons to herself, both to promote religious fellowship and for self-improvement. Reading and writing to Esther Burr were means with which to improve character. The same could be said of the whole network of "female Freemasons" who surrounded Sally Prince in Boston. In their adoption of literary pursuits, in their quest for moral improvement, even in their identification with the masons, a secular club noted for its dedication to moral and secular improvement, the female Freemasons were participating in a feminized version of the provincial Enlightenment.[3]

It should be obvious from those cases that the Enlightenment in America was a varied affair that affected diverse classes of people from different backgrounds and regions. We will notice more about those variations in the next three chapters. Until recently, one rarely found the term "Enlightenment" applied to America at all. The Enlightenment was considered essentially a European, especially French, affair, comprising the efforts of such prominent *philosophes* as Voltaire, Diderot, Montesquieu, and Rousseau to substitute critical reason and the scientific method for scholasticism and credulity—in short, an age of reason for an age of faith—until their optimistic presumptions succumbed to the violence of a French Revolution they were alleged to have brought about. An infant America had few philosophers of the stature of those French-speaking thinkers or even of their British or German counterparts. Americans therefore were deemed to have participated only marginally in the Enlightenment and to have contributed even less—at least until the enlightening of political principles associated with the American Revolution. Indeed, so closely were conceptions of an American Enlightenment identified with the thinking of the most prominent Revolutionaries—when it was considered at all—that a major collection of documents published under the title *The American Enlightenment* was divided into five sections, titled simply "Benjamin Franklin," "John Adams," "Thomas Jefferson," "James Madison," and "Alexander Hamilton."[4]

In recent years, historians have taken a broader approach to the Enlightenment in general. If the Enlightenment produced some of the most renowned intellectuals in the history of the Western world, those thinkers, we can now see, were less far removed from the cultures in which they lived than previous generations have supposed; below the level of the most renowned of the *philosophes*—or literati, as they are often called in English—was a reading public that was largely and deeply interested in and affected by Enlightenment ideas. The literati were also more widely distributed than has been previously emphasized, with representatives not only in France but in Scotland, England, Ireland, Germany, Switzerland, the Netherlands, Poland, Sweden, and America, among other places, with considerable strength in the provinces as well as in the cultural capitals.[5] America's political enlightening of the Revolutionary generation can now be seen to have been integrally related to the broader culture of the Enlightenment.

The Enlightenment, so conceived, was not the affair of a small group of leaders but of a much broader array of citizens in many places. In addition to the "High Enlightenment" of the *philosophes*, historians now write of a "Low Enlightenment" in the world of the middling and lower classes and of the vast expansion of printed works directed at such people. They also have written of a moderate Enlightenment, of radical and skeptical Enlightenments, of genteel and evangelical Enlightenments, and of Enlightenments of the province and the village, of the aristocracy, of the tradesmen, and of women. Scholars now pay much more attention to the institutional manifestations of Enlightenment in the clubs and lodges and associations of the eighteenth century rather than just in the isolated musings of individuals. Enlightenment, in this view, was a cultural movement of widespread, if somewhat imprecise, appeal.[6]

When Enlightenment is conceived this broadly, then provincial Americans—like the Enlightened citizens of such provincial European cities as Edinburgh, Dublin, Geneva, and Göttingen—can certainly be seen to have participated in the culture of Enlightenment. Moreover, in certain areas of inquiry, such as natural history, political economy, and the moral philosophy of everyday life, provinciality offered special possibilities and a particular slant to Enlightenment inquiries, allowing provincials to become not just participants in but active contributors to Enlightenment culture. In fact, the Enlightenment constituted an important underpinning for the meaning of provinciality itself, as we shall see. Conversely, the culture of the province strongly influenced the nature of the American Enlightenment as well as that of several other countries.

What Was the Enlightenment?

The question "What is Enlightenment?" was first posed by the German philosopher Immanuel Kant near the end of the eighteenth century. It has not been an easy question to answer. To Kant, Enlightenment was a search for truth, the freeing of human knowledge from the chains of suppression and superstition with which it had long been bound; Kant did, however, distinguish what was attained in the actual "age of Enlightenment" from the pure idea of Enlightenment itself. To him, *"Dare to know!"* was the "motto of the Enlightenment."[7]

To subsequent writers, the eighteenth century was the "age of reason"—the title, in fact, of one of the works of the international revolutionary Thomas Paine—in which rational knowledge replaced credulity and superstition. But as twentieth-century scholars have pointed out, the Enlightenment was not an uninhibited celebration of reason; indeed, some of the most renowned of the literati, such as David Hume, made their reputations by emphasizing reason's limits. Nor are present scholars as convinced as were the *philosophes* of the reasonableness of their decidedly optimistic conception of the progress of knowledge.

In the broadest sense, the Enlightenment can be identified with a particular version of a progressive view of history that emerged during the seventeenth and eighteenth centuries, one in which progress represented not the movement toward an otherworldly paradise but rather cumulative advances in intellectual, cultural, technological, and even moral affairs on earth. That such a view was closely related to earlier Christian millennial visions was pointed out early in this century by the historian Carl Becker, in his *Heavenly City of the Eighteenth-Century Philosophers* (1932).[8] Indeed, the *philosophes'* call for the removal of impediments to the advancement of knowledge paralleled in important respects the effort by Reformation Protestants to destroy all barriers to attaining scriptural truth. At the heart of both movements lay the assumption that with the destruction of wordly corruptions the truth itself could be revealed. Remove the barriers and the people would see.

As the historian Henry May has argued, the Enlightenment in America intersected religious belief at almost every point. Many among the literati did not regard their secular goals as incompatible with Christian and even millennial visions; on the contrary, they believed that the two could be rather easily fused, as we shall see. The difference was one of emphasis: those we call Enlightened did not view faith and faith alone as the key to human progress but insisted on the necessity of rational striving in order to surmount the blinders to human knowledge imposed by arbitrary authorities—whether of church, state, or mere ancient tradition—and put knowledge on a new and more secure footing.[9]

Another way of looking at the Enlightenment is to consider it as partly an effort to work out the ramifications for human society of the scientific revolution of the sixteenth and seventeenth centuries. The significance of that movement was substantial indeed. During the very same centuries when Europeans were establishing footholds and colonies in the Americas, scientific thinkers in Europe were dramatically revising their manner of comprehending the world around them, undermining the philosophical edifice known as scholasticism, calling into question much inherited opinion about the world and its place in the cosmos. The implications were certainly not grasped all at once; nonetheless, from early in the seventeenth century, a varied group of scholars began suggesting some newer methods—in some cases, a whole new intellectual project—for reconceiving that place.[10]

American colonization occurred at a particular juncture in the history of the European mind. When the first European explorers set out for the Americas, and, some believe, even when the first English colonists arrived at Jamestown and Massachusetts Bay, they still possessed a substantially medieval view of their world. The sense of providential mission many of them held to was buttressed by the fact that in their intellectual universe, the earth still stood at the center of the cosmos. It was surrounded by a sun and moon and stars and by the heavens, all of which looked directly down on human affairs, the principal focus of attention from above. Such a view was supported by Scripture, the foundation of all truth; it was confirmed as well, or had been until very recently, by the authority of science and by common observation. The blending of those different authorities was scholasticism, which combined classical knowledge derived from Aristotle with the dictates of medieval Christianity and extended them both by a series of logical deductions.[11]

Even as Europeans began expanding their influence across a wider portion of the earth, much of the basis for those endeavors, and the foundations of knowledge itself, were beginning to alter. The astronomy of Copernicus, Kepler, and Galileo argued—against vigorous opposition from the Catholic Church—that it was the earth that moved around the sun and not the other way around. If that were true, the biblical story of creation, in which God places a sun and moon and stars in the sky, would seem to some to possess a different status, requiring, in a way that it had not before, a measure of explanation and interpretation. Moreover, the belief that the heavens surrounded the earth, and the centrality of the earth itself, no longer seemed quite so certain.

Events on earth only added to that uncertainty. The mass of data that Europeans suddenly confronted in the age of exploration about the varieties of human society that inhabited the earth made even the assumption of the centrality to human history of the spread of Christianity less self-evident than it previously had been. Moreover, the violent religious wars of the sixteenth and seventeenth centuries suggested to some observers that certainty itself was dangerous to civil society, a point confirmed in England and its neighbors by the emergence of sectarian radicalism and the turbulence it created in the revolution known variously as the English Civil War or—taking account of its effects in Scotland and Ireland—the "War of the Three Kingdoms."[12]

To some, those developments posed a stark challenge to the intellectual moorings of the age, reflected in the famous lament by the English poet and Anglican clergyman John Donne early in the seventeenth century that a "new philosophie calls all in doubt" with "all coherence gone." At almost the same time his countryman Francis Bacon devised an ambitious program to recast human knowledge through a new, experimental method in order to place it on a more secure empirical foundation. But the greatest step toward establishing a new foundation for knowledge occurred in the last third of the century with the scientific work of Sir Isaac Newton, which strove to identify general laws of nature that would rest on the certainty of mathematical proof. Nothing in Newton's work was meant to contradict religion; on the contrary, Protestant writers long celebrated Newton for providing the clearest understanding of the workings of God's laws in the natural world.[13]

What is called the Enlightenment was, in one sense, the continuation of that effort to place knowledge on a firmer footing. So impressive was Newton's achievement in reducing all of the varied motions of the universe to a system of uniform laws that for a century and more, philosophers of all sorts attempted to follow up his discoveries in the natural sciences by attaining a similar certainty through the discovery of an underlying system of natural laws in the social world. That international effort to establish such a foundation for the study of human society without depending on either the dubious assumptions of scholasticism or the ambiguities of Scripture is much of what we know as the Enlightenment.

The effort to study human society scientifically carried with it certain assumptions that were characteristic of Enlightenment thinking. One was that if empirical observation provided a valid approach to the study of human society, then human nature itself must be, in essence, everywhere the same. The behavior of people in different societies might vary from one to another; their natures could not, or else the quest for a science of humanity would be in vain. Thus much of Enlightenment inquiry consisted of a search for general principles that could explain all of the wide variations in human behavior in diverse societies. Some, such as the French *philosophe* Montesquieu, looked to variations in climate to explain diverse human adaptations to their environments. Others proposed that human societies differed according to their relative stages of development. The latter theory led to the creation of a four-stages theory of civilization, popularized by French and Scottish writers, which traced human evolution from a primitive hunter-gatherer state through the intermediate stages of pastoral and agricultural economies, culminating in modern commercial society. All human societies, it was supposed, fit into one of those categories. The analysis of those stages and the manner in which societies progressed from one to another provided the foundation for what we today know as the various social sciences.[14]

The name for such a broad-based approach to human affairs was cosmopolitanism, the belief in promoting the interests and concerns of all of humanity rather than following mere local, regional, or national concerns. Cosmopolitanism constituted another distinguishing feature of the Enlightenment. The *philosophes* were citizens of the world, an identity later claimed and lived by the English-born Thomas Paine when he supported political revolutions in America, France, and Britain and endorsed the goals of liberty, progress, and prosperity for all humanity.[15]

Paradoxically, the Enlightenment's very cosmopolitanism gave it a particular resonance in the provincial world. In common language, cosmopolitanism and provincialism are virtual opposites. The former implies the broad, urbane, even universal perspective achievable by those whose sights are influenced by the wide range of affairs visible to the inhabitants of the city; the latter connotes a narrowness of vision, localism, and particularism. Yet as the eighteenth century evolved, cosmopolitanism and provincialism—or provinciality, in a less pejorative form of the word—became considerably less opposed to one another. As provincial citizens gained confidence in their economic and cultural resources, they became increasingly aggressive in their claims for political and cultural equality with their countrymen from the metropolis. Within that context, provincials would come to regard claims for metropolitan supremacy as narrow and particular while supporting provincial claims with increasingly generalized arguments about the political and cultural competence of provincials—what might be called, in short, a cosmopolitan form of provinciality.[16]

Provincial participation in such discussions calls into question some earlier views of "The Enlightenment in America," the title used by Henry May for what is still the principal account of that event.[17] The implication was that the Enlightenment was essentially a European phenomenon, to which provincial Americans attended with some interest but without really affecting its nature. Yet if we look at the Enlightenment not simply as the intellectual construction of a small number of rarefied minds but as a culture of inquiry and intellectual involvement, then in a number of areas—in political ideals, in the world of science, and in the establishment of a moral philosophy of everyday life—provincials would be more than just consumers. Even as Enlightened culture spread through the reading public of provincial America, provincials offered their own sets of ideas that made them into active participants in the transatlantic culture of the Enlightenment and, in certain key respects, essential contributors to it.

Anticipations of Enlightenment

The age of Enlightenment is most often identified with the eighteenth century. Few such movements are without earlier anticipations. We can trace the origins of the Enlightenment in America at least to the later Restoration years and to the growing involvement of British elite groups with the colonies, which brought to the New World a number of individuals who would play significant roles in instigating interest in Enlightenment in America, including such gentlemen as William Penn, such merchants as James Logan, such educators as Charles Morton, and the families of such clergymen and tradesmen as Benjamin Colman, Benjamin Franklin, and James Blair.

In the sources of the Enlightenment in America, two groups in particular require special notice for their influence. One was the circle of moderate Anglican academics and clerics associated especially with Cambridge University in the second half of the seventeenth century, referred to as "Latitude-men" or, more generally, Latitudinarians; the other was a similar group of moderate Scottish Episcopalians connected to the universities at St. Andrews and Aberdeen. In fact, the term *Latitudinarian* has been applied to both groups. They shared the desire to transcend sectarian strife by de-emphasizing the significance of the forms and doctrines belonging to particular sects and denominations in favor of a more broadly based Protestantism. In short, they allowed Christians greater latitude to differ over small matters.[18]

Latitudinarians in general were suspicious of particularity and certainty in spiritual matters. They disliked and distrusted any form of religious "enthusiasm," or the belief in direct revelation that was found among some radical sectarians in the middle years of the seventeenth century; the sense that one had special instructions from God made individuals less amenable to moderation or compromise, or to reason itself. Latitude-men also disavowed those such as the rigorous "High Church" party among the Anglicans who enforced in a high-handed manner conformity to the particular practices and creeds of the religious establishment. Latitudinarians preferred a religion based on moderation, balance, and order, one that conformed in general to the natural order of things rather than to the particular prejudices of any one group. They were, in short, prominent representatives of the "Moderate Enlightenment," the predominant form of Enlightenment that existed in provincial America.[19]

Although the origins of Latitudinarianism have been traced to the academic circle at Cambridge University surrounding Henry More, whose ethical writings became standard in American university curricula, the term is most often reserved for the ministers, such as John Tillotson, who became Archbishop of Canterbury after the Glorious Revolution, Edward Stillingfleet, and Joseph Glanvill. Many of the Latitudinarian preachers came from Puritan family backgrounds and shared with their predecessors a fervent Protestantism and a distaste for the narrow creed demanded by High Church Anglicans; they were equally opposed to the rigidity of Puritan codes of worship and the instability and disruption those had caused. Instead, those men favored a broad approach to doctrinal matters, de-emphasizing extensive formal creeds and promoting common Protestant themes. Tillotson, probably the most widely read author in America in the early eighteenth century, was acclaimed for his genteel or "polite" style of preaching and for his emphasis on Christian morals. He was admired even by some Puritans who had far less tolerant religious views than his own.[20]

Along with their friend and contemporary the philosopher John Locke, Latitudinarian preachers participated in a dramatic shift in the definition of religion, away from both the Catholic view of religion as an integrated life of works, worship, and ritual and the Protestant focus on scriptural truth and saving faith. Instead, the Latitude-men followed Locke in maintaining a sharp distinction between what they considered the essentials of religion, defined principally as faith personally held and manifest in a commitment to Christian morals, and everything else, which came to be labeled, from the time of Locke, "things indifferent." Their goal was to achieve a consensus on religious matters organized around fundamental Protestant beliefs that would draw moderate Puritans into a broadly based Anglican Church.

Latitudinarians also helped shift the focus of preaching. Tillotson's sermons attained popularity in part because he preached at length on the benefits of religion, what religion could do for men and women, not only in the afterlife but in this world as well. In a sermon on "The Advantages of Religion to Particular Persons," Tillotson discussed the importance of religion for salvation. For Puritan writers, that would have been the whole of the subject, but Tillotson went on to consider other advantages. Religiosity, to Tillotson, had worldly benefits as well, such as improved understanding, health, and contentment.[21] In other sermons Tillotson set out to demonstrate the contributions of religion to the public welfare, to governments, and to the happiness of human societies.

In their attempts to forge a consensus on religious matters, Latitudinarian preachers also shifted the grounds of their defense of religion. Rather than relying on biblical command—which had led to generations of sectarian warfare, in their view—Latitudinarians defended religion by showing its conformity to nature and to reason. Much of the impetus for scientific discovery in the late seventeenth and early eighteenth centuries came less from the promise of technological benefits, which were still far from being realized, than from its potential to uphold religious truth by demonstrating the grand design that underlay nature, a perfection that seemed inconceivable without the constant exertions of providential will. "Natural religion," as that form of religion came to be called, would be among the foremost intellectual movements in the British world in the eighteenth century.[22]

Their interest in nature led Latitudinarians to develop a considerable interest in science. Several of those who came to be known as Latitude-men were among the leaders in establishing the Royal Society of London for the Promotion of Natural Knowledge in 1662, the first scientific society in England. Several men with Latitudinarian principles participated in the famous Boyle lectures at the end of the century, instituted by a legacy from the renowned scientist Robert Boyle. Those lectures helped disseminate among the public the Newtonian idea of a universe that conformed to fixed laws, but their underlying motive was to promote religiosity by demonstrating the basic conformity of nature to God's law. Several published works that grew out of that effort would be widely read and cited in America, including William Whitson's *New Theory of the Earth* (1696), Samuel Clarke's *A Discourse Concerning the Unchangeable Obligations of Natural Religion* (1706), and William Wollaston's *Religion of Nature Delineated* (1722). Whitson and Clarke had both been Boyle lecturers.[23]

The other important group associated with the Latitudinarians derived from the moderate Episcopal community in and around the Scottish universities at Aberdeen. They included the famous bishop Gilbert Burnet, who left the tumult of ecclesiastical conflict of Restoration Scotland to assume a bishopric in England; Burnet became Bishop of Salisbury after the Glorious Revolution. From his English post he helped direct a number of Scottish Episcopalians to the colonies, including the Virginian James Blair. Those Scots manifest a politically more conservative form of Latitudinarianism that would have a pronounced influence in Virginia and several other sectors of provincial society, as we shall see.[24]

The appeal of the Latitudinarians in America was extremely broad. In England, their goal of incorporating moderate dissenters into a broadly based church had produced only mixed results. In the provinces, where a dominant church hierarchy was lacking everywhere, it had a wide resonance, appealing both to the dissenting majorities in most northern colonies and to the gentry-dominated, Low Church establishments to the south. Moreover, Latitudemen such as Tillotson established conclusively that even a religion of conscience could be preached in language fit for polite company, which was especially suitable to the religious temperament of the emerging southern planter class; William Byrd, for example, read his sermons regularly.[25]

Another reason for the Latitudinarians' appeal to provincials was that although they spoke as members of an established church, the implication of their preaching was to locate the ultimate authority in religion not in the church but in the mind of the individual. Like their Puritan predecessors, and unlike their High Church colleagues among the Anglicans, Latitudinarians addressed their listeners' consciences directly. In attempting to demonstrate the conformity of religion to the natural order, they assumed that hearers were to judge for themselves rather than take the pronouncements of the church for granted.

The First American Enlightenment

One of the earliest manifestations of the Enlightenment in America emerged at Harvard during the last 15 years of the seventeenth century, during the presidency of Increase Mather. Mather combined his presidency with other duties, including his ministry in Boston's North Church and a prolonged mission to England from 1688 until 1692 during which he attempted to restore the Massachusetts Charter. In Mather's absence, Harvard was led by its tutors, John Leverett—who would become president of the college in 1708—and William Brattle. Those younger teachers helped to direct the college's curriculum away from its former reliance on scholastic texts and toward those of the new philosophy, including the ethics text of the Cambridge Platonist Henry More and the natural philosophy work of the English Dissenter and educator Charles Morton, who emigrated to Massachusetts in 1686.[26]

Among those trained by Leverett and Brattle in Mather's absence were a group of Puritan clergymen who came to be known as "Catholicks" for their

A Prospect of the Colledges in Cambridge in New England

Harvard College circa 1725 by William Burgis, 1743. *I. N. Phelps Stokes Collection, Miriam and Ira D. Wallach Division of Art, Prints and Photographs, The New York Public Library, Astor, Lenox, and Tilden Foundations.*

tolerant, or catholic, approach to religious practice. They included a number of men who became prominent ministers, including Benjamin Wadsworth, Thomas Foxcroft, Ebenezer Pemberton, and most important, Benjamin Colman of Brattle Street Church. Together, they did much to modernize Puritanism and to bring New English religion closer to British norms.[27]

In their support for the new learning and for a new approach to religion, New England Catholicks did not abandon Calvinist orthodoxy. What they left behind were aspects of New English Puritanism that were particular to the region and that distinguished it from other Protestant and even from Reformed denominations or sects. At the Catholick Brattle Street Church, the congregation discontinued the most particular New English church forms, such as a strictly Congregational ordination and a church membership restricted to those deemed visible saints. In their place they instituted rituals that brought them closer to the Presbyterian and even to the Episcopal Churches, such as Presbyterian ordination, communion open to all moral members of the community professing faith, and the practice of reading from the Bible during religious service without comment or explanation by the minister, a practice that earlier generations of Puritans had referred to as "dumb reading."

Perhaps the most important contribution of the Catholick preachers in New England was in the realm of religious psychology. Puritanism, in most of its forms, had been rooted in a particular version of what was then the prevailing way of understanding the human mind, called the faculty psychology. Briefly stated, most seventeenth- and eighteenth-century observers divided the workings of the mind into various functions or faculties, among which were the will, the intellect, and the various passions. There was considerable disagreement about many of the particulars, such as exactly how many faculties there were or whether the will or the intellect was supreme. Nearly everyone agreed that it was incumbent on reasonable beings to employ both the will and the intellect to check the passions, which were associated with the baser instincts of humankind.[28]

By the latter part of the seventeenth century, some analysts had begun to adopt a less rigid view of the passions. As Latitudinarians and others began to move toward the view that the natural world should be analyzed for its role as the product of God's will, so some would come to regard the human mind as among the greatest of the divine creations. In that view, all of the human faculties must have had necessary and even beneficial functions. Proponents of such ideas came to consider the emotions less as signs of human frailty and legacies of original sin than as divinely mandated and necessary contributors to the welfare of human society. For the derogatory term *passions*, they would increasingly substitute the less pejorative *affections*.

In accepting a broader view of the functions of human nature, the Catholicks, without abandoning Calvinist doctrine, strayed a long way from Calvinist emphases on human depravity. If blind passions prevented women and men from following the dictates of human reason, benevolent affections could motivate people to pursue a reasonable and moral course of life. Whereas the goal of earlier Puritan preachers had been, in effect, to induce their hearers to suppress their corrupted natures, the goal of Colman and his allies was more nearly to improve them.

Catholick preachers such as Colman were pioneers in adopting such a view of the affections in religious discussions. One of Colman's first publications, for example, was a sermon on *The Government and Improvement of Mirth* (1707), which was hardly the sort of subject one would have found in the preaching of an earlier generation of Puritans, who insisted that religion required a sober temper and suppressed levity. As Colman wrote, "Mirth may be decent and good, since it is a shadow of heaven."[29] Mirth contributed as well to sociability, also a positive good. Colman's sentiments were influenced, in turn, by the writings of the great English Dissenter Isaac Watts, whose psalms and hymns were among the century's most popular religious works, and the religious poet Eliza Singer Rowe, both of whom he had befriended in England. Both Watts and Singer were noted for looking for ways to attach the natural affections to spiritual matters.

One of the manifestations of that altered sense of the affections was the attempt to reform musical worship in Puritan New England during the third decade of the eighteenth century, in which Colman and other Catholicks played an important role. Traditionally, the singing of psalms in Puritan worship had been a chaotic affair, characterized by highly individualistic forms of singing as expressions of the spirit. Beginning in the 1720s, proponents of what came to be called "regular singing" campaigned to reform the practice, to teach singing to congregations and to impose the use of regular harmonies rather than random expression, a position articulated in such pamphlets as John Tuft's *Introduction to the Singing of Psalm-Tunes*. Such reform was resisted by many congregations, who saw the movement both as a grasp for control by the clergy—which it was—and as a step backward toward a highly ritualized and uncritical form of worship of the sort they associated with Roman Catholics and Anglicans.[30]

In one sense the movement for regular singing was part of a broader Enlightenment effort to impose order on congregations and communities; the Enlightenment goal of finding the general laws that underlay the varieties of human behavior also included a considerable desire to impose order and regularity. Indeed, the "Moderate Enlightenment" consisted largely of an attempt to reduce human behavior to order and regularity and balance. For the colonial gentry, that meant curbing much of what they perceived as disorderly tendencies among the lower classes, whether manifest through radical or spiritual styles in religion, riotous politics, or disorderly ceremonial behavior.

Although regular singing was a means with which to impose order, its advocates were also concerned with the nature of the music itself and its effects on the mind. The effort to reform church music also implied a particular view of religious psychology, in which the beauty of the music could serve as a motivator for spiritual worship. The affections the music inspired were to serve as instruments of evangelical appeal. A similar view underlay the adoption of Isaac Watts's enormously popular versions of psalms and hymns.[31]

Catholick preachers did much to transform preaching in New England. Colman was noted for his elegant preaching style. His style emulated that of Isaac Watts, who in the words of Samuel Johnson "taught the Dissenters to write and speak like other men, by shewing that elegance might consist with piety." Thereafter, concerns with style would stand alongside doctrinal exposition in the composition of sermons.[32]

Catholick preachers, like the Latitudinarians before them, demonstrated a marked interest in the new science and in using science and the observation of nature to supplement Scripture. The Catholick approach to science was evident in 1727, when New England was struck by an earthquake of major proportions. As in the past, New Englanders faced with such unusual events resorted to fast days and prayer, but some reactions to the earthquake differed considerably from earlier pronouncements. Throughout the region, but especially among the Catholicks, the sermons included often-elaborate explanations of the natural causes of earthquakes, of nature's workings beneath the surface. Such explanations were intended not to replace providential ones but rather to amplify them: God worked through a wondrous creation. It was still He who set the causes in motion and He who allowed them to happen. Resorting to the natural was intended not to eliminate God's providence but to extend it by demonstrating how thoroughly and masterfully God manipulated the world.[33]

Preachers such as Colman read God's providences differently than had Increase Mather, for example. Whereas Mather had devoted himself to recording "illustrious providences," the focus among Catholick ministers shifted from the unusual to the usual. Whereas deviations from the course of nature had in earlier times represented the principal evidence of the workings of the divine hand, ministers were now as likely to examine the regular course of nature, finding in that very regularity convincing proof of divine power. Although God might transcend the general laws of nature at any time, he did so only rarely. Nature itself and not its disruptions became an increasingly powerful demonstrator of the divine will.

A few ministers went further. To Connecticut's Samuel Johnson, the appeal to nature and the new learning suggested some of the inadequacies of the New England way. Following in the path of those Puritans who had come to see purely Congregational forms as conducive to disorder, Johnson was one of a group of six Yale graduates who stunned the New England community in 1722 by defecting to the Anglican Church. Johnson defended their course through biblical citation; at least as important to that avid follower of the new learning was its consistency with order in church and in society. Johnson also followed such Enlightened English churchmen as Samuel Clarke in exalting reason above revelation as a guide to the divine order, although the New Englander would later repent the rashness of that position.[34]

Few New Englanders followed Johnson. Most continued to adhere to a Calvinistic faith in an all-determining providence even as they redefined the manner in which his will was to be read. In that shift, New English ideas resembled nothing so much as those of the English dissenting community, led by such men as Isaac Watts, who were increasingly absorbed with matters of natural religion, the religious affections, and the quest for Protestant unity. New Englanders also began to promote Protestant unity, following the 1691 Heads of Agreement that outlined a union—in practice more like an alliance—between English Congregationalists and their Presbyterian neighbors to form a "United Brethren." Both Mathers promoted the plan as closely resembling in practice the actual workings of New England Congregationalism, but they continued to resist the moves toward Presbyterian forms that appeared in Brattle Street and elsewhere. But the drift toward enhanced clerical authority and Presbyterian consolidation continued in the region, culminating in negotiations of a Plan of Union that would eventually ally American Congregationalists with their Presbyterian neighbors to the south.[35]

The Inner Light and the Moral Sense

New Englanders were not the only provincials influenced by Latitudinarianism, the new science, or the new learning of the early Enlightenment. Colonists to the south and west of the Hudson River began to adopt other kinds of Enlightened approaches to intellectual life. The sources of those approaches were more diverse than in New England. Although many colonists elsewhere also were influenced strongly both by Tillotson and by their contacts with English Dissenters, their communities were also influenced by their growing contacts with Scotland and the Protestant north of Ireland. Especially important among those contacts were the Scottish Episcopalian community associated with Bishop Gilbert Burnet and the Presbyterian academic community extending from Glasgow to Protestant Ireland. Burnet's influence was particularly significant; among those with ties to Burnet were Commissary Blair and other Episcopal clergymen in Virginia and elsewhere, the bishop's son William, governor of New York and of Massachusetts, and such Quakers as Robert Barclay, George Keith, and James Logan in the mid-Atlantic.

By the middle of the eighteenth century, Philadelphia ranked as probably the most Enlightened city in America. At its founding in 1682, there had been little reason to think that such growth would come about. The city on the Delaware had been established by Friends as part of William Penn's "Holy Experiment" to establish a Quaker homeland. Those early Quakers, with their lower-class origins, their radical agenda, and their visionary experiences, hardly seemed to anticipate the Enlightenment. Yet eventually strong affinities emerged between Quaker thought and some of the leading ideas of the Enlightenment, so much so that such eighteenth-century observers as the French *philosophe* Voltaire, the French-born American writer J. Hector St. John de Crèvecoeur, and even Benjamin Franklin offered Quakers as model figures who exemplified the provincial Enlightenment.[36]

In William Penn's generation, Quakerism itself began to change. A society that had been dominated at the outset by poor farmers and tradesmen began to attract gentlemen and merchants also; Penn himself was a wealthy landowner, Oxford educated, and the son of an admiral and important Restoration politician. Without abandoning their core beliefs, Penn and other second-generation Friends moved Quakerism away from its most radical spiritual elements and toward an emphasis on the manifestation of spirituality in the world, creating in the process what would become a powerful social philosophy with important implications for community, family, and society. The leading Friends of Penn's generation were closely associated with some of the principal luminaries of the day, including the philosopher John Locke and the political martyr Algernon Sydney.[37]

At the heart of Quaker belief was the doctrine of the "inner light," the light of the spirit within everyone. Like the Puritans, Friends rejected the efficacy of mere ritual and outer forms in religious life, but they went a good deal further than most Puritans in insisting on the inner presence of the spirit, a belief not unlike that of individuals the Puritans called Antinomians. Quakers joined the Puritans in denying divine authority to any human church and resting instead on the authority of Scripture, but Friends went further and asserted that even the Bible did not represent God's final word, which was constantly renewed through the inner light. In the words of Robert Barclay, author of the famous *Apology for the True Christian Divinity of the People Called Quakers*, Scripture represented only "the declaration of the fountain and not the fountain itself."[38] Their rejection of biblical finality led orthodox Protestants of other denominations, whose first principle was scriptural truth, to deny that Quakers were in fact Protestants at all.

Quakers joined other Protestants in denying the efficacy of priests and spiritual mediators, but again Friends took matters a step further than other Protestants and abolished an established ministry altogether. That action brought some among the early Quakers to the verge of spiritual anarchy. But by Penn's day, the inner light was not leading most Friends to an unbridled individualism. Instead, like other Protestants, they concluded that God conveyed a common message to all humankind. Thus Quakers came to rely on a consensus among believers—the "sense of the meeting"—to determine contested matters.

Some Friends wanted the society to go even further toward the regulation of the inner light. One such person was George Keith, a Scottish Quaker from Aberdeen, who was a former student of Bishop Burnet and a friend of the Cambridge philosopher Henry More. Keith was originally welcomed to Pennsylvania, but he soon grew troubled by some of the practices he saw there. He argued that Friends there were insufficiently attentive to Scripture—"Ranters and airy Notionists," Keith called some of them—and also too willing to turn disciplinary matters over to a formal hierarchy of meetings controlled by prominent Friends. Keith had many followers, but only a minority in Pennsylvania, and in 1692 he and they were disowned by the Philadelphia Yearly Meeting.[39]

In the aftermath of the schism, Pennsylvania's Quakers consolidated their position against Keith's challenge. Rejecting the adoption of a formal, scriptural creed, Quakers conducted their business through a highly structured and hierarchically arranged system of local, monthly, and yearly meetings that prevented excesses deriving from the internal voice of the spirit. The unique combination they effected of a religion based on the spirituality of the inner light and on the voluntary discipline of a highly developed organizational structure allowed the Quakers to establish a far more stable foundation than did other radical sects of the era.

In relying on what was, in effect, the common or shared sense of the meeting, Quakers prefigured what would become one of the characteristic Enlightened idioms, the appeal to the common sense or understanding of humankind. Such an appeal rested on the belief that humanity shared a common moral sense, an internal predilection for apprehending immediately and unambiguously that which was just and right that was not unlike a secularized form of the inner light. Barclay described the inner light as an "inward illumination . . . which is evident and clear of itself, forcing, by its own evidence and clearness, the well-disposed understanding to assent . . . even as the common principles of natural *truths* move and incline the mind to a natural assent."[40] For both Quakers and devotees of the provincial Enlightenment, that emphasis on the common sense of humankind provided an important alternative to a reliance on traditional and established forms of social authority. And although orthodox Quakers denied that the inner light could be reduced to any natural and inborn moral sense without the assistance of the spirit, for some eighteenth-century Quaker moralists the difference came to seem a matter more of theory than of practice.

The most sophisticated and learned of the Quaker moral philosophers was James Logan, another Scottish Friend, who arrived in Pennsylvania in 1699 to serve as Penn's personal secretary. Like his countrymen George Keith and Robert Barclay, Logan was, on the whole, more bookish than his English counterparts. He was an avid book collector and created one of the largest libraries in colonial America. His tastes were diverse: he read religion, science, philosophy, law, history, classics, and nearly every other form of literature. His circle of friends and correspondents included a group of Scottish literati in the colonies: Cadwallader Colden, like Logan a native of Scotland's southeast by way of Ireland, and the governors Robert Hunter, Alexander Spotswood, and William Burnet—the bishop's son—as well as Benjamin Franklin.[41]

Like the Latitudinarians and like the Catholick preachers of New England, Logan saw close connections between the realms of religion and both natural and moral philosophy. He had a special interest in science and was among the first Americans to master Newton's *Principia*. He conducted original experiments in botany, which he published in the Royal Society's *Transactions*. He also sponsored the early careers of a number of young scientists in early Philadelphia, including Thomas Godfrey, a glazier, mathematician, and inventor, and the young botanist John Bartram.

In 1735, Logan became one of the first colonists to use the new learning to write on the subject of ethics. Following the English theologian William Wollaston's popular *Religion of Nature Delineated*, Logan began a work entitled "The Duties of Man Deduced from Nature." Logan started with the concept of the "moral sense," articulated most clearly by the Presbyterian minister Francis Hutcheson of Ireland and Glasgow, one of the most influential moral philosophers of the age. According to Hutcheson, all men and women were possessed of a moral sense, something like a general approbation of benevolence, that functioned somewhat like the aesthetic appreciation of beauty. It was written in their hearts by a benevolent deity. We shall have more to say about Hutcheson and the moral sense shortly, but it is important to note the similarities between the moral sense and the inner light, at least in their practical effects. Logan argued that the rules of ethical conduct, to which the moral sense attached itself, were drawn from observation of the natural world. To the mathematically inclined Logan, such rules could even be calculated in arithmetic form, an idea he shared with Hutcheson and even Benjamin Franklin.[42]

Logan's intellectual career in many respects resembled that of an English virtuoso, with his wide-ranging interests, his passion for collecting books in diverse fields and for contributing to as many of those as possible, even as he continued his principal occupation as politician and agent for the proprietor. Much the same could be said for some in his circle of correspondents: Colden, Hunter, and the English Quaker Peter Collinson, as well as such other Philadelphia grandees as Isaac Norris and Logan's literary son-in-law, John Smith. Yet Logan's goals always leaned toward practical applications, as in his research on the sexuality of plants, which he used to test the fertility of corn. So did his efforts to sponsor promising young men of modest means, such as the glazier Thomas Godfrey and the aspiring botanist John Bartram, who would be the most assiduous collector of plants in the British colonial world. Bartram's penchant for collecting certainly had much in common with the style of the virtuoso.[43]

The concern for practical improvement was widespread on both sides of the Atlantic, as we shall see. Yet several features of Quaker Pennsylvania were distinctive in the provincial world. One was the opposition to war and violence for which Friends became famous. They sought, whenever possible, to negotiate with their Indian neighbors rather than rely on brute force, and William Penn, by and large, kept relatively good relations with his native neighbors. Quakers in general advocated the rules of civility and law over violence, concerns that would be characteristic of the provincial Enlightenment.

Quaker civility was only partly the result of their benevolence. A story Logan told concerning his first voyage to Pennsylvania may suggest another part. When the Quakers were sailing from England for America, another ship was sighted on the ocean. As the seamen prepared for possible attack, Penn and the other Quakers retreated below, but Logan remained on deck to fight. The ship turned out to be friendly, and Penn scolded his young secretary for his willingness to engage in the battle. To that Logan supposedly replied, "I being thy servant, why did thee not order me to come down? But thee was willing enough that I should stay and help to fight the ship when thee thought there was danger."[44]

True or not, the story suggests something about the ability of Pennsylvania Friends to maintain peace. They were able to live peaceably with their neighbors partly because of some delicate negotiations that imperial representatives undertook on behalf of British interests in America at the imperial diplomatic center at Albany, along with a balance of power that was maintained by British might and the relative weakness of Penn's Indian neighbors.[45] Several Pennsylvanians, including Logan and Governor William Keith, were especially active and effective in that branch of imperial diplomacy.

For nearly three-quarters of a century, the Quaker-dominated government in Pennsylvania managed to finesse the issue of warfare, appropriating sums of money for the king's use and leaving it to non-Quakers to fight and conduct the province's defense. By the middle of the century, that strategy began to unravel in the face of the severe threat to the security of the British colonies. By that time, Quakers formed only a small percentage of the colonies' inhabitants, and the Society itself was losing adherents who were reluctant to accept its stringent demands. Faced with a new crisis over the outbreak of war during the 1750s, Friends withdrew from active participation in politics, leaving such worldly matters to non-Friends. Quakers instead increasingly channeled their energies into spiritual reform, including a variety of benevolent enterprises.[46] To some, the most important of those was opposition to slaveholding, a second area in which Friends manifested distinctive and enlightened attitudes.

Quaker views of slaveholding had not been so clear at the outset. Pennsylvania at its founding was surrounded by colonies where Africans worked as slave laborers, and Quakers, possessed of substantial estates and important commercial connections, quickly joined their neighbors in purchasing slaves. For much of the colonial period, slavery remained an important source of labor in the Delaware Valley, and Friends, who prospered as farmers and as merchants in the city, were as active as any group in slaves' employment. Between 1731 and 1753, for example, more than 60 percent of Quaker representatives to the Philadelphia Yearly Meeting were slaveholders.[47]

From the beginning, some Friends questioned the practice. Even before Pennsylvania's founding, Quaker missionary William Edmunson visited Barbados and denounced the practice of slaveholding as he found it there. So did a group of four Friends in Germantown, Pennsylvania, as early as 1688, and a group of followers of George Keith five years later. Quaker testimonies against slaveholding, or at least against the slave trade, appeared with some regularity thereafter. The most uncompromising, such as the merchant Ralph Sandiford's charge that slavery was the work of the devil, or Benjamin Lay's accusation of apostasy against slaveholders, caused division within Friends. Both men were disowned by their meetings for their contentiousness. But the persistent, methodical, and moral antislavery campaigns conducted by such men as the New Jersey tailor John Woolman and the schoolmaster Anthony Benezet finally helped induce the Society to prohibit slave trading by members in 1758 and slaveholding a decade and a half later. For those men, the religious imperatives of the inner light blended almost imperceptibly into broader humanitarian concerns.[48]

Quaker opposition to slavery derived from two principal sources. One that was consistently important was their opposition to violence: the slave trade was founded on violence, and slavery itself relied on the ultimate rule of force. Friends taking such a position were largely motivated by their own desire for purity and their determination to follow the rule of the inner light; they did not necessarily manifest much concern for the plight of the slaves. Friends who opposed slavery on other grounds, such as the Quaker belief in the equality of souls before God, did. Not all Friends agreed that spiritual equality precluded slave owning; many insisted that the spiritual and social realms were entirely different and that Quakerism did not mandate social reform. But increasing numbers of Friends disagreed. Quakers who opposed slavery on such grounds were more likely to exhibit a real humanitarian concern for the plight of the slaves and of freedmen, and a few expressed their opposition in phrasing sounding very much like that of natural rights.

In questioning slavery, Quakers were almost unique during the first half of the eighteenth century. As the historian David Brion Davis has explained in his book *The Problem of Slavery in Western Culture*, the eighteenth century witnessed a profound moral revolution. Before that time, questions about the morality of slaveholding were virtually absent from Western culture. Sympathetic observers might pity the lot of the slave; *very* few questioned the essential morality of the system. Slavery was as old as the Bible and seemed to be sanctioned by that sacred book. Moreover, few observers before the middle of the eighteenth century envisioned the possibility of any real alternative. Poverty and hard labor seemed inevitable parts of the human condition, and few thought that their societies possessed sufficient productive capacities to eliminate them. Although it might be possible for individuals to escape from poverty, the reality was that in most societies a significant portion of the population could never expect to live beyond the level of bare subsistence. Thus people traditionally reserved their charitable sentiments for those with whom they were most closely connected, such as family, clan, neighbors, and friends.[49]

Only in the later seventeenth century and after did such perspectives begin to change. Davis lists four significant trends in eighteenth-century thought that contributed to the beginnings of antislavery sentiment: Quakerism and the sectarian tradition, the emphasis on sentiment and the affections, Enlightenment rationalism, and natural law. We shall have more to say about those subjects later, but the most important point may be how closely they became intertwined among Quakers and others. Quaker emphasis on the inner light and the philosophy of moral sense shared the belief that God had implanted an inner voice or a moral sense in everyone, one that was present but weak and in need of cultivation, one that would follow the dictates of universal benevolence and natural law. When John Woolman kept a journal of his inner struggle against slaveholding, he was at once confronting sin, cultivating the conscience, and applying rational rules of benevolence to the treatment of all humankind.

The moral revolution that antislavery represented was not easily effected even among the Quakers. For most of the colonial period, Friends' initiatives against slaveholding encountered ardent resistance from wealthy Quaker slave owners, who prevented a consensus against the institution from developing. That Woolman, Benezet, and other opponents of slavery eventually succeeded in accomplishing their goal was the result both of their assiduous campaigning and of Friends' changing positions in the colonies. As the leading Quaker families solidified their positions in Pennsylvania, their relative numbers in the Society declined, in part because of the loss of many of their children to other, less stringent faiths. In the process, the power of the rural meetings rose, meetings that had less stake in slavery and more of an interest in humanitarian aims.[50]

The triumph of antislavery in the Society of Friends after mid-century, like the eventual restriction of slavery in the North in general, was thus the product of a moral revolution that depended both on cultural trends and on changing economic and social relationships in the colonies. It was also part of a larger, international movement held together by Quaker merchants and Quaker meetings on both sides of the Atlantic. In the late 1750s, the London Yearly Meeting also took up the question of slavery, leading to the disowning of slave traders some four years later. Thereafter, the transatlantic Quaker connection was the central axis in the rise of humanitarian movements that would eventually reach far beyond the Society of Friends.[51]

Quaker humanitarianism led in other directions as well. Friends played an active role in the creation of benevolent institutions, such as almshouses and hospitals. Moreover, Quaker benevolence provided a greater role for women than did most active movements in eighteenth-century America, usually through women's meetings, in which women could proffer charity and conduct business. Those women's meetings provided one of the most important early forums for women's involvement in movements related to the Enlightenment.[52] It was not the only one, as we shall see.

Quaker humanitarianism constituted an important provincial contribution to the Enlightenment. Colonial Friends maintained broad and regular contacts with networks of Friends in Europe, with whom they corresponded about such matters as the testimony of peace, antislavery, and benevolent causes generally. Out of that ongoing discussion the Society of Friends on both sides of the Atlantic emerged as a leading promoter of reforms and of the values of organization, humanitarianism, and institution building. In the process, the Quaker women and men of provincial America functioned as important participants in the work of Enlightenment.

The Moral Sense and Moral Education

Quakers were not the only channel for the conveyance of ideas of the moral sense in America, or even in Pennsylvania. Among the other conduits were some in the Presbyterian clergy, such as Francis Alison, a native of Ulster, graduate of Scottish universities, and longtime leader of the "Old Side," an antirevivalist faction of the Presbyterian Church in America. At Glasgow University, Alison first encountered Francis Hutcheson, who was also an Ulster native and Presbyterian clergyman as well as one of the leading spokesmen for what would become the moral sense school. Alison came to America in 1735 and served as head of the Presbyterian academy at New London, along the Maryland-Pennsylvania border, and later as vice provost of the newly founded College of Philadelphia.[53]

In Ireland, Alison had been associated with the Presbyterian party known as the New Lights, a group that opposed that Church's policy requiring candidates for the ministry to formally subscribe their names to the doctrines of the Church as enunciated in the Westminster Confession. The terminology is confusing; in America, the term "New Light" would be applied to supporters of the religious awakening of the 1730s and '40s, especially in New England, a very different position from that adopted by the tolerant and usually antirevivalist New Lights of the Irish and Scottish Presbyterian Churches, as we shall see. During the 1740s, Alison became perhaps the leading spokesman for Old Light, or Old Side, Presbyterianism in America.[54]

The leading figure among the Irish and Scottish New Lights was Francis Hutcheson, who was a third-generation Presbyterian minister in Ireland. He had been educated at Glasgow University, to which he returned in 1729 as professor of moral philosophy. Building especially on the insights of the essayist Lord Shaftesbury (1671–1713), who had contended that all men and women possessed an inner moral sense, the gratification of which led to pleasure in much the same way that beauty gratified the sense of aesthetics, Hutcheson extended, systematized, and popularized Shaftesbury's ideas, converting them into a general approach to moral philosophy that attracted adherents throughout the British world and became an essential part of the moral philosophy that distinguished in particular what has come to be known as the Scottish Enlightenment.[55]

Part of Hutcheson's appeal derived from the fact that he was a clergyman, unlike Shaftesbury, whose supposed Deistic leanings made his philosophy suspect among the orthodox. Yet in his pursuit of moral philosophy, Hutcheson sought to establish a new basis for morality beyond that of a blind obedience to religion or authority. His philosophy avoided both extremes: the mere reassertion of scriptural dogma, on the one hand, and the scandalous notions—associated with such philosophers as Thomas Hobbes and Bernard Mandeville—suggesting that all morality could be reduced to mere self-interest on the other. Much of Hutcheson's work consisted of demonstrating how an innate moral sense led to moral acts that could not be reduced to disguised expressions of interest.[56]

Hutcheson conceded that, in actual practice, moral behavior was far from universal. Yet he attributed that not to the absence of a moral sense but to the influence of stronger passions, such as self-interest. Even sinners, he contended, recognized the depravity of their actions; they were simply unable to resist competing temptations. Thus the goal of Hutcheson's philosophy was to cultivate the moral sense, in much the way that Quakers advocated attending to the inner light. Hutcheson the moral theorist was never far removed from Hutcheson the moral preacher.

Hutcheson's philosophy represented a considerable softening of the rigid Calvinism of his Presbyterian ancestors. The concept of a moral sense, in tone if not necessarily in substance, was considerably at odds with a Calvinistic emphasis on the natural depravity of humankind. His philosophy differed from that of his predecessors also in that he drew his moral lessons from experience with minimal regard to Scripture. And although Hutcheson was determined to establish a foundation for morality that was consistent with religion, it was not dependent on any particular variety thereof.

Hutchesonian philosophy had substantial links to its Reformed Protestant antecedents. In particular, Hutcheson shared with his Protestant predecessors a notion of moral virtue much more substantial than what had been typical in pre-Reformation Christianity, in which virtue had essentially been identified with moral behavior; a virtuous person was one who performed moral acts. Reformed Protestants insisted on a deeper understanding of virtue, in which good actions were meritorious only if they derived from a proper inner principle. For them, that principle was a Christian virtue that derived only from divine grace, of which the remnants of a natural human conscience in fallen humankind provided but a pale imitation.[57]

What made British moral philosophy so compelling to Anglo-Americans of the eighteenth century was that it retained the Protestant emphasis on the indwelling principle of virtue, although its foundation shifted from the supernatural to the natural. To Hutcheson, it was not grace itself but rather a natural faculty that had been graciously implanted in humankind that led to morality and benevolence. The affinity between the Hutchesonian philosophy and some versions of the inner light should be apparent.

It was no coincidence that the moral sense philosophy originated in Scotland and Protestant Ireland; such a philosophy was well suited to the needs of emerging provincial societies. Among its principal effects was the transfer of moral authority from traditional institutional forces in church and state to the collective and common sense of an informed citizenry, much like the transfer the *Spectator* attempted in the realm of manners and taste. The figure of the impartial spectator, introduced by Adam Smith, stood as the principal representative of the philosophical reasonings of the Scottish moralists.[58] The providence those philosophers envisioned worked not in opposition to nature but through the natural benevolent and harmonious instincts implanted in all men and women. The implication was to minimize the restrictive and coercive forces of established authority in favor of the moral influence of communities of citizens. The moralists established as their principal goal the cultivation of the moral sense through religious instruction and moral education.

Francis Alison, along with a number of other American educators, incorporated the Hutchesonian philosophy into his lectures, first at his New London
Academy and later at the College of Philadelphia. There he taught an illustrious group of students, including the clergymen John Ewing and Matthew
Wilson, both noted educators with expertise in science, mathematics, and philosophy; doctors such as David Ramsay, who became famous as a historian of
the American Revolution; such political leaders as Charles Thomson, one of
the founders of the American Philosophical Society and secretary of the Continental Congress; and Thomas McKean and Hugh Williamson, the former a
signer of the Declaration of Independence, the latter a member of the Constitutional Convention.[59] All demonstrated broad intellectual interests.

Alison and his party were not the only sources of Enlightenment moral
philosophy at the College of Philadelphia. The year after Alison's appointment, Benjamin Franklin recruited another educator to head the college, a
recently arrived Scottish Episcopalian named William Smith. Smith had been
educated at Aberdeen during an important period of change at that city's two
universities. During the 1750s, the universities at Aberdeen had abandoned
the old way of teaching, called regenting, under which a single teacher, or
regent, was responsible for the entire education of each class, in favor of a pro-
fessorial system of specialized instruction. The introduction of that system
was accompanied by curricular reforms intending to make education there
less scholastic and more practical, de-emphasizing the classics and devoting
increased attention to science, mathematics, history, and moral philosophy.[60]

In important respects, the Aberdeen reforms evidenced a continuity with
the educational traditions of Bishop Burnet in striving for a broadly based,
humanistic education. Yet Aberdonians developed a particular variety of
moral sense philosophy that differed in emphasis from that preached by
Hutcheson. As developed by such figures as George Turnbull, Alexander
Gerard, and especially David Fordyce, the Aberdeen literati devoted considerable attention to the implications of moral sense philosophy for educational
theory, especially through Fordyce's *Dialogues Concerning Education* (1745), a
book that greatly impressed Benjamin Franklin, among others. Those writers
de-emphasized the aesthetic component of the moral sense that Hutcheson
and Shaftesbury had outlined and emphasized its rational and reflective component. In that representation of the moral sense, the possibilities for education stood out: through proper instruction educators could direct the rational
faculty that was the moral sense toward suitable ends and thereby inculcate
proper moral values.[61]

The Aberdonian version of Scottish moral philosophy that Smith imported had implications that were rather less democratic than those of Hutcheson's philosophy. Although the Aberdonians agreed that moral sense was
implanted in all men and women, not everyone had an equal capacity to apply
it. Rather, it was perfected through rational reflection rather than through the
attachment of the affections. The capacity for such reflection differed consid-

erably among individuals, a position that William Smith would maintain throughout his career.[62]

When Smith arrived in America, he settled first in New York, which was just beginning to contemplate the establishment of a college. Smith joined the discussion by publishing a pamphlet entitled *Some Thoughts on Education* (1752), which he followed the succeeding year with another, fictional work entitled *A General Idea of the College of Mirania*. The latter work was modeled largely on the newly revised Aberdeen curriculum, which advocated a practical education designed especially to provide moral instruction. The pamphlet attracted the attention of Franklin, who invited the Aberdonian to Philadelphia to head the new Philadelphia academy.[63]

William Smith was a man of wide-ranging interests, from religion and education to politics and polite letters. Although his fictional college at Mirania placed special emphasis on practical education, Smith also promoted the classics at the Philadelphia College, which was not always to Benjamin Franklin's liking. Franklin preferred practical instruction suitable to a broad range of citizens to classicism that appealed only to a small group of men of letters. Smith and Franklin eventually clashed over politics as well, since Smith was a proponent and Franklin a staunch opponent of the Pennsylvania proprietors.

William Smith was among the principal promoters of a genteel literary style in Pennsylvania. In 1757, he sponsored the publication of the *American Magazine*, a literary journal composed largely by Smith's circle of associates from the Philadelphia College and devoted to cultivating the public's taste for polite letters. In that journal, Smith published the literary efforts of his friends and associates as well as literary news and criticism designed to keep provincials abreast of the latest productions abroad. Smith's circle included such up-and-coming Philadelphia literary figures as the writer Francis Hopkinson, the doctor and educator John Morgan—one of the founders of the first medical college in Philadelphia—and the painter Benjamin West. The *American Magazine* was among the principal expressions of the High, "polite," or genteel Enlightenment in America.[64]

The College of Philadelphia was only one of several colonial institutions with roots in the Episcopal Enlightenment. Another was Kings College in New York, an Episcopal institution headed by the New England–born and –educated Samuel Johnson, whose encounter with the new learning at Yale had helped persuade him to abandon Congregationalism for the Church of England. By the time he succeeded to the presidency of Kings in 1754, Johnson had retreated from his earlier glorification of reason above revelation, but he continued to advocate toleration—a sentiment amplified by his experience as a member of a religious minority in Connecticut—and to include works of the Latitudinarians and other representatives of the new learning in the curriculum.[65]

Still another institution of the Episcopal Enlightenment was William and Mary, dating from James Blair's long tenure as president. Blair was not alone;

one of his early successors was William Stith, a native Virginian, graduate of the college, and Episcopal minister whose interests ranged from politics to Virginia history (about which he published a book in 1747). Stith was a true Latitudinarian in sentiment and in 1753 preached a sermon on "The Nature and Extent of Christ's Redemption," in which he questioned the Calvinistic belief in the inevitability of the damnation of the bulk of humankind, a fate he deemed too inhumane for a benevolent God. That position spurred a response from Stith's Presbyterian neighbor Samuel Davies, who defended the Calvinist position, although Stith's death while he was preparing his answer precluded the publication of Davies's letter.[66]

A more famous instructor at William and Mary was the Aberdonian William Small, who would become renowned as the teacher of Thomas Jefferson; the future president remembered Small as "a man profound in most of the useful branches of science, with a happy talent of communication, correct and gentlemanly manners, and an enlarged and liberal mind." Small arrived in Virginia in 1758 as professor of mathematics and soon occupied the vacant chair in natural philosophy. The following year, he founded a society in Williamsburg for promoting scientific experiments. Jefferson credited Small with providing his "first views of the expansion of science, and of the system of things in which we are placed" and described him as the first at the college to give regular lectures in "Ethics, Rhetoric, and Belles Lettres"—all traditional components of the moral philosophy curriculum. Small later returned to England and became a leader of the renowned Lunar Society of Birmingham, which included among its members such luminaries as James Watt, Joseph Priestley, and Erasmus Darwin.[67]

The Natural History Circle

The literati of the early provincial Enlightenment were also interested in natural history, especially the field of botany. Unlike abstract Newtonian philosophy, whose complicated mathematics were beyond the comprehension of many colonials, natural history was of interest to a broad range of educated provincials. It appealed to clergymen interested in examining the works of God's creation. It attracted virtuosi interested in collecting specimens to display in their homes and gardens. It gained the attention of physicians interested in biology and herbal medicines. It was interesting as well to all attentive to the wonders one could find in America.

Beginning in the later years of the seventeenth century, natural history was an especially popular subject in the Chesapeake. Several of its key students were Anglican clergymen, such as John Banister and Hugh Jones. Natural history was also of considerable interest to such gentleman as William Byrd and John Lawson, author of *New Voyage to Carolina* (1709). Perhaps the most important of all was Mark Catesby, Royal Society member and author of the

Natural History of Carolina, Florida, and the Bahama Islands, who collected specimens over a number of years in Virginia as well as in the colonies listed in that
work. In exchange for their patronage, Catesby sent seeds and specimens to
wealthy English men of science for their private gardens and served as one of
the focal points for the transatlantic botanical exchange.[68]

During the first quarter of the eighteenth century a new group came to the
fore in natural history circles: the physicians, such as Cadwallader Colden,
William Douglass, and John Mitchell, followed by the Carolina circle of John
Lining, Lionel Chalmers, Alexander Garden, and others. Nearly all of those
men were Scots and had had either Scottish or Continental educations. They
formed an important part of a transatlantic natural history circle, at the center
of which stood the English Quaker John Fothergill, another doctor with a
Scottish medical education, and the Quaker merchant Peter Collinson; the latter maintained an extensive correspondence with members of the Scottish,
colonial, and Dissenting communities, which served as the closest thing
provincials had to a network for scientific communications. In addition to the
Scots physicians, the leading colonial contributors were the Quaker James
Logan—also a Scot—and the Quaker naturalist collector John Bartram.[69]

The prevalence of Scots among those physicians had a substantial history.
After 1737, with the creation of Edinburgh's medical school, that city rose to
prominence in medical education, but Scots' achievements in colonial medicine preceded that date. Their reputation grew out of Scotland's place as a
poor and backward nation on the fringes of Europe that had a large population
of skilled and educated young men who needed to make their places abroad.
For centuries Scotland had sent its surplus to the European Continent, especially to Leyden, which attained preeminence in medical education by the
early years of the eighteenth century. Scottish physicians in the seventeenth
century found positions in such places as the Continental Regiments; in the
years after the Union of 1707, those same classes of educated Scots would seek
their fortunes in the emerging British empire.[70]

Before 1700, there were few trained medical men in the colonies. As late as
1721, during the inoculation controversy in Boston, William Douglass was the
only Boston physician with a medical degree. That was part of the controversy, as Douglass resented the assumption of medical authority by such clergymen as Mather and his uncertified ally in the medical community, Zabdiel
Boylston. Douglass, having studied at Edinburgh and Leyden, represented a
new breed of university-trained doctor. He criticized mere "empirics" who
had no more than a practical knowledge of medical procedure. Douglass and
most of the other educated physicians also had a broader theoretical knowledge as well as much more wide-ranging interests in the fields of politics, letters, and natural and moral philosophy, as befit the university men they were.
How far that knowledge benefited their patients is open to dispute. Douglass
himself contended that the Boston populace was safer staying away from that
city's physicians. The gibe was aimed at the nonuniversity men among the

medical community; whether the treatment Douglass provided was more effective remains an open question.[71] Nonetheless, Douglass and his fellows would come to represent one of the more prominent manifestations of the genteel Enlightenment.

Those doctors' interest in natural history followed logically from their knowledge of medicine and biology and from their use of herbal medications. Cadwallader Colden studied the classification of plants, established a horticultural garden at his estate at Coldengham, and shipped New World seeds and plants to his European correspondents. Exportation was later taken over by his daughter Jane, who became known as the most active and perceptive female botanist in America. Physicians John Mitchell, John Lining, and Alexander Garden also made noteworthy contributions to the field of natural history, which appealed to them also because they were men of the Enlightenment. With the introduction of the Linnaen system of classification, natural history became the most orderly field of natural philosophy, a system of order par excellence. On their own, and through the medium of Peter Collinson, several colonial naturalists corresponded with Linnaeus.[72]

In general, colonial naturalists looked more toward the discovery and classification of species than at the theoretical underpinnings of that classification; Cadwallader Colden was a major exception. There is nothing surprising about such a tendency. Once Linnaeus provided a scheme of classification, the essence of Enlightenment science was to consolidate the scheme and to demonstrate its validity. A generation ago, historians portrayed colonial science as particularly practical in nature. If that was true of American science in this period, it was true of British science as well; a recent study of both American and British articles published in the *Philosophical Transactions of the Royal Society* in the eighteenth century has found no distinction between the essentially practical nature of their contributions.[73]

The Organization of Provincial Science

The members of the natural history circle organized not only their science but themselves. The eighteenth century has been cited as a period of organization in the field of science, and that was abundantly true in America. Cadwallader Colden is often credited with the first suggestion to create an intercolonial scientific association, which came to fruition in 1743 as the first American Philosophical Society, organized by Franklin and Bartram. William Douglass organized Boston's first medical society. In a larger sense, the greatest organizer of all was Peter Collinson, who introduced many of the colonial science enthusiasts not only into European scientific circles but to each other as well.

The creation of scientific societies was one of the characteristic features of Enlightenment science in America and Europe.[74] The establishment of such societies in America signifies also the efforts of the provincial literati to advance the level of their culture in an effort to catch up with the state of learning and development among their metropolitan countrymen. Such aspirations marked a significant change for colonial scientists. Their goal was no longer to be adopted individually into European circles of learning, as Cotton Mather, for example, had attempted to do with his frequent submissions to the Royal Society. Rather, it was to establish provincial science on a sound and significant footing.

Probably the greatest colonial scientist, and certainly the most recognized in European circles, was Benjamin Franklin, who retired from his print shop in 1747, leaving the business in the hands of his partner David Hall, in order to devote himself full time to scientific experiments and public service. Franklin had studied Newton's works by that time, especially his *Opticks*, which provided a model for an experimental scientist to follow, and Franklin set out to conduct a series of his own experiments. His particular interest was electricity, a subject that a number of experimenters had opened up in the eighteenth century and that ranked at the time principally as a curiosity. Franklin's great contribution to that subject was to reduce the material to order, by his theory of charges and countercharges and especially by his insightful law of the conservation of charges, which still has considerable meaning today. His success in framing a set of general laws for what had previously seemed merely curious and irrational phenomena was his principal claim to fame, in European as well as American literary circles. It led the British philosopher and man of science Joseph Priestley to compare Franklin to Newton, in that the latter's reputation also rested on his ability to explain the diversity of natural phenomena through a system of general laws.[75]

Franklin's experiments helped to confirm Francis Bacon's proposition a century and a half earlier that scientific experiments would have practical benefits. Until that time such an assertion was more an article of faith than a demonstrated fact; indeed, for long after, Franklin's experiments were cited as the principal proof of the benefits of scientific experiments. What made his work useful was that he managed to link his experiments to natural phenomena: the current his Leyden jar produced was the same, many times reduced, as the one lightning produced in the sky. Out of that discovery came such practical inventions as the lightning rod. An even greater benefit was his ability to explain a set of natural phenomena and replicate them on a controlled scale.

Franklin's scientific work is a good example of the interchange between the American and European scientific worlds. Franklin developed his interest in electricity from European experiments, including the American tour of lectures and experiments on electricity the Edinburgh doctor Archibald Spencer conducted in the 1740s. But Franklin was no mere consumer of European ideas, nor was his goal simply recognition from metropolitan audiences. He exceeded his teachers in the latter regard and made himself a scientific contributor of the first rank. His election in 1756 to the Royal Society represented more than a provincial's willingness to provide data to the Society, as Mather, for one, had done. Europeans learned from, and respected, the man who took on the persona of the provincial scientist.

Natural History and the Divisions of Humanity

Another area of inquiry to which the provincials in the New World had special access was the study of humanity, what we today would call ethnology or anthropology. Again, physicians in particular contributed to that study. Colden and John Mitchell were among those who provided significant contributions to ethnology, which were incorporated into the work of such European writers as the Scotsman Lord Kames and his countryman the historian William Robertson.

Colden's *History of the Five Indian Nations Depending on the Province of New-York in America* proved especially important.[76] Colden wrote at a time when imperial-minded elites in the colonies had begun to envision a conflict between Britain and France in the western territories as the key to all of North America. To such elites, the support of powerful Indian nations such as the Iroquois seemed vital to the outcome. Colden's method was that of the historian: he gathered documents from both English and French sources and compared them in an attempt to provide a coherent narrative of Indian affairs. He gave his history a particular slant. He proclaimed the Iroquois to be British dependents; he labeled their league a confederacy, a particular European concept of relations among equal nation states, a label that has been employed in describing the Iroquois ever since.

Colden praised his Indians for their loyalty and heroism, in part to contrast them with the French, whom Colden criticized for being Christians evidencing less humanity than the Iroquois. Colden's praise, which was part of a growing tendency to view Indians as "noble savages," was also consistent with Enlightenment ideas: Europeans began to romanticize primitive cultures even as they were theorizing about a sharp separation in civilization between their own cultures and others. It was all part of the general effort to classify humanity according to the various stages of civilization; Scots and French writers in particular outlined the four-stages theory in which all human societies were seen to have progressed from primitive states of savagery, succeeded by periods of pastoral and then agricultural subsistence, until they reached a modern form of commercial civilization. In such a view, Indians were like Europeans of an earlier time, and although Enlightened thinkers might extol the benefits modernity offered in the form of comforts, achievements, and liberties, they also noted the older, heroic virtues that the moderns had evidently lost. Such depictions of the native, although useful tools in social criticism, were hardly an advantage to Native Americans, however, since the depictions emerged at about the same time that Indians were disappearing from the most settled

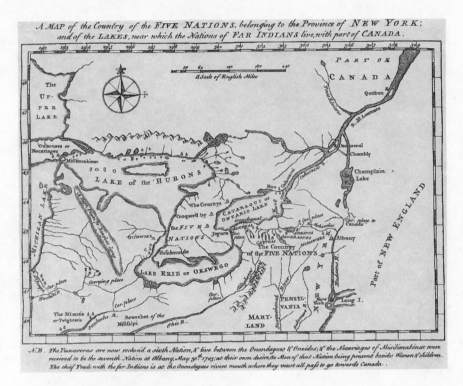

Map from Cadwallader Colden's *History of the Five Indian Nations. Courtesy of the Library of the State University of New York at Stony Brook.*

parts of North America. In some respects, romanticization served as a substitute for intellectual confrontation.[77]

The Virginian Mitchell's work on race was more anthropological and biological in nature. Mitchell took as his subject the by then long-debated question of the causes of racial differences in humankind, which he offered in an essay printed by the Royal Society in 1745. He explained these differences, in Enlightenment fashion, with reference especially to differences in climate, as well as in diet and lifestyle. Most notably, he argued that what distinguished white and black humans was not the different colors in the skin but rather a greater or lesser ability to show color through the skin, owing, he argued, to the fact that Africans' skin had greater density than Europeans'. White and black were not colors, he argued, citing Newton's work on the subject, but rather the presence or absence of all colors. The races of humanity differed from one another only in the relatively small matter of light's ability to penetrate the skin.[78]

The most significant aspect of Mitchell's essay may be what he did not argue. Neither he nor any of his peers thought that racial differences reflected

John Mitchell's map of North America, 1755. *Geography and Map Division, Library of Congress.*

fixed differences in human nature, either as the result of providential decree—which was an earlier assumption—or of innate difference; the latter was largely a later idea, as we shall see. Mitchell assumed that whatever differences existed had a natural and environmental explanation.

Mitchell's assumptions were those of the Enlightenment. Humankind, Enlightenment thinkers assumed, possessed an essential nature that was everywhere the same. In part that assumption was rooted in their desire to establish general laws for humanity on the Newtonian model; the key to Newton's achievement, in this view, had been to comprehend physical movement by positing a uniformity to all matter. A science of humanity would have been precluded at the outset by any assumptions of innate racial differences in human nature. Such beliefs were also products of their Christian inheritance and of the faith in a single creation. Even in the nineteenth century, Christian theologians in America would be among the last holdouts against racialist views of human nature that posited essential and invariable differences among the races of humanity.[79]

Underlying Enlightenment anthropology were the concepts of civility and civilization, and in particular the four-stages theory. Provincials had little doubt where they ranked on that scale, of course, or that Africans and Native Americans were in a lower stage of civilization. Yet because those differences were assumed to result from social and environmental causes rather than from differences in biology or human nature, they were not assumed to be fixed and unchanging. Rather, it was understood that societies progressed at different rates in different places.

Not until the 1780s, in Thomas Jefferson's famous *Notes on the State of Virginia*, would one find anything closely resembling an argument for innate biological differences among the races. The argument Jefferson offered there was highly tentative, and the Virginian certainly allowed the possibility that his evidence was inadequate. Nonetheless, the future president concluded that even accounting for the differences in condition between Africans and Europeans in the New World, the mere fact of enslavement did not account for what he regarded as monumental differences in learning and achievement between the races. He concluded instead that such differences could result only from the Africans' lesser capacities.[80]

It is easy today to see the deficiencies in Jefferson's argument. Although he employed the Enlightenment method of reasoning only from closely observed phenomena, his idea of fair conclusions strikes the modern reader as peculiar, to say the least. After noting what he regards as Africans' inability to follow complicated reasoning, Jefferson observes that it would be "unfair to follow them to Africa for this investigation"; rather, for the sake of fairness, they should be judged "here, on the same stage with the whites." Whether the colonies in fact were a fair stage for a trial, given the slave population's subordinate position and lack of opportunities, he never thought to ask. Indeed, Jefferson believed that the situation of African-Americans provided them with real advantages because they were situated where "they might have availed themselves of the conversation of their masters. . . . and even lived in countries where the arts and sciences are cultivated to a considerable degree."[81]

Jefferson excepted Native Americans from such criticisms. He found them to possess artistic abilities and a gift for "sublime oratory"—Jefferson here linked American Indians to other natural "primitives." But in Africans he found himself unable to locate any such virtues. Indeed, the ability to study the races as subjects for natural history provided Jefferson with a further rationale—if he still needed one—for keeping the races separate.

Jefferson's argument points out one of the ironies of racial thinking during the Enlightenment. For if Enlightenment methods were founded on the concept of human sameness as essential to the scientific study of humankind, that methodology, in turn, provided Jefferson and his successors with the tools for inventing and developing a conception of racial difference that has remained with us to the present day. Jefferson did not simply distinguish between the achievements of Europeans and Africans, as earlier generations of colonials had done; he formulated those distinctions into a theory based on an ostensibly scientific method. His main point was not simply the different result he saw between whites and blacks but different results that seemed to him to have no other natural or social explanation. What he was led to, then, was a theory of racial difference, of an innate difference in human nature, an argument that could hardly have been conceived without the methods of the scientific study of humankind.

Jefferson's conclusions are rendered doubly ironic by the fact that as he was writing, some African-Americans were just beginning to enter into the world of letters. Those included the scientist and mathematician Benjamin Bannecker and the poet Phillis Wheatley, who published her first collection of verse in 1773.[82] Jefferson would deny her achievement, considering her poetry inferior, which was certainly true if Wheatley were compared to the great masters but hardly if she were compared to some of the sentimental poets of the century that he admired. That Jefferson would not recognize blacks' achievements and did not appreciate the tremendous barriers that social conditions in the Americas posed to such attainments suggests some of the limitations of the provincial Enlightenment. A movement that could credit the achievements of an artisan who raised himself through force of character and could recognize the inhumanity of enslavement in a progressively prosperous provincial world retained a considerable blindness to the humanity of those who remained subordinated.

Americans would continue to confront such issues for generations, of course. Their formulations concerning race would provide one of the most persistent, if also most troubling, influences of their peripheral location on the character of the provincial Enlightenment. Still another irony of that Enlightenment was that it was on the peripheries that Europeans found themselves most closely confronted with the varieties of humanity that formed so large a part of the Enlightenment inquiry. There also they found unprecedented opportunities for wealth. Together those features underwrote much of Europe's progress beyond the level of mere subsistence and led to the systematic development of those institutions of exploitation that posed the most serious challenge to emerging notions of humanity, benevolence, and natural law.

Thus there was much for the Western world to ponder in the provinces and on the periphery. There they discovered botanical novelties that allowed for the development of an orderly system of biological classification. There they encountered the varieties of humanity and the diversity of human cultures that provided the material for speculation about a science of humankind. There they confronted the task of establishing imperial dominion over maturing and thriving provincial societies. There they witnessed the fabulous riches that could be produced by brutally exploited slave laborers.

Gradually, provincials moved toward the forefront of those inquiries. From simple collectors of botanical specimens, provincial scientists would begin to enter into the forefront of natural history discussion. From mere observers of the peoples of the periphery, provincials would begin to report and describe and even theorize about the governments and cultures of their Indian neighbors and about the races of humankind. More than just profiting from those encounters, provincial groups led by the Quakers would begin to strive for a goal of civility in crosscultural relations and for the universal liberty of men and women.

The Enlightenment also provided an important framework for provincials to understand their societies and themselves. Through a science of society that looked for the underlying principles of progress and prosperity, and through a moral sense philosophy that located ethical authority in the collective opinion of the citizenry, the Enlightenment helped provincials articulate their claims to political rights and the worthiness of their communal judgments. Thus if the situation of the provinces contributed much to the enquiry that we call the Enlightenment, so also would the Enlightenment—with its notions of humanity and universality, and its analytic approach to humankind—do much to define and to legitimize provinciality.

four

Religious Awakening
in the Provincial World

In the year 1738, even as the provincial Enlightenment was taking hold among early American elite groups, a youthful but immensely popular Anglican preacher named George Whitefield ventured as a missionary from England to the new colony of Georgia, where he worked to promote an orphan school with which he became associated. It soon became apparent that the preacher's goals extended beyond so limited a conception of charity. In October of 1739, after a year of preparation back in England, Whitefield returned to America and began a spectacular preaching tour of the British colonies that took him as far to the north as New England and as far south as Georgia over a full year, during which he preached to numerous excited crowds along the way. At Philadelphia, the evangelist was met by a crowd that he estimated to be 6,000; at nearby Germantown, 5,000; at Neshaminy, 3,000; and back in Philadelphia, 10,000; and on it went. Encouraged by the evangelist, thousands asked themselves the question "What must I do to be saved?" In numerous congregations, from Massachusetts to Georgia, the tour caused either the outbreak of a religious revival or the furthering of one already under way.[1]

Whitefield's American tour of 1739–1740 represented the high-water mark of what contemporaries would refer to as a "Great and General Awakening" in the colonies. The English preacher attracted followers of all sorts, from established clergymen, such as Benjamin Colman and James Blair, and such younger preachers as Samuel Davies and the demonstrative James Davenport to hordes of ordinary men and women, all denouncing a cold and formal religion and the loss of a vital spirit. In the process, the Awakening divided the

American religious community and caused schisms that rent congregations and denominations from north to south.[2]

The occurrence of such a revival during the high tide of the Enlightenment may seem somewhat surprising at first: the event was accompanied by such seemingly unenlightened behavior as visions, swoons, apparently uncontrolled body motions, and hysterical fits. Moreover, it included a widespread denunciation of mere book learning, a notorious episode of book burning in Connecticut, and the preaching of total dependence on supernatural aid, all of which seemed to conflict with the Enlightenment's foremost principles. Indeed, so contradictory have those movements seemed that chroniclers from the time of the Awakening itself have viewed the event as having marked the division of American religion into two permanently opposing camps: one that was orthodox and evangelical and another that was enlightened and liberal, the latter progressive and rational, the former revivalist and supernatural. The evangelicals were dubbed the "New Side" or "New Lights," in reference to their supposed new access to divine truth through evangelical conversion; the others were called "Old Lights" or "Old Side," or—in some cases—Liberals, which referred to their supposed freedom from undue prejudice in favor of inherited opinions.

In fact, with the exception of the most extreme positions on both sides, the differences between Old Lights and New Lights can easily be exaggerated. Although it hardly seemed so during the height of the Awakening, the two had more in common than they recognized. Both accepted the redefinition of religion as faith personally held, and both insisted, in rather different ways, that the experiential side of religion took precedence over inherited doctrines and disciplines, thus reinforcing the primacy of individual conscience, a necessary ingredient of provincial identity. Both were substantially immersed in the transatlantic culture of commerce and letters. Both were shaped by and, in turn, contributed to provincial culture, and both helped to unify the American colonies and to highlight some of their cultural distinctiveness. One of the Awakening's principal legacies was to further expand the reach of transatlantic culture in provincial America. In that sense, as we shall see, the spread of evangelical culture in America constituted one of the principal mechanisms for disseminating some of the attitudes and ideas associated with the provincial Enlightenment.

Premonitions of Revival

When Whitefield began his preaching tour in 1739, the movement that became known as the Awakening was already well under way in several parts of America. What may be the Awakening's best-known event had taken place several years earlier, in the Connecticut River Valley in New England, under the leadership of the Northampton minister Jonathan Edwards, successor to his grandfather, the eminent Solomon Stoddard, a man with no small reputation as a revivalist himself. In 1734 and 1735, Edwards led a revival of religion in that town in part by preaching a distinctly Calvinistic sermon on the doctrine of "Justification by Faith Alone." That sparked an awakening that affected more than 300 persons in the community and that spread to neighboring towns up and down the valley in what the Northampton preacher called a "surprising work of God in the conversion of many hundred souls." The Connecticut Valley revivals ended several years before Whitefield's visit reignited the New England Awakening, but it became a well-known and celebrated event on both sides of the Atlantic, largely through Edwards's widely circulated *Faithful Narrative* of the affair. Jonathan Edwards and the town of Northampton were identified with the Awakening ever after, and Edwards's description came to represent the classical revival narrative. Over the next few years it was republished many times in England, Scotland, America, and Europe. In the words of historian C. C. Goen, once Edwards's narrative "of the surprising work of God" had appeared, "the simple fact is that no revival could ever be a surprise again."[3]

If the Northampton minister penned the work that was to stand as the symbol of the revival, from its very beginnings the promotion of that revival was a transatlantic undertaking. Edwards began by writing a short account to Benjamin Colman, which the latter included in a letter to a Dissenting minister in London, John Guyse. Both Guyse and his colleague Isaac Watts had been attempting to promote the revival of religion among the English Dissenters for a number of years, and Colman first published a version of Edwards's letter and then solicited the longer narrative at their suggestion. The two English ministers then arranged for the publication of the full description, which appeared in London in 1737. Watts and Guyse continued to ask Colman to send additional information about the revival, citing requests from a large group of correspondents in both England and Scotland and initiating what would become a long and voluminous transatlantic communication about such matters.[4] Thus the letter that became the prototypical revival narrative was in every sense the product of the joint efforts of a transatlantic evangelical community and was a response as much to the needs of the British as to American promoters of revival.

The revival was not surprising because it was unprecedented. To the contrary, there were distinct and long-standing revival traditions in New England, Britain, and western Europe. Edwards's grandfather Stoddard had conducted at least five religious "harvests" in Northampton during his long ministry, and Scottish, English, and New English ministers had all pleaded for a revival of religion for many years. It was surprising only in the sense that its location and timing were unforeseen: ministers before that time prayed for revivals but never knew if or when their prayers would be answered.

The Connecticut Valley revivals were not even the first of the decade in the American colonies; similar movements, inspired chiefly by immigrant preachers, were already under way in the Middle Colonies. During the 1720s, a min-ister of the Dutch Reformed Church named Theodorus Frelinghuysen, who had been educated in traditions of European Pietism, which emphasized per-sonal faith and a life of devotion, had initiated a series of local revivals in the vicinity of his Dutch congregation in New Brunswick, New Jersey.[5] Perhaps more important, the Dutch pastor's example had influenced his Irish-born Presbyterian colleague in New Brunswick, Gilbert Tennent, who had adopted a similarly evangelical preaching style with some success. Gilbert Tennent was one of a family of Presbyterian clergymen in the region, including his three brothers and their father, the Reverend William Tennent of Neshaminy, Penn-sylvania. Together, they formed the most important family of evangelical cler-gymen in the Middle Colonies and, quite possibly, in America.

The elder Tennent was a native of Ulster who had been educated in Scot-tish universities and ordained as a minister of the Irish Episcopal Church. Upon arriving in America in 1718, Tennent applied for admission to the Pres-byterian Synod, citing as his reasons what he called the laxity in doctrine and the "anti-scriptural" practices of the Episcopal Church, which aligned him per-fectly with Presbyterian tradition. At Neshaminy, he began to train his sons for the ministry, and then about a dozen others, almost all Ulster immigrants like himself, most of whom became evangelical ministers. His opponents derided his school as a "Log College," and the name stuck; the Tennents and the Log College circle became the core group of Middle Colony revivalism.[6]

The Log College revivals began as early as 1730. In that year, the third son, John Tennent, recently settled in an old Scottish congregation in Freehold, New Jersey, began a course of preaching on the doctrine of regeneration. That led to consternation within the congregation and concern for their souls. The minister, barely 23 years old, was already ill when the revival broke out. When he died in 1732, he was succeeded by his elder brother, William Tennent Jr., and the grieving congregation experienced another stirring of revivalism. Both Tennent brothers had reputations for having mystical experiences—especially William, whose conversion included a period of four days in a trancelike state. The brothers used the drama of their experiences, along with their illnesses, to excite their congregations and promote the revivals.[7] By the mid-1730s, a Presbyterian awakening was in full swing from central Jersey to southeastern Pennsylvania.

The Presbyterian revivals in the Middle Colonies had a distinctive charac-ter, one that was rooted in Scottish and Irish evangelical traditions. In theol-ogy it was Calvinist, but in practice it was a good deal more activist than tradi-tions found among New England evangelical preachers before the Awakening. The Presbyterian style was best represented by Gilbert Tennent, a tireless preacher and party leader. In the winter of 1740–1741, at White-field's suggestion, he followed the Englishman to New England, where he embarked on a rigorous schedule of preaching throughout the region for sev-eral months, until he retired in a fit of depression and exhaustion.[8] Tennent was no less willing to rush his ideas into print to mark almost any occasion. He published close to 100 sermons during his lifetime, along with a number of longer essays and tracts. Tennent was contentious, brash, and emotional, his preaching active and loud, leading Whitefield to refer to him as a "son of thunder." His exertions made the Presbyterian Awakening a far less "surprising" affair than that which accompanied the preaching of the austere Jonathan Edwards.

Tennent's sermons were in keeping with his preaching style. Rather than organizing his lectures according to the traditional structure of text, argument, and improvement, the Presbyterian's preachings were all action. Doctrine and exegesis appeared not in advance of persuasion but in the service of it. Tennent was particularly known for his employment of what came to be known as "searching"; he would address his hearers on the necessity of the new birth and attempt to seek out and destroy the various strategies they used to persuade themselves of their safety. He was fond of images of aggression and violence; among his first published sermons was one entitled *The Necessity of Religious Violence in Order to Obtain Durable Happiness* (1735). Another, *A Solemn Warning to the Secure World, from the God of Terrible Majesty* (1735), called for Christians to take heaven by storm. His message in all was essentially the same: convert *now*.

A Great and General Awakening

Not until the Englishman Whitefield's spectacular American tour were those diverse local movements knit together into a larger intercolonial revival. A particularly vivid account of one stop on Whitefield's journey has been left to us by a Connecticut farmer named Nathan Cole, whose rather ordinary life was transformed by Whitefield's appearance. Let us attend first to the sounds and images Cole uses to describe the day that the itinerant first arrived in his vicinity:

> Now it pleased God to send Mr. Whitefield into this land; and my hearing of his preaching at Philadelphia, like one of the old apostles, and many thousands flocking to hear him preach the Gospel, and great numbers were converted to Christ, I felt the Spirit of God drawing me by conviction; I longed to see and hear him and wished he would come this way. . . . Then on a sudden in the morning about 8 or 9 of the clock there came a messenger and said Mr. Whitefield preached at Hartford and Wethersfield yesterday and is to preach at Middletown this morning at ten of the clock. I was in my field at work. I dropped my tool that I had in my hand and ran home to my wife, telling her to make ready quickly to go and hear Mr. Whitefield preach at Middletown, then ran to my pasture for my horse with all my might, fearing that I should be too late.

Having my horse, I with my wife soon mounted the horse and went forward as fast as I thought the horse could bear; and when my horse got much out of breath, I would get down and put my wife on the saddle and bid her ride as fast as she could and not stop or slack for me except I bade her, and so I would run until I was much out of breath and then mount my horse again, and so I did several times to favor my horse. . . . [A]s I drew nearer, it seemed like a steady stream of horses and their riders, scarcely a horse more than his length behind another, all of a lather and foam with sweat, their breath rolling out of their nostrils every jump. Every horse seemed to go with all his might to carry his rider to hear news from heaven for the saving of souls. . . . [A]ll along the 12 miles I saw no man at work in his field, but all seemed to be gone.[9]

It was all quite heady stuff. Implicit in the description is one of the keys to Whitefield's success. Although Cole's neighbors experienced the Englishman's arrival one morning "on a sudden," there was very little that was spontaneous in the event's planning. Neither Cole nor his neighbors were taken unprepared. Nearly all of the fervor the farmer described actually took place prior to Whitefield's arrival, before the Connecticut audience had ever seen the evangelist or heard him preach. Well before Whitefield set foot in Connecticut, Cole heard that Whitefield had preached with success before excited crowds in Philadelphia, then that he was in the Jerseys, then on Long Island, then in Boston, then in Northampton, and then, finally, in Hartford. Someone was spreading the news of Whitefield's celebrity and of his approach. *Then* Cole and his neighbors heard of his upcoming visit to Middletown. "Spontaneous" excitement was preceded by weeks or months of active promotion.

That work was performed by Whitefield himself and by his principal promoter, a wealthy Englishman named William Seward, both of whom devoted unprecedented energies to publicizing the minister's travels and to spreading word of his successes. Whitefield wrote and had published lengthy journals in which he described his visits to various communities and the reactions of excited crowds; those journals were always sent out before his arrival. He befriended printers wherever he went and made himself into a major story in all of the colonial papers, including Franklin's in Philadelphia; in spite of Franklin's general skepticism about revealed religion, the two men developed a lifelong friendship of great benefit to both. Indeed, Whitefield's sermons were among Franklin's most profitable publications. Although he and other printers publicized the evangelist's travels in order to help sell their newspapers—Whitefield was becoming big news—that coverage in turn was integral to the preacher's success.[10]

There is an illuminating comment about the hype concerning Whitefield in Henry Fielding's novel *Joseph Andrews*, published early in 1742. It concerns the attempt by a solid and virtuous clergyman named Parson Adams to have his sermons published. The bookseller with whom he converses responds that in the present day, sermons in general are "mere drugs" in the market. The trade is so well stocked with them, and they attract so little interest, he continues, "that really unless they come out with the name of Whitfield or Westley," they will not sell. He continues, "I am no enemy to sermons but because they don't sell: for I would as soon print one of Whitfield's, as any farce whatever."[11]

The comparison of the evangelist's sermons to farce suggests another aspect of Whitefield's celebrity: he was not simply a born actor but an experienced one as well. Drawing on an early interest in acting and the theater, which he had since come to condemn (as had most orthodox ministers), the preacher-actor would mesmerize crowds with a strong voice, an intense stare, and the acting out in the pulpit of vivid scenes that re-created the great dramas of the Bible and of human salvation.[12] If Edwards was principally a preacher of rarefied intellect and Tennent a preacher of action and terror, Whitefield was essentially a dramatic preacher holding forth on the themes of sympathy and love.

Another feature of Whitefield's style was his ability to set himself up as a victim of persecution by church authorities. Wherever he went, the Anglican field preacher became embroiled in controversy, often with the leadership of the Anglican Church, a fact that had a particular appeal to provincial audiences that were composed largely of Dissenters but also of Anglicans resistant to authority emanating from the metropolitan leadership of that church. Whitefield's appearance encouraged such reactions, as he wore a surplice and carried the Anglican Book of Common Prayer wherever he went.

Whitefield seemed to go out of his way to provoke controversy. In one of his published letters, he criticized the Latitudinarian Archbishop Tillotson, a revered figure among Anglicans, for having no more knowledge of the new birth than "Mohamet." In another, he attacked the current bishop of London. It was hardly surprising when the authorities of that church denounced Whitefield in turn. In opposing Anglican authorities, Whitefield established himself as a champion of Dissenters and provincials.[13]

As the revival took hold, a number of itinerants followed Whitefield in his journeys. The first was Gilbert Tennent, who undertook his own preaching tour of New England at Whitefield's urging. Soon others were imitating their practices, beginning with James Davenport of Southold on Long Island, descended from one of early New England's most famous preachers but who lacked the sound judgment of his ancestor. His preaching in fact combined the most controversial aspects of the styles of Tennent and Whitefield. He followed Tennent in condemning unconverted ministers and did so not only in general, as had his predecessor, but by name in the towns that he visited. He followed Whitefield in exuding emotion, extending the style to include what were thought to be unruly actions, such as singing in the streets, an action widely considered inconsistent with proper Christian deportment. Davenport's behavior was widely condemned, not only by opponents of the revival but even by evangelicals in both New England and the Middle Colonies. A chastened Davenport would soon disavow his errors, but a number of other radical evangelicals would prove less submissive to the injunctions of their clerical colleagues.[14]

Whitefield's revivals affected communities from New Hampshire to Georgia, yet they did not strike everywhere. The New York colony was largely bypassed, outside of the city itself and the communities of Long Island, which were culturally an outgrowth of New England. Nor was there much impact in Maryland other than near the Pennsylvania border, or in Tidewater, Virginia. The Society of Friends was largely unaffected, as was the Church of England, with a few notable exceptions.[15] In contrast, the revival was strong in much of New England, especially in eastern Connecticut, the Connecticut River Valley, and some areas near Boston. The Middle Colony corridor from New York to Philadelphia was also strongly affected, as was the Virginia backcountry. And everywhere the Awakening made its greatest impact in the principal Dissenting communities, whether Congregational or Presbyterian.

In the middle of the Awakening, in the summer of 1741, Jonathan Edwards delivered one of the most famous and dramatic sermons in American history, entitled "Sinners in the Hands of an Angry God." It is probably Edwards's most famous work, although it was hardly the most characteristic production of a minister noted for his powerful logic and broad knowledge. Its power derived largely from his ability to apply cold logic to an aroused audience; indeed, it has become a classic example of restrained rhetoric used to produce emotional force. Based on a phrase from Deuteronomy, "Their foot shall slide in due time," the sermon's theme was that unconverted men and women were not merely awaiting the future judgment of heaven on them; that judgment was already delivered and waiting for them, to be carried out at any moment. Only instant repentance could forestall it.[16]

In one of the most often cited passages in the history of preaching, Edwards compared the sinner to a spider, a "loathsome insect" suspended over an eternal fire, a "bottomless pit, full of the fire of wrath," held only by a slender thread that at any moment might give way. Perhaps the sermon's most affecting aspect resulted from the passivity of the "angry God." God's wrath required no further provocation, nor was there any necessity for divine action. On the contrary, unrepentant sinners would not be thrown into hell but would be allowed simply to fall of their own weight to those depths, where they would endure eons and eons of exquisite torture that would not, and could never, be relieved, in Edwards's frighteningly powerful portrayal of the meaning of the infinite. Only the hand of God held sinners up from the pit of eternal misery. When God withheld support, they fell. They were condemned already.[17]

The New Light

Whatever their differences in preaching style, the revivalists shared some elements of style and endorsed several common themes. One was a considerable willingness to address their hearers' emotions rather than simply their intellects. One did not exclude the other, of course. Edwards's sermons certainly addressed understanding, and many revivalists took great care to see that converts clearly comprehended the doctrines of regeneration after their initial awakenings. But they almost invariably assumed that the first stirrings of conversion were more likely to arise in response to emotional appeal rather than to rational argument, regardless of whether the particular passion touched was pathos or fear.

The most characteristic aspect of revival sermons was an intensive emphasis on the doctrine of the new birth. All preached on the "nature and necessity of regeneration" in order to obtain salvation. There was of course nothing new about the message itself, which had always comprised an important element of Reformed theology. But during the revival, evangelical preachers often made personal conversion the sole theme of their preaching, to which all others were subordinated.

In their own way, the revivalists, as much as Locke or the Latitudinarians, relied on the redefinition of religious life. Like those earlier scholars, revivalist preachers separated the components of the religious life into one category of religious essentials and another of things indifferent. But whereas moral preachers of the Enlightenment emphasized the moral impulse over what they portrayed as mere technical distinctions in religious doctrine and ecclesiastical order, their evangelical counterparts emphasized the act of conversion, which they placed above both doctrinal niceties and moral behavior.

One of the results was that Whitefield and some—though by no means all—revivalists de-emphasized doctrinal preaching almost as much as had the Latitudinarians. They did devote considerable attention to the doctrine of the new birth, but even there their purpose was more persuasion than instruction. Most revivalists emphasized how *little* doctrinal knowledge was necessary for regeneration. Indeed, the most frequent criticism of Whitefield's preaching was that its doctrinal focus was limited and that it contained inconsistencies that resulted from his emphasis on persuasion over exposition.[18]

In one respect, revivalists also followed the Latitudinarians in their attitude toward Scripture. Of course they all insisted on the Bible's infallibility and on the importance of following scriptural practice, contending that the way of the Bible was the only road to salvation. Yet implicitly they also sought external standards for measuring the sanctity of what they were doing, standards consistent with, but not intrinsic to, Scripture. Some assumed that outward behavior constituted the best indicator of internal change; in the frequently cited words of the Presbyterian Samuel Finley, "[W]hen he that was formerly a Drunkard, lives a sober Life: When a vain, light and wanton Person becomes grave and sedate: When the Blasphemer becomes a Praiser of God: When Laughter is turned into Mourning; and carnal Joy into Heaviness; and that professedly on account of their Soul's Condition: When the Ignorant are filled with Knowledge of divine Things. . . . When such as never minded any Religion, do make Religion their only Business," then one could surely discern the hand of God.[19]

To Edwards, the true "distinguishing marks of the work of the spirit" were ultimately judged by holiness, the attachment of the affections to all that was godly. For others it was the emotional release that one felt upon the achievement of assurance, a mark that both critics and moderate defenders of the revival castigated as Antinomian. Even when the excitement of the revival inspired some proponents to anticipate and predict a millennial conclusion, in all but the rarest cases it was the progress of the Awakening itself—that is, the realm of experience—rather than scriptural prophecy per se that provided the data for the argument. In that sense, evangelicals accepted some of the most important implications of the scientific revolution, which had redefined issues of certainty, relying less on ancient texts and more on the realm of observation.

Evangelicals also joined other eighteenth-century ministers in de-emphasizing the subtleties of religious doctrine. During the Awakening and in its immediate aftermath, nearly all American evangelicals remained committed to an essential Calvinism. In other words, salvation was wholly the work of God and not of man. That belief distinguished them from such English evangelicals as the Methodist organizer John Wesley, Whitefield's former friend and ally, who combined his message of salvation by faith with the Arminian assertion that it was within the sinner's power to work toward its achievement. But aside from their adherence to such essentials, most American revivalists required few particulars in doctrine and paid far less attention than their predecessors had to the details of what separated Presbyterians from Anglicans, for example, or to particular beliefs about worship or the sacraments, or to other matters that they considered "things indifferent."

Yet their Calvinism distinguished American evangelicals from Arminians such as Wesley more in theory than in practice. All evangelicals insisted that it was the sinner's duty to strive toward salvation, even if the Calvinists among them denied that it was within the individual's power to effect it. Instead there emerged a certain catholicity, or tolerance, among evangelicals in regard to religious doctrine—albeit a tolerance that they confined to evangelicals. As Samuel Finley expressed it in his sermon *Christ Triumphing and Satan Raging,* the "breaking down of Bigotry"—the holding of communion with godly persons belonging to different religious societies—was itself a sure mark of the working of the spirit.[20]

Evangelicalism also transcended the bounds of denomination and locale; one of the Awakening's principal issues was the revivalists' overt defense of the itinerant, the traveling preacher unconnected to a particular congregation who visited and even trespassed on the domains of other ministers, spreading the Gospel as well as disruption. Indeed, nothing better illustrates the revivalists' acceptance of a segmented religious life than their endorsement of itinerant ministries, including that of Whitefield, the "grand itinerant."[21] Whitefield preached conversion to a different crowd almost every day, leaving the remainder of the minister's job to other clergymen, a criticism that opponents of the revivals made repeatedly.

During the height of the Awakening, some began to view the event as a harbinger of better days to come, of the restoration of pure religion on earth and of the approaching reign of Christ—in short, of the millennium. The most famous such pronouncement came from Jonathan Edwards, who in 1739 offered to his congregation a series of lectures that was later assembled and published posthumously under the title *The History of the Work of Redemption*. In those lectures, Edwards set out to display the divine plan for humankind in the history of the world, punctuated by a series of progressive reformations unfolding in periods when learning was at its height but religion was in decay. The implication—or hope—was that another grand reformation was ensuing, or about to ensue. And in an influential work published at the height of the Awakening, entitled *Some Thoughts Concerning the Present Revival of Religion in New-England*, Edwards's logic led him to the conclusion that the millennium was likely to begin in America.[22]

In the midst of their excitement, revivalist preachers and revived laymen and laywomen increasingly attacked those who opposed the revival outright or who were merely lukewarm in support. Whitefield of course was a master at making himself the center of controversy, which generated publicity in the papers and interest among the provincial audience. Despite his Anglican ordination, he managed to provoke opposition from that church's officials in New York, Philadelphia, Charleston, and Boston and was denied the use of their pulpits in all of those places. James Davenport met with ministers in many of the parishes he visited and proclaimed in public his opinion of their spiritual states. Such procedures did much to turn wavering ministers against the revival.

What may be the most famous controversy involved Gilbert Tennent, who, in the town of Nottingham along the Maryland-Pennsylvania border in the winter of 1740, preached his most famous, or notorious, sermon, *The Danger of an Unconverted Ministry*. He used the story of the Pharisees to imply a condemnation of the opponents of the revival as unconverted and worldly men more interested in maintaining their own privileged positions in the church than in spreading the Gospel or ministering to the needs of their hearers. "All the Doings of unconverted Men," he said, "not proceeding from the Principles of Faith, Love, and a new Nature . . . but flowing from, and tending to Self, as their Principle and End; are doubtless damnably Wicked . . . and do deserve the Wrath and Curse of a Sin-avenging God." It was the hearers' duty to shun such persons and seek out ministers who gave direct evidence of personal conversion. More than any other revivalist sermon, *The Danger of an Unconverted Ministry* stood out for the Old Side as the symbol of everything that was wrong with the revival.[23]

At the peak of the revival, its rhetoric took on an anti-intellectual tone. Whitefield, upon visiting Harvard, criticized the institution for teaching such secular and moralist writers as Tillotson and Samuel Clarke rather than evangelical writers. Gilbert Tennent described those studies as "meer criticks." And Davenport staged a massive book burning at New London, which included works not only by Tillotson but even by Boston's Benjamin Colman, who combined his Latitudinarian sentiments with warm support for the revival.[24]

Davenport was extreme; most of the prominent revivalists were not in fact anti-intellectual at all in spite of their heated rhetoric. Many were firm supporters of education. The New Side Presbyterian minister William Tennent had set up an instructional school for ministers at the "Log College," where his training included not only theological materials but also the classics. Several Log College graduates in turn set up academies of their own, including Samuel Blair, Robert Smith, and Samuel Finley; we shall discover in the next chapter just how vital those academies were to the advancement of learning in provincial America. The Awakening was a great impetus to the creation of educational institutions in America, and the origins of both the College of New Jersey (later Princeton) and the New Hampshire college that became Dartmouth can be traced to the revival.[25]

Attacks such as those staged by Whitefield, Tennent, and Davenport provoked a swift counterattack by those who questioned the godliness of the revival and the spirit of its proponents. The most widely publicized at the time involved Whitefield and Alexander Garden, Anglican commissary of South Carolina, which was reported in the papers of that colony and others. Upon hearing of the evangelist's uncharitable attacks on Anglican authorities, Garden summoned him before an ecclesiastical court. There Whitefield, in a tone that markedly contrasted that of his publications, denied Garden's authority over him but attended the court anyway, portraying himself as a humble and persecuted defender of the truth, a position that earned him widespread sympathetic coverage from the press. Garden had a point. Whitefield was preaching under the Anglican banner, with license from church authorities, even as he attacked them.[26]

In opposition to Whitefield, Garden set forth a clear exposition of the alternative Anglican position. His principal target was the evangelicals' conception of conversion as something certain and immediate that can be known and felt. Such conversions were not susceptible to rational discussion; those who questioned them were viewed simply as lacking in experiential knowledge. In sharp contrast, Garden sketched a view of regeneration in which God dealt with humankind as "moral agents," incorporating into conversion both "the Law and the Gospel," repentance and reform. Above all, true conversion

required reason as well as emotion and a proper ordering of the mental faculties: "Suffer not your passions to be moved," he preached, "but as your minds
are instructed." The commissary was certainly on the mark in noting the
source of the evangelist's popularity: it was his voice, "that enchanting Sound!
. . . It was not the Matter but the Manner, not the Doctrines he delivered, but
the Agreeableness of the Delivery. . . . Take away this Cause, no more Multitude after the Preacher!"[27]

The dispute between Whitefield and Garden pitted Anglican against
Anglican, but in fact most of the controversy the Awakening generated took
place within the dissenting denominations: Presbyterian, Congregationalist,
and Dutch and German Reformed. In 1741, the American Presbyterian
Church divided over the issues the revival caused and the animosity it engendered; the evangelical party allied with the Tennents withdrew from the "Old
Side" synod in Philadelphia to form a separate "New Side" synod in New
York, a split that would last for 17 years. Each side had rival Presbyteries and
even opposing congregations in certain areas, and each claimed the mantle of
the true Presbyterian Church.[28] The Congregationalists avoided an organizational split only because their church had no formal organization to divide.
With no sanctioned structure above the gathered congregations, New Englanders divided at the level of individual towns and churches, leaving a trail of
fractured congregations throughout the region.

In their charged rhetoric, the revivalists often gave the impression that the
Awakening pitted the poor against the rich, the meek against the powerful.
How far such a contention conformed to reality remains unclear. Certainly
the revival had some well-to-do adherents among the merchants of Boston,
New York, and Philadelphia and among country gentlemen in many
colonies—although in most places, larger numbers of those groups probably
opposed rather than endorsed the Awakening. Many others were at least in
comfortable circumstances. By contrast, in what was then the poorest section
of the mid-Atlantic, the backcountry frontiers of Pennsylvania and New York,
the revival found only a limited appeal.

In other areas of early America the revival found at least a measure of support among those of modest means. Much of the constituency for the Awakening in Boston and Philadelphia apparently came from poorer, if not the
poorest, elements of the population. In established New England towns, it
appealed to some in less secure circumstances. And everywhere the leading
opposers came from the most respectable elites, who condemned the revival
in particular as a threat to proper order and decorum. To the extent that the
revivalists' message did attack elements of the established religious order,
which it certainly did, it inevitably drew the ire of at least a portion of the
most respectable persons and families.[29]

Opponents of the revival also contended that the event appealed in particular to women and children. They had their own reasons for that contention, as
we shall see; to a limited degree revivalists conceded the point. Again, the

degree to which that assertion was true is less than clear. In some towns and villages affected by the event the revival drew more women than men, but in others it did not. The larger point is that by the beginning of the Awakening, women already outnumbered men in almost all of early America's denominations, the result of what has been called the "feminization" of American churches. Thus in some parishes, in New England in particular, where there was already a high rate of church membership, the revival could awaken only those who were not already in the churches, which meant an available pool that was predominantly male. Nonetheless, after a brief surge of male converts, the larger trend toward feminization continued almost unabated.[30]

It is clear, however, that the Awakening was identified with women regardless of the actual proportion of converts. In many places, the revival appealed disproportionately to relatively powerless portions of the population—women, children, and young men who had not yet made their way in the world. The revival even drew in some Indians in the "praying villages" of New England and in the Middle Colonies, and some African-Americans in both the South and the North, slaves as well as free people; the Awakening, in fact, would do much to spur evangelical missions to the Indians sponsored by evangelical leaders on both sides of the Atlantic.[31]

Historically, movements that relied on direct access to the Spirit have appealed to the powerless more often than have traditional churches, most of whose forms have tended to reinforce the social hierarchy and to connect religious attainment with social position. Conversely, those movements that have claimed direct access to the Spirit have provided a means with which to bypass traditional sources of power.[32] That was true of many of the movements opponents of the Awakening associated with the revival, most of which had a substantial female presence: the Antinomian controversy in early New England, the radical sects of the English Civil War, and the visionary movement known as the "French Prophets."

Edwards versus Chauncy: The Great "Debate"

Among the many confrontations the Awakening provoked, one in particular has stood out both for the eventual fame of the participants and for lucidity of argument: that between the Northampton revivalist Jonathan Edwards and the Old Light minister Charles Chauncy of Boston, which evolved in a lengthy series of pamphlets and tracts that appeared in the public press between 1741 and 1743. In fact, their so-called debate was not really a debate at all; Edwards never directly addressed his adversary, and much of his argument was devoted to repudiating not the positions of his Bostonian opponent but the even more problematic arguments of Edwards's supposed allies among the radical New Lights. But Chauncy did address Edwards's arguments directly, especially in his *Seasonable Thoughts on the State of Religion in*

New England (1743), which ran to more than 400 pages. Not only the title of that work but also its organization and topics were meant to counter Edwards's *Some Thoughts Concerning the Present Revival*, which had appeared the previous year.[33]

The later differences that emerged between the two preachers should not obscure the fact that at the start of the Awakening, and for a considerable time thereafter, the two demonstrated considerable agreement. Both expressed reservations about the emotional excesses the revival was then producing, as we shall see. Both expressed confidence as well that beyond those excesses New England was in the middle of a movement containing real vital religion and that people had been converted in the process. And as late as 1742, some of Chauncy's sermons contained an evangelical strain almost as strong as that found in Edwards's famous *Sinners in the Hands of an Angry God*. In June of the previous year, Chauncy's sermon on *The New Creature Described* contained the following call to conversion:

> *Who hath bewitched you,* O sinners, that you are thus lost to all sense of your own safety and interest! Be convinced of your danger. You are certainly in a state of dreadful and amazing hazard. You are the persons marked out, as it were, by name, in the revelations of God, for an exclusion from the kingdom of heaven: And if you live and die in your present condition, you will surely be made miserable without mercy and remedy. It is no tale I am now telling you; No, but *the very truth of the true and faithful God*. O realize it to be so! and awake out of your security. Awake thou that sleepest, and call on thy God![34]

Nor was Edwards without doubts about the course of the Awakening. He expressed those as early as 1741 in a sermon delivered at Yale, published as *The Distinguishing Marks of the Work of the Spirit*, which would become the principal theological defense of the revivals on both sides of the Atlantic. In that sermon the Northampton minister set out to defend the Awakening by disowning its most unruly side effects, such as visions, faintings, and other bodily symptoms, as unnecessary parts of the revival. Where he parted company with the Old Lights was in his contention that if the appearance of such symptoms did not prove the divine origins of the event, as the most radical of the New Lights had suggested, neither did it disprove them. It was not surprising that so visible a display of divine power was accompanied by an excess of emotion, even if that display was not part of God's work.[35]

Chauncy would go a good deal further. In a 1742 sermon entitled *Enthusiasm Described and Caution'd Against*, the Boston preacher launched a direct attack on the revival. Whereas Edwards defended the Awakening by attempting to separate the wheat from the chaff, Chauncy saw only chaff, which he viewed as not merely ancillary to but an essential part of the revival. The presence of so much disorderly behavior—and the Boston pastor, as we shall see, was extremely concerned with disorder—rendered the whole unworthy of the Spirit and therefore certainly not of divine origin, and dangerous as well.[36]

To Chauncy, the key term in all of the discussion was *enthusiasm*, the belief—or false belief, as the term was commonly used—that one was possessed of a direct inspiration from the Spirit. That contrasted directly with orthodox Calvinist teaching that revelation was complete with the New Testament and that claims of direct communication after biblical times were not only false but blasphemous, in that they challenged the adequacy of scriptural revelation. They were also dangerous to the good order of society; persons who believed they had direct guidance from the Holy Spirit would not be constrained by the rule of reason or by the ordinary constraints of common life. Chauncy linked the Awakening to past enthusiasts such as the communitarian Anabaptists of sixteenth-century Munster, the Antinomians of seventeenth-century New England, and the mystical French Prophets, all of which had constituted direct threats to order and morality as well as to true religion. Moreover, enthusiasts could never be reasoned out of their false beliefs, since they did not subject their experiences to rational discussion or to the test of empirical proof. To them, the voice of the Spirit constituted an authority superior to that of rational debate.[37]

In place of what he deemed to be enthusiasm, Chauncy offered the outline of a very different kind of religious experience. He criticized preaching whose principal goal was to stir passions, arguing that reason rather than passion was the hallmark of true religion. The spirit of God, Chauncy asserted, affected people as reasonable creatures. In nothing did enthusiasm more clearly reveal itself, in his view, than in the disregard to the "dictates of reason." True religion, he continued, was "a sober, calm, reasonable thing," prepared by conviction and repentance rather than mere terror and raised affections.[38]

Chauncy condemned Whitefield's preaching in particular. The evangelist's goal, according to Chauncy, was to move the passions rather than to inform the reason. That he had succeeded owed less to the force of his arguments than to the target of his appeal, which was the "raw, illiterate, weak and conceited young men, or lads" for whom the example was set by "one or two weak women." The result was visions, trances, and other hysterical symptoms, the very opposite of the "sobriety" and "decency" one found in true religion, where understanding governed the passions, a state the Bostonian referred to as "moral holiness."[39]

Chauncy's stance in general drew upon the Moderate Enlightenment, which valued moderation, order, sobriety, civility, and decency. It was rationalist rather than voluntarist, emphasizing the understanding over the will and especially the necessity of governing the passions. Chauncy shared his suspicion of enthusiasm with his Latitudinarian predecessors; they, like the Bostonian, had viewed rational religion as the reasonable alternative to the instability and violence that resulted from the exclusive reliance on direct revelation and unrestrained passions.

Order and authority were central themes in Chauncy's criticism of the Awakening. The practice of itinerancy—the dissemination of preachers into distant parishes with or without leave from local pastors—impinged on order, as did encouraging parishioners to leave the ministries of "unconverted" clergymen. So also did the stirring up of the passions to frenzy, the sanctioning of visions and personal revelations, and the encouragement of individuals to speak freely of religious matters regardless of age, gender, or station. One of the "main ends" of religion, to Chauncy, was "to dispose and enable People to behave as Christians in their various Stations, Relations, and Conditions." Religion to Chauncy should be a "reasonable thing" conforming to the Enlightened times in which he lived, and an orderly thing as well. Chauncy condemned in particular "the disorder of EXHORTING, and PRAYING, and SINGING, and LAUGHING" as unseemly and a clear "breach upon common order and decency."[40]

Decency was a matter of particular concern to Chauncy, and he repeated the term often. He criticized the Awakening for producing heights of passion and for discouraging gravity of countenance. Nor did the revival produce much in the way of Christian "charity," which according to Chauncy was surely lacking in the abrasive and contentious preaching of Whitefield and Tennent and in the frequent attacks on respected figures in the religious establishment. Charity, according to the Boston minister, was "the grand work by which Christians are to distinguish themselves from others" and "the grand criteria for judging whether the Spirit dwells within."[41]

In important respects, Jonathan Edwards had the more difficult task. As a leader of the 1734–1735 Connecticut River Valley revival and an early proponent of the Awakening, Edwards was committed to disproving Chauncy's characterization of that event as mere enthusiasm. Yet Edwards was as much a man of the eighteenth century as was Chauncy. He also was familiar with, and strongly influenced by, the new learning, which he had first encountered during his college days at Yale at a time when the Yale curriculum was moving ever further into the transatlantic world of learning. Such a progression was especially evident in the aftermath of the college library's 1714 acquisition of more than 700 new volumes, financed with a gift from the London merchant and colonial agent Jeremiah Dummer, which included works by Locke, Shaftesbury, Newton, and others; the study of those same volumes would help persuade another Yale student, Samuel Johnson of Connecticut, to abandon his Puritanism entirely for a more Enlightened Anglicanism of the sort that derived from the Latitudinarians.[42]

The effect on Edwards was different. Although he remained firmly committed to his ancestral faith, he came to realize that the mere reiteration of faith or the allusion to special providences would not satisfy a literate eighteenth-century audience. He sought to explain his beliefs in ways that would persuade a generation inclined to view the natural, civil, and spiritual worlds in accordance with the principles of order and reason. He recognized that the revival's more spectacular symptoms—the crying out, the falling down, the reliance on individual visions and providences—would no longer inspire certainty among a large portion of the public. Thus the Northampton pastor had to explain those symptoms not as manifestations of the Spirit but rather as natural events that could be understood in an orderly way as the direct results of human nature and human psychology. The result would be the creation of some of the most notable and influential works in early American theology and philosophy, works that became standards in a substantial portion of the British world.

Most interpretations of the Edwards-Chauncy debate ultimately derive from Perry Miller's brilliant but often unreliable intellectual biography, *Jonathan Edwards*.[43] To Miller, Edwards was a perfect modern, the individual who brought Puritanism into the modern age by pouring its age-old beliefs into the mold of the new empirical philosophy of Newton and Locke. That Edwards was influenced by the new learning is beyond question, but he was hardly the lone scholar in the wilderness that Miller portrayed, in an age in which Enlightened science and literature were becoming staples of eighteenth-century education and discussion. Moreover, Edwards's primary goal in utilizing the new learning was to combat its seemingly secular implications and to preserve as much as possible of the theocentric perspective of early modern Calvinism.

One area in which Edwards was certainly influenced by modern ideas was psychology. Like his correspondent Benjamin Colman, Edwards made considerable use of the psychology of the affections, a subject he addressed in all of his revival works and completed in his *Treatise Concerning Religious Affections* (1746).[44] He also borrowed from the British moralists the association of virtue with beauty—the representation of virtue as an inner principle not subject to prior rational conviction but manifest in an aesthetic sense, a relish for doing good. But Edwards's goal was certainly not that of Francis Hutcheson, to derive a purely natural ethics supported by religious motivation. Rather, he hoped to demonstrate that one could attain true virtue—which he defined as a selfless benevolence, or the love of being in general—only through regeneration and grace.

In Miller's view, Edwards—but not Chauncy—moved beyond the older faculty psychology, which assigned the mind's principal attributes to different faculties, such as the intellect and the will, and offered instead an integrated psyche in which will and intellect functioned together. That allowed Edwards to present regeneration as a simultaneous change in all of the faculties and to portray the revival's more violent emotional symptoms as natural byproducts of a radical change in one's nature rather than as irrational passions. Yet Chauncy was no backward defender of the old psychology. The faculty psychology did not disappear with Locke's newer sensationalist psychology but combined with it to produce the typical Enlightened psychology of ordered faculties of the reasons and the affections. Chauncy's portrayal of a rational faculty ordering and controlling the lower appetites was standard fare in the Moderate Enlightenment and even among moderate Revolutionaries in the America of the 1770s and 1780s and on into the nineteenth century. The whole movement to polish and refine British and provincial culture, associated with Addison and Steele, the novelists, and genteel elements in the colonies, assumed such a model of the human psyche.[45]

In some respects Chauncy's theology was conservative, supportive of the social order. The Bostonian criticized the revival for its appeal to "*Children, young People,* and *Women,* whose Passions are soft and tender, and more easily thrown into a commotion." Elsewhere he referred to the "raw, illiterate [and] weak," including "weak women" who were affected.[46] His love of order was reflected in his assertion that a revival, if it were truly a work of the Spirit, would work to reinforce the inclinations of individuals to remain within their stations in society, whether as wives, children, employees, or tenants.

Edwards's theology, by contrast, appealed directly to those without standing in the social order, to women and the young. In the *Faithful Narrative,* Edwards offered two examples of converts whose natures had been sanctified by conversion, both young girls. His *Thoughts on the Revival* contained a much more extensive discussion of the nature of true piety in the example of his wife, Sarah Pierpont Edwards, although he was careful to disguise not only her identity but her gender. (He later offered the world an even fuller portrayal of a male convert, the Indian missionary David Brainerd.)[47] The kind of appeal to the affections Edwards endorsed was often identified with women; true religion, according to the Northampton pastor, was exemplified in selfless behavior that placed the interests of religion, of others, of "Being" in general, above one's own. Women were often expected to behave just so in the family and in society.

Yet there was more to Chauncy's hostility toward disorder than simple elitism, although that was certainly one of its elements. He did criticize unbridled passions, but he did not reject all appeals to the affections. In one sermon, he sounded much like Edwards in describing regeneration as "not meerly an assent of the mind to gospel truths" but an entire change in orientation, an "inward, strong persuasion" affecting not only the reason but a true religious "joy."[48] It was a "universal change." The "whole inner man is altered," so that converts had "neither the same apprehensions, nor resolutions, nor affections as they had before."[49]

The largest difference between Chauncy's view of conversion and that of his rival was its results. Although Old Lights were often called moralists, mainstream New Lights such as Edwards were no less concerned that converts adopt a saintly lifestyle. Indeed, for both, anything less than moral behavior was considered a pretty good sign of the lack of saving grace. Where they differed was in the nature of that behavior. Although both believed that conversion resulted in a new attachment of the affections, the objects of that attachment differed. To Edwards, the legacy of regeneration was an altogether altered attachment of the affections, away from the selfish and worldly attachments they had held before and toward the love of God and of all being. Such a belief was manifest in a selfless and holy deportment. By contrast, Chauncy believed that the affections were altered in a manner that attached them more fully to the normal duties of common life, to one's role in the family, the church, the community, the colony, and the nation. Regenerate affections were directed primarily not toward the other world but toward the soundest, most virtuous ends of this world.

To a degree, Chauncy's views made him a conservative; he was unalterably opposed to subverting the proper and moral order of civil society. He opposed allowing the young, the poor, and the female to preach publicly outside of their proper stations. Yet he did not oppose all expressions of public discontent. When Chauncy later saw a British king and Parliament infringing on what he considered the just rights of their colonial subjects during the 1760s and '70s, he did not hesitate to support resistance, rebellion, and ultimately revolution.[50]

Moreover, the Bostonian molded his view of conversion into an unusually broad evangelical tool, to be *"poured out,* both upon *pastors* and *people,* upon high and low, rich and poor, male and female, bond and free, old and young." Because his view of conversion did not require abandoning the ordinary course of common life, Chauncy could later extend his sentiments into a defense of the doctrine of universal salvation. On such matters his positions were far less exclusive than those of Edwards or of other New Light Calvinists.[51]

In recounting the drama of Chauncy and Edwards's debate, we ought not to lose sight of the many similarities that Chauncy and Edwards shared both as New England ministers and as men of the eighteenth century. Both were born into the families of clergymen during the first decade of the eighteenth century; both were educated in New England's colleges at a time when those institutions were altering their curricula as the result of the new learning. Both considered themselves loyal to New England's peculiar religious traditions, and both shared the belief of most of their colleagues that Puritan practices required modification to make them more effective in the modern age.

Despite Chauncy's categorization as an extreme religious liberal or Edwards's as a modern, both men were theists, in the sense of believing in an all-powerful providence that controlled human destiny. Although Chauncy is often classified among New England's Arminians, the label is not wholly accurate. His ideas retained significant Calvinist elements, such as the absolute sovereignty of God and the incapacity of humankind to effect its own salvation, the principle Arminian position. Indeed, it was the irresistible force of the divine will that would ultimately lead to the universal reformation and salvation of humankind. Chauncy as much as Edwards continued to espouse the doctrine of regeneration; they differed less in their view of its necessity than of its manifestations. Both defended the sanctity of Scripture: indeed, the Boston pastor argued that it was the influence of the Holy Spirit on the

Bible's recorders, rather than the alleged direct inspiration felt by contemporary converts, that rendered it the one true and infallible guide.[52]

For both Chauncy and Edwards, religion required new explanations in an Enlightened age. Both were influenced by the quest for order and regularity and natural laws that followed the scientific revolution, and both applied that explanatory effort to the subject of religion. Edwards was no more willing than Chauncy to root religious assurance in the sort of individual, personalized experience of direct revelation that so many subjects of the revival exhibited. The Northampton clergyman joined his Bostonian colleague in cautioning against believing fortuitous circumstances, or apparent providences, to be certain rules for conduct or reliable signs of regeneration. Both regarded the phenomenon of enthusiasm and even the religious experience itself as subjects for analysis. Both ultimately looked for confirmation of beliefs and experiences not in signs or providences or prophecies but rather, in the Enlightenment manner, in human nature—in a proper ordering of the human faculties, as Chauncy viewed it, or as Edwards argued, in a proper attachment of the affections.

Both men also recognized the necessity of arguing from observation and experience to persuade an eighteenth-century audience. Thus Edwards used the case of his wife, of David Brainerd, and of several other converts to display empirical manifestations of the new birth and its effect on religious affections. Chauncy spent several months traveling in New England observing conversions and noting firsthand counterexamples that could be used to demonstrate the enthusiastic nature of most of the alleged conversions. Thus neither writer ultimately relied on Scripture to make his case. Both implicitly agreed with the Latitudinarians that the many attempts in human history to create social orders based upon scriptural models had produced ambiguity and discord, and so both looked beyond the Bible for the means with which to shore up its message.

As sons of New England, Chauncy and Edwards both invoked their Puritan ancestors to support their positions. To Edwards, the Awakening represented a revival of the vital piety of earlier generations, and he argued from personal experience that the revival conformed exactly to the celebrated religious harvests of his famous grandfather, Solomon Stoddard. Chauncy cited the condemnation of Anne Hutchinson by the Puritan founders as proof of their ancestors' hostility to enthusiasm.

Even as they rooted their positions in New English traditions, both Edwards and Chauncy conducted their debate for a transatlantic audience. In addition to citing New England precedents for the Awakening, Edwards relied heavily on examples cited in the Scottish Presbyterian minister Robert Fleming's classical *Fulfilling of the Scripture*. Edwards's original narrative, as we have seen, was published in London at the instigation of English Dissenting ministers. Thereafter, the two men continued to address an English and, increasingly, a Scottish audience, as that country also became embroiled in contentions over local religious revivals. Edwards's *Distinguishing Marks of the Work of the Spirit* was published in England and in Scotland (twice) the same year it appeared in Boston. Both Scottish and American ministers began publishing religious periodicals devoted to spreading revival news to a transatlantic audience.[53]

Even after the Awakening abated, the transatlantic discussions it engendered continued apace. Edwards, in his *Thoughts on the Revival*, had suggested the likelihood that the revival was a harbinger of the millennium, which, he projected at that time, was to begin in America. Then, with the outbreak of a similar evangelical movement in western Scotland in 1742, the Scottish minister John Erskine amplified Edwards's idea and speculated that the Scottish and American revivals might together signify the coming of the millennium. By 1745, the American Awakening having lost its momentum, Edwards himself, in a letter to a Scottish correspondent, suggested that perhaps it was not America at all but rather Scotland that was destined to lead the evangelical movement. Thereafter, evangelical ministers in Scotland and America maintained an extensive and intimate correspondence about religious affairs, one manifestation of which was the launching of a transatlantic "Concert for Prayer" in 1747, an attempt to get Christians in both countries to pray simultaneously for a reinvigoration of the British-American revival movement. Edwards's collection of millennialist sermons, *The History of the Work of Redemption*, was first revised and edited for publication in Edinburgh by John Erskine.[54]

Revival opponents were equally active participants in transatlantic discussions. One of Chauncy's first attacks on the Awakening appeared in a published letter to Edinburgh's George Wishart.[55] Subsequently, not only Chauncy's works but several other tracts by opponents of the revival were republished in Glasgow by those opposed to the Scottish evangelical movement. Conversely, both pro- and antirevival sermons and pamphlets written in Scotland were quickly republished by printers in Boston and Philadelphia.

It should be noted that this was a very particular kind of transatlantic debate; both Old Side and New corresponded principally with their religious colleagues in the Presbyterian Church of Scotland. That was partly because Scotland was immersed in controversy over its own revival during the early 1740s that began in the western parish of Cambuslang.[56] In part it was because of the Church of Scotland's association with Calvinist or Reformed religion. In the aftermath of the revival, evangelicals on both sides of the Atlantic would identify Scotland and America as the principal homes of the Awakening and of true religion.

In the aftermath of the Awakening, Jonathan Edwards became the most articulate defender of the revivals in the British world. During the remaining 15 years of his life, he composed a remarkable series of theoretical works defending its principles. In his *Treatise Concerning Religious Affections*, Edwards further depicted the influence of regeneration on human psychology. In *Freedom of the Will* and *Doctrine of Original Sin Defended*, Edwards set out to counter philosophers' articulation of an enlarged picture of human capabilities and of human goodness and presented what would become the standard Calvinist defense of predestination in an Enlightened age. He argued that although God was the creator of all humankind, and even of the human will, men and women still sinned voluntarily—that is, in sinning they followed the dictates of their own wills and were therefore culpable. In that sense their wills were free and sinful and worthy of damnation. Finally, in *The Nature of True Virtue*, Edwards returned to the subject of benevolence, arguing against the moralists that true virtue—an inner sense of benevolence altogether without selfish motives—could not be found in natural man but only in the entirely redirected and reconstructed will and affections associated with regeneration.

Ironically, Edwards did not fare as well at home as he did in the larger transatlantic evangelical world. After concluding that a consistent doctrine of regeneration required him to abandon the practice his eminent grandfather had initiated at Northampton in allowing all professing Christians of good behavior into full communion in the church, in 1748 Edwards, against the wishes of some of his congregation's most prominent members, began to restrict communion within his parish to those who offered a clear profession of faith, reasserting the minister's discretion in the process. In the ensuing battle, Edwards was dismissed from his congregation and left for the Indian mission in the frontier town of Stockbridge, where in relative isolation he wrote his most prominent philosophical works. His eminence continued to attract support: he was offered a pulpit in Scotland and in 1757 accepted a call to the presidency of the new Presbyterian College of New Jersey at Princeton, but he died from an adverse reaction to a smallpox inoculation after barely a month in office.[57]

Chauncy's career was in many respects more successful. He achieved international recognition, although not to the extent of his rival. He was awarded an honorary doctorate in divinity from Edinburgh University in 1742. He continued to minister to Boston's First Church for the remainder of his long career and continued to grow in popularity. During the 1750s and '60s, he was among the leaders of those American clerics who campaigned against the efforts of the colonial Anglican Church to establish an American bishop in the colonies by act of Parliament. A decade later he spoke articulately against the Stamp Act, linking America's religious freedoms to its civil liberties.[58]

Radicals and Separates

If Edwards's position on church membership remained outside the mainstream of the established church, it closely resembled that of many who left the establishment during the revival. One of the principal effects of the Awakening in New England was to reopen the whole question of church membership, which had long been a particular concern in the region. For half a century, under the leadership of such ministers as Solomon Stoddard, New England churches had been moving away from the restrictive membership practices of the founding generation and toward a more open policy. Now, responding in part to the preaching of Davenport and of other radical evangelicals who proclaimed their assurance of salvation on the basis of the experience of grace in their souls, multitudes of New Lights departed from churches that allowed the saved and the damned to intermix. They joined instead purer visible churches like those of the first New Englanders or of the English Separatists that denied communion to mere moral men and women who were unable to testify to the work of the Spirit on their souls. In fact the position of the new Separates was quite different from that of New England's Puritan founders, who had viewed their congregations of visible saints as religious establishments. The Separates, by contrast, rejected that establishment along with all others and set up their churches on the basis of voluntarism.[59]

A good example of a center of Separatism and New Light radicalism was eastern Long Island, settled in the seventeenth century by New Englanders and especially by groups with Separatist traditions, from either Rhode Island or the more orthodox Puritan settlements. From the beginning, eastern Long Island was home to a variety of sectarians: Quakers, Separatists, and others who participated in a transatlantic network of Puritan radicals together with other New Englanders across the sound in Rhode Island and eastern Connecticut. In 1740, Southold was home to James Davenport (whose principal offenses were committed across the water in New London), and eastern Long Island would soon house such other radical itinerants as Elisha Paine, Jonathan Barber, and Samuel Buell.[60]

Among the difficulties faced by Separates was the shortage of ordained ministers and the absence of institutions to train Separate preachers. During the height of the Awakening, a number of the separated churches were led not by ministers but by laymen—and occasionally laywomen—such as church elders and other community leaders but occasionally by people with no greater claim to spiritual authority than the workings of the Spirit. Those were the sort of leaders Charles Chauncy condemned, and their position was the kind of abuse of formal church authority and of the tradition of an educated ministry that respectable evangelicals such as Edwards, Benjamin Colman, and Thomas Prince fought against. Out of those movements emerged some important religious figures, such as the future Baptist leader Isaac Backus, from a Separate congregation in Connecticut.[61]

Not all lay exhorters were as uneducated or illiterate as critiques by the Old Lights suggest. Some, such as Elisha Paine of Windham, Connecticut, were well established in their communities. Paine was a highly respected lawyer before becoming a Separate. Following his conversion during the Awakening, Paine felt the call to preach and applied to the county ministerial association for a license. The association accepted his qualifications and offered him a license, provided that he would subscribe to the still-controversial Saybrook Platform, which rendered local congregations subordinate to a clerical association, a step away from the independence of New England tradition and toward Presbyterianism. That he refused to do.[62]

What Separates did agree on was the primacy of the call of the Spirit above mere book learning and the related aspects of ordinary ministerial education. That was evident in one of Paine's descriptions of a Separate meeting:

> I preached from Ez. 14.3 and from Rev. 2.21. After service we sang a hymn. I felt the Spirit of the Lord come upon me. I rose up and exhorted and persuaded them to come to Christ; and immediately there was a screeching and groaning all over the multitude.[63]

Early Separate meetings were rife with perfectionism, enthusiasm, and Antinomianism. They emphasized the necessity of particular faith—doctrines believed personally by individual members and implanted by the Holy Ghost —more than of broad church confessions. The confession of the Mansfield Meeting took matters even further, boldly stating that "we believe that we are of that Number who were Elected of GOD to eternal Life, and that Christ did live on Earth, die and rise again for us in particular." Antinomian tendencies were also evident in that document, which proclaimed the members "[j]ustified in the Sight of GOD, for the sake of Christ"; God made them believe "by sending . . . the Holy Ghost into our Souls" so that they were now "Partakers of the Divine Nature."[64]

A good example of a Separate layman was Nathan Cole, the Connecticut farmer who left so vivid an account of Whitefield's appearance at Middletown. Cole waited for a number of years to become a Separate, during which time he was tormented by visions and fears of hell. As was typical, a vision— in this instance an image of the gate of heaven "as plain as ever I saw anything with my bodily eyes in my life"—started him toward his resolution to separate. He cast about and debated about which church to join, until one day in 1763, "as my mind was following the footsteps of the flock in the bible; I came right upon Mr. Frothinghams Congregational [Separate] Church in Middletown." Another Connecticut Separate, Hannah Heaton, recorded a religious life composed of bouts with Satan in visions and dreams and a spiritualized natural world of comets, thunderstorms, and other remarkable providences. The Separate laity seems far removed from the world of the Enlightenment.[65]

For many Separates, the journey was not yet complete. Many would eventually abandon that communion as well for the Baptists, who refused to grant the privileges not only of church membership and communion but even of baptism either to infants or to any who were unable to offer convincing testimony of their faith. By 1760, New England would house as many as 30 Separate-Baptist congregations.[66]

There were economic as well as spiritual reasons for that change. The arrival of toleration in New England had entitled members of dissenting Protestant congregations to withhold their tax payments to the standing order and to direct them instead to their own congregations. Separates were classified as Congregationalists, however, and were therefore denied the exemption. Those who went over to the Baptists could claim it. (By contrast, on Long Island, where there was no religious establishment, a few Separate congregations continued to flourish.) In general, there is considerable evidence that Baptist adherents hailed disproportionately from marginal areas of New England towns—from river valleys and mill sites—and had less involvement than the rest of their townspeople with the integrated aspects of communal life. They lived farther from the meetinghouses and had less desire to contribute to them. They preferred an ideology of voluntarism.[67]

Outside greater New England, sentiment in favor of any sort of separatism was much weaker. Middle Colony evangelicals came predominantly from state church traditions and had little inclination toward separatism or toward congregational purity. Thus although the Presbyterians divided into rival Old Side and New Side synods, each claimed to represent the true Presbyterian Church. In that region, the most radical outgrowths of the Awakening took place among the German sects of Pennsylvania, especially the Moravians, whose claims to a direct and supernatural revelation were denounced as heretical and enthusiastic by almost every other group in the region.[68]

There were also radical New Lights in the southern colonies, principally in the Carolinas. In South Carolina, the planters Hugh and Jonathan Bryan, aroused by Whitefield's preaching and inspired by his denunciations of the ill treatment of slaves in the colony, demonstrated to the entire planter class just how dangerous religious enthusiasm could be in a slaveholding colony. Hugh Bryan began by establishing a school for the religious education of Negroes. Soon large crowds of slaves were meeting at his plantation for religious education, a sight that inspired fear in a colony that had recently faced a major slave rebellion. Rumors spread that Bryan had gone beyond Whitefield's warning about their un-Christian treatment of their slaves and was prophesying that slaves would destroy the colony, a charge Bryan later admitted to Carolina authorities.[69]

The affair ended more peacefully than might have been anticipated. Bryan's visions reached their zenith when he believed that he, like Moses, could part the waters before him, an experiment that nearly drowned him before he was rescued. He then began to recant his prophesies, which allowed the planting class to close ranks around him without further damage. The Bryans continued to sponsor evangelical churches and the religious education of slaves; like Whitefield, they never suggested that Christian slaves need be anything but slaves. Anglican and dissenting churches would grow side by side in the colony, without posing any apparent threat to the social order.

Such religious radicalism emerged much more slowly in Virginia, which had a far stronger Anglican establishment under firm planter control. The Awakening of 1739–1740 barely affected the Old Dominion; not until the middle of the decade did a true New Light group emerge, and those were moderate Presbyterians, first under lay leadership and eventually under the ministries of several clergymen, including Samuel Davies. Virginia Presbyterians long retained their moderate profile, campaigning for religious toleration but otherwise offering little challenge to the standing order in either politics or religion.[70]

That challenge was left to the Baptists, who emerged after 1760, especially in the southern backcountry, where they provided a far more radical dissent from planter religion and from the dominance of genteel planter values in the Chesapeake. The Baptists opposed the conspicuous displays of wealth and personal power common among the gentry of the region, along with dancing, gambling, horsemanship, and other planter amusements. In cultural style, the early Baptists represented the very antithesis of the planter ideal. Baptists and, still later, Methodists would form an important component of the religious life of the small farmer population of the southern backcountry, with a spiritual emotionalism and rough egalitarianism that contrasted markedly with the hierarchical, genteel, and enlightened sensibilities of the gentry.[71] As the Anglican missionary Charles Woodmason described them, they were "Rude—Ignorant—Void of Manners, Education or Good Breeding—No genteel or Polite Persons among them. . . . The people are of all Sects and Denominations—A mix'd Medley from all countries and the Off Scouring of America."[72]

Liberal Theology

If the Awakening led evangelicals to push their positions to further radical extremes, it had a similar effect on those called Liberals, especially in New England. Although Edwards and other revivalists had attacked opponents of the Awakening as Arminians, after the Dutch theologian Jacobus Arminius, who had advanced the position that grace was not irresistible, that men and women had the power to choose faith or not, for most opponents the label was inaccurate. Criticizing the revivalists for implying that only a personal feeling of assurance, rather than its manifestation in a sanctified lifestyle, was the mark of conversion, most opponents denied that such a lifestyle was in any sense a cause of their salvation. Chauncy, for one, explicitly denied any such implication, insisting instead in orthodox fashion that conversion was invariably the work of God. But in the years after the revival, in reviewing what they deemed the dangerous and disorderly ramification of enthusiasm, an increasing number of clergymen in and around Boston, led in particular by the celebrated Jonathan Mayhew of that city's West Church, moved increasingly away from orthodoxy altogether and maximized their views of the capabilities of human nature and the achievements of reason and natural religion. Thus they began the process that would turn Liberalism into Arminianism and Arminianism into Unitarianism, the ultimate rejection of what had been the orthodox doctrine of the Trinity.*

Many of the Liberals only hinted at a move towards Arminianism, if they went that far at all. Perhaps the first to do so explicitly was Lemuel Briant, in a sermon preached from Jonathan Mayhew's West Church pulpit in 1749 on *The Absurdity and Blasphemy of Depreciating Moral Virtue*. Briant put the case bluntly: "Either our Righteousness is of some Use and Significancy in the Affair of our Salvation, or it is not. Either it has some Connection with, and actual Influence on our Happiness, or it is of no real Necessity as to us." The latter statement, of course, was pure Antinomianism, which he rejected out of hand. In essence, Briant agreed with the most rigid Calvinists in disavowing any middle ground between endorsing and categorically denying the efficacy of virtue for salvation; he differed from them in avowing the Arminian choice.[73]

Most Liberals did not go that far during the middle years of the eighteenth century. Charles Chauncy was too much a descendant of New English traditions to wholly disavow ancient doctrines of salvation by faith. Nor did he ever abandon or even temper traditional Calvinistic notions of an all-determining providence, as did some of his Arminian friends. Instead, he extended that doctrine in an altogether different direction, eventually challenging the equally significant doctrine of election. By the 1750s, Chauncy's biblical studies combined with his eighteenth-century view of a benevolent deity moved him in the direction of universalism, causing him to doubt that a God devoted to the good of humankind would irrevocably doom even a portion thereof to eternal torment. "A more shocking idea can scarce be given of the *Deity*," he wrote, "than that which represents him as *arbitrarily dooming the greater part of the race of men to eternal misery*."[74] Rather, an omnipotent creator would certainly use his power to compel sinners to repentance during a lengthy but impermanent period of suffering—a view his critics compared to the Roman Catholic doctrine of purgatory. Such a view seemed too harsh a challenge to orthodoxy in New England in the middle of the eighteenth century, and the Boston pastor kept his ideas private, awaiting a more "seasonable" moment. That moment would not arrive until the 1780s.

In their tendency toward Arminianism, New England's Liberal preachers followed the example of their English Presbyterian counterparts. By the second half of the eighteenth century, orthodox English Calvinists considered many of the Presbyterian clergy to be unsound in doctrine, as they departed

---

*Unitarianism combined the older heresies of Arianism and Socinianism, both of which rejected the doctrine of the Trinity by denying either the divinity of Jesus or his equality with God the father.

from such doctrines as predestination in favor of positions more consistent with voluntarism and free will. Their questioning did not end with the doctrine of predestination but extended to attacks on the doctrine of the Trinity and of the divinity of Christ. Such Unitarian positions, which would be proclaimed in Liberal New England circles as well before long, would culminate in the next century in the controversy surrounding the appointment of Henry Ware as Professor of Divinity at Harvard in 1805.[75]

Few other colonial ministers went as far as New England's Arminians. In the mid-Atlantic, Presbyterian Old Side ministers split with their New Side colleagues over the Awakening, not over the basic tenets of Calvinism. Most Old Side preachers in that region adopted positions similar to that of the most Enlightened faction in the Presbyterian Church of Scotland, with whom they often identified, if they went even that far.[76] If they sided with Chauncy in denouncing as enthusiastic the excessive emotionalism of the revival and preferred more rational and decent expressions of piety, few among the clergy doubted that religion was in need of reviving and that preaching the word and striving for repentance were the ways to achieve it. The largest number of provincials in the mainstream denominations continued to endorse a broad religious middle ground that avoided the extremes of Separatism and Unitarianism.

Protestants and Provincials

True Liberals and authentic Separates remained rare in the colonies; they were outnumbered almost everywhere by a Protestant mainstream that forms the subject of the next chapter. Yet the evangelical revival as a whole contributed to provincial culture in several important ways. The first was that everywhere it expanded the reach of the transatlantic community, bringing into personal contact or correspondence groups that had not been so involved before. Whitefield himself certainly played a key role in personalizing that community. Just as important were the series of evangelical periodicals that grew out of the revival: the *London Weekly History,* the *Glasgow Weekly History,* Thomas Prince's *Christian History* from Boston, and the *Christian Monthly History* of Edinburgh, along with their successors, each of which carried news of the revival from the whole of the British world. Although the papers themselves were short-lived, the correspondences they began were not. The reports in the papers took the form of letters written by firsthand observers, often ministers, to the editors of the papers. Many of those correspondences across the bounds of the province and the ocean lasted for decades.[77]

One significant result of those transatlantic connections was an increasing identification of provinciality itself with evangelical religion and with Dissent generally, at least in the northern colonies. Both Scots and Americans of Reformed denominations came to identify Scotland and America as the principal homes of the revival and of religious orthodoxy. Many of the correspondences that grew out of the revival linked American evangelicals with Scottish Presbyterian ministers, such as John Maclaurin, John Gillies, and especially John Erskine of Edinburgh. Erskine maintained an active correspondence with leading evangelicals throughout the British world for more than six decades and did much to nourish a united evangelical front that extended beyond purely religious matters to the realms of politics and moral reform. Collectively, those evangelical correspondents in both places created an image of a provincial evangelical community working jointly to defend the cause of true religion against interference from intrusive authorities in church and state.[78]

The revival also increased the political assertiveness of provincial congregations. As the Awakening divided American denominations, those who resisted the prevailing order were forced to defend their dissent on the basis of such concepts as individual conscience and minority rights, coupled with a Latitudinarian view of religious essentials. New Side Presbyterians, for example, in the process of dividing the Philadelphia Synod, contended that it was the duty of minorities to give way to majorities in the church—unless the majority attempted to impose inessentials or "circumstantials" on the consciences of the minority. Such tyranny necessarily led true Christians to "obey God rather than Man."[79]

Some of the most heated debates took place in Congregationalist Connecticut, where Old Light preachers aligned with magistrates to pass strict laws preventing itinerancy, denied religious exemptions on taxes to separating New Light congregations, and then removed from office all who failed to enforce the laws with vigor. Such stridency called forth much discussion, the most eloquent being former clergyman Elisha Williams's *Essential Rights and Liberties of Protestants* (1744).[80] In that pamphlet, indebted heavily to Locke's *Letter on Toleration* and to his contract theory of government, Williams contended for the liberty of all Protestants to worship in whatever manner seemed necessary to them from their reading of Scripture, independent of the authority of church or state. Civil authority was not to infringe on the rights of private conscience.

The audience he was addressing in colonial Connecticut hardly noticed that the liberties he endorsed belonged not to people but to *Protestants*. Williams followed a considerable line of authors in contending that Catholics did not merit such rights, because, as he wrote: "tho' the principles of a consistent Protestant, naturally tend to make him a good subject in any civil state, even in a popish one . . . yet that is not the case with the papist: for by his very principles he is an enemy or traytor to a Protestant state: and strictly speaking popery is so far from deserving the name of religion, that it is rather a conspiracy against it, against the reason, liberties, and peace of mankind."[81] Williams was referring, of course, to the argument that the principal allegiance of Catholics was to the pope rather than to the nation and that as such they were sworn to undermine Protestant states. Williams believed that Catholicism was not a religion but "a conspiracy against it" because he followed Protestant practice in defining religion as belief personally held and arrived at, which Catholic teaching did not necessarily promote.

So striking was the libertarian rhetoric of some of the evangelicals that several historians have portrayed it as the fountain of American democratic tradition, from which the American Revolution and its aftermath derived. Such a view has tended to portray religious Liberals as the true conservatives of the day, as they endorsed the hierarchical aspects of the colonial social order while resisting its leveling tendencies. It has cast evangelicals as forward-looking advocates of egalitarian principles.[82] Although there is certainly much support for such an argument, it is, in the end, far too simple. Evangelicalism in the eighteenth century was a mix of sentiments, some democratic but others far less so. Conversely, although Liberals on the whole strongly supported order, they were far from illiberal on many other issues, including the Revolution itself.

We should also remember that the evangelical movement was not originally or uniquely American and cannot, by itself, account for what became distinctive about American culture. It had close connections with the related revival movements in England, Scotland, and Wales and even with a variety of Pietist movements on the European continent. Participation in the evangelical movement was itself a measure of the involvement of provincial Americans with transatlantic culture. Moreover, the Awakening greatly furthered such involvements. Thus the revival movement of the eighteenth century both reflected and contributed to the development of provincial identities.

five

_____

Piety, Virtue, and Character

One of the more unusual friendships to grow out of the revival movement was that which linked the evangelist Whitefield, the pious, charismatic, and emotional saver of souls, with the practical, secular, and skeptical printer Benjamin Franklin. On the surface the contrast could not have been greater: the Englishman sacrificed any prospect for material acquisition to a lifelong quest to spread the Gospel; the provincial printer questioned the efficacy of any such effort, adopting as his motto the principle that the way to serve God was to serve the needs of men and women in this world. Yet the friendship that they maintained during their lives was real. Franklin uniformly praised the Englishman's numerous charitable efforts and defended him against the many false charges that he appropriated the proceeds of those efforts for his own benefit; Whitefield prayed for Franklin's conversion and conversed with him regularly about matters of religion and benevolence. At Whitefield's death in 1770, Franklin eulogized him as one whose "integrity, disinterestedness, and indefatigable zeal" he would "never see exceeded."[1]

Part of that friendship can be attributed to motives of self-interest. Whitefield the itinerant depended on the lavish publicity that Franklin and his fellow printers provided in order to attract his audiences; printers, in turn, relied on the evangelist's popular appeal to attract readers to their newspapers and to the many sermons they printed. Whitefield, in fact, was as much a publishing phenomenon as a religious one; hundreds of his works were published during his lifetime, in Britain and in America. Between 1737 and 1750, British and American publishers issued something like 400 editions of the evangelist's writings.[2] Franklin the protocapitalist would have been ungrateful indeed to have treated so profitable an author with anything less than amity and respect.

Yet it would be uncharitable on our part to find nothing more than personal interest in a friendship that lasted for several decades. The two men shared something else as well: an intense devotion to the betterment of humankind. Each in his own way was a tireless worker for the cause of humanity. That they differed in their view of the proper means to that end may, in the final analysis, be less important than their common effort.

Nor were the means they employed as different as one might suppose. Both employed the mechanisms of the market and of the expanding culture of communications in highly innovative ways in pursuing their causes. Both were fervent advocates of a multitude of charitable enterprises. Both believed that the betterment of human society depended on the betterment of the individual. Indeed, although both men participated in considerable institutional innovation, they devoted the bulk of their efforts to inspiring the independent individual rather than to reforming society by revamping its structure. In that, the two friends worked in a manner well suited to the goals of a provincial citizenry attempting to project an identity of competence and confidence. In short, from the varying perspectives of religious and secular culture, both men focused their attention on the building of moral character. For Whitefield and for Franklin, and for the broad range of provincial citizens in the mainstream of American religious culture in the decades after the Awakening who shared those concerns, their efforts to improve moral character placed them squarely in the camps of both evangelicalism *and* the Enlightenment.

From Religious Revivals to the Revival of Religion

What has been called the "high tide" of the Great Awakening came during and just after Whitefield's American tour, when his travels to New England were followed by the appearance there of a host of radical itinerants, from the Presbyterian Gilbert Tennent and his younger colleague Samuel Finley to such homegrown products of the region as Eleazar Wheelock, Samuel Buell, and James Davenport. It was Davenport who began to turn the tide against the revival. As he charged through New England's parishes, Davenport demanded the support of the local ministers and condemned as corrupt and unregenerate those who refused. The most divisive act of all came in New London, where he and his followers built a large fire in which they burned a variety of worldly possessions as well as what they considered heretical books. In the process, they threw into the fire the works not only of such usual evangelical targets as Charles Chauncy but even those of Benjamin Colman, an active proponent of the revival. Finally, Davenport withdrew amid a slew of charges of enthusiasm and, faced with denunciations even from his former friends, recanted his "errors."[3]

Davenport's actions not only alarmed opponents of the revival but threatened to bring the entire Awakening into disrepute. In 1742, an assembly of ministers from Boston and Charles-Town, including several who warmly supported the revival, collectively condemned his activities as imprudent, irregular, and "tinctur'd with a Spirit of Enthusiasm" and closed their pulpits to him. In Connecticut he was placed on trial before the General Assembly of the colony, judged to have been under the influence of "enthusiastical Impressions" and "disturbed in the rational Faculties of his Mind," and deported from the colony. Even such former allies as Tennent and Wheelock dissociated themselves from his practices.[4]

Davenport's actions were only one of several incidents that caused supporters of the revival to pause. Another was the preaching of the Moravians in Pennsylvania, a German-speaking sect led by Count Nicholas von Zinzendorf and formerly allied with Whitefield and John Wesley. Tennent castigated the Moravians for their reliance on sensory perceptions in the work of grace and charged them with enthusiasm. The Moravian "errors" also facilitated a retreat by such Middle Colony evangelicals as Gilbert Tennent and Samuel Finley from uninhibited support for the Awakening. Henceforth, their preachings employed more measured tones, balancing support for conversion and awakening with the need to uphold order, decorum, and moral behavior.[5]

The titles of some of Gilbert Tennent's published pulpit sermons illustrate the change that took place in his thinking. His aggressive and even abusive *Danger of An Unconverted Ministry* (1740), delivered at the height of the Awakening, was followed four years later by the more humble *Danger of Spiritual Pride*. One of his early and strident calls for revival, *The Necessity of Religious Violence* (1735), was succeeded by *The Necessity of Holding Fast the Truth* (1743)—his attack on the Moravians—and then, at the close of the Awakening, by *The Necessity of Studying to Be Quiet, and Doing Our Own Business* (1744). By the end of the decade, Tennent the controversialist was earnestly preaching unity and reunion, in *Brotherly Love Recommended* (1748), *Irenicum Ecclesiasticum, or a Humble Impartial Essay upon the Peace of Jerusalem* (1749), and finally, *The Blessedness of Peace-Makers Represented* (1759). Tennent may well have been thinking of his own earlier rashness when, in a 1744 sermon, he denounced "ignorant Novices in Religion" who "pronounce sentence against the spiritual states of others rashly and without sufficient foundation."[6]

What emerged in the aftermath of the Awakening was a broader kind of evangelicalism that was concerned less with grand and demonstrative religious revivals than with the revival of religion in common life, a position on which most Old Side and New Side ministers could agree. Such a focus, common among mainstream evangelical groups on both sides of the Atlantic, originated in the preaching of such English Dissenters as Isaac Watts, whose *Humble Attempt towards the Revival of Practical Religion among Christians* (1731) called for the use of all tools at the ministers' disposal to revive personal religion, and Philip Doddridge, whose works included "Free Thoughts on the Most Probable Means of Reviving the Dissenting Interest" and *Rise and Progress of Religion in the Soul*. Those works influenced a wide range of religious leaders on both sides of the Atlantic. Their approach to revivalism was summed up by a Scottish evangelical preacher named James Stoddart, a close ally of American evangelicals, in a sermon entitled simply *The Revival of Religion*. There Stoddart emphasized the necessity of combining piety with "natural parts," "useful learning," and "consummate prudence" to spur the revival, a long way indeed from earlier views of religious revivals.[7]

A good example of the newer approach to revivals was the awakening that broke out at the College of New Jersey in 1757, led by the Reverend Aaron Burr. Although participants and observers eagerly reported on the progress of religion at Princeton, they were just as careful to emphasize the regularity of the revival and the efforts undertaken to moderate the passions. When the awakening first began, the president sent for assistance from nearby Presbyterian clergymen, including the Reverend William Tennent Jr., brother of Gilbert, whom Esther Burr described as "not attal like Gilbert but as prudent a Man in Conducting affairs of relegion as ever I saw in my life. He hates noise." Eventually brother Gilbert did turn up at Princeton eager to preach, and Aaron Burr had to "manage" the evangelist so as to prevent "irregularities" without offending him.[8]

All depictions of the revival were careful to emphasize its rationality and regularity. Esther Burr commented on "the propriety and [decorum] that subsists amongst the scholars. . . . There is nothing in the Whole affair but what is desireable." Aaron Burr described it as a work "carried on by the still voice of the Spirit; no boisterous methods; no special pathetic addresses to the passions." He informed a correspondent that the revival had not disrupted the work of the college and that no religious exercises had at any time been carried on in the hours appointed for study." Words such as *solemn, prudent,* and *decent*—some of Charles Chauncy's favorite terms—dominate the descriptions. Only Anglicans remained aloof from the revival, and several withdrew their sons from the college.[9]

One aspect of the newer evangelicalism, indicated by the title of Isaac Watts's sermon, was increased public attention to the realm of what was referred to as practical religion—personal devotion, moral behavior, and family worship. Thus Esther Burr described in her journal her husband Aaron's preaching in Newark in February of 1755:

> At meeting all day. Mr. Burr is still insisting on a reformation in famalies, and tells the people they must expect that this will be the burthen of his sermons until he sees reformation beginning. He has been remarkably stired up to be fervent in his preaching of late.[10]

The reference to her husband's "stired up" and "fervent" preaching about family reformation suggests that Aaron Burr was engaged in something other than a simple reversion to the sort of cold moralist preaching that the Puritans had so roundly condemned. This was no Arminian call to a life of good works.

Rather, it was part of an effort to promote piety by inducing a change in disposition, to instill what Samuel Davies referred to as "evangelical virtue or true Christian morality," to link piety tightly to virtue.[11]

A good exposition of that style of evangelical preaching can be found in the work of the New Side Presbyterian John Blair, graduate of the Log College and brother of the leading New Side revivalist Samuel Blair, who preached first in Pennsylvania and later in New York and served as Professor of Divinity at the College of New Jersey. Blair preached and wrote extensively about the processes of regeneration and of the new birth, but he defined them in ways far removed from the emotional and sensory descriptions of the most radical New Lights. Conversion, to Blair, was evidenced through moral behavior but not simply in the fact of a moral life. Rather, one examined one's behavior as a guide to one's inward temper or disposition. Blair described regeneration as an inward principle, a "settled determination of the mind to right activity towards spiritual objects." Its attainment became evident only through "a course of experience" characterized by "strictness, spirituality, and holiness." Words such as *habitual* and *constant* in reference to the avoidance of sin were among the most frequent that Blair and his associates used in their descriptions of the regenerate.[12]

If one of the principal goals of evangelical preaching was to persuade hearers to avoid sin, Blair's motive was to induce morality not for its own sake but rather as a first step toward repentance. Such moral preaching relied on the assumptions of the faculty psychology and on particular eighteenth-century understandings of the passions. In the view of such preachers, sin was not simply wrong in itself; it was also detrimental to conversion. In the process of sinning, one gratified powerful passions, which had to be overcome to make way for repentance and for an altered disposition. Just as moral sense philosophers insisted on the controlling of the passions as a prerequisite to the refinement of the weaker moral sense, so evangelical moralists insisted on the controlling of sinful passions before one could begin to repent. Thus John Blair advised his hearers not to harden their hearts against conversion "by giving loose reins to your lusts and sinful practices."[13]

As committed Calvinists, those evangelicals were careful to maintain that mere striving for morality would not suffice; "evangelical repentance" went far beyond common moralism. It was the sinner's obligation to strive nonetheless; as John Blair's brother Samuel put it, a sinner "never practices any thing like repentance till he comes to this: to forsake entirely his sinful courses, withstand all snares and temptations to them, and wrestle against the inward corruptions of his heart."[14] That may seem a long distance from the criticism of moral preaching by Blair's fellow Log College graduate Gilbert Tennent in his *Danger of an Unconverted Ministry* during the height of the Awakening, which he characterized as "Driving, Driving, to Duty, Duty." Yet it was a road that Tennent himself would travel. By 1744 that preacher, in a sermon on *The Necessity of Keeping the Soul*, would also loudly advocate "the earnest and constant use of all appointed means" in order "to keep the soul from sins."[15]

Presbyterianism and Provincial Union

Such a position was especially prominent within the Presbyterian Church, which was the most rapidly growing provincial denomination during the first half of the eighteenth century and whose position in the colonies was becoming increasingly central. In fact, the term *Presbyterian* was used somewhat broadly in the eighteenth century to refer not simply to those affiliated with the Presbyterian Synod but, more generally, to Dissenting groups who favored government by Presbyters or ministers rather than by bishops and hierarchies: in short, to churches that insisted on the right to govern themselves. Presbyterians established important working relationships with several other religious groups, including the Dutch Reformed and the Congregationalists. They would even establish cooperative relationships with colonial Anglicans in the colleges.[16]

Geographically, the Presbyterians' position was literally central, anchored in the heartland of the New York to Philadelphia corridor and extending throughout the Middle Colonies. Its principal governing body was the synod, located in Philadelphia but dividing in 1741 into an Old Side synod in that city and a New Side synod in New York. Its educational center was the College of New Jersey, which was founded at Elizabethtown in 1746 and moved to Princeton a decade later.[17]

In form, Presbyterianism was well suited to provincial society. During the seventeenth century, the Presbyterian presence in the colonies had been minimal; the first American presbytery was not even formed until the last decade of the century. Instead, most of the communions that took root there represented either local offshoots of European religious establishments, as in the case of the Anglican and Dutch Reformed Churches, or sectarian faiths with strong Separatist leanings, such as New England's Congregationalists and the Quaker and Baptist meetings that sprang up in the mid-Atlantic. Presbyterianism fit somewhere in between. Rejecting, with other Dissenters, the hierarchical structure and metropolitan orientation of the Anglican Church, Presbyterians were equally resistant to the extreme localism and lay control that was found among the sects. Instead, a combination of ministers and lay elders together governed the Presbyterian Church. It was, therefore, neither centralized and metropolitan nor wholly congregational and local. If authority was dispersed into presbyteries, those were linked together, in turn, in larger groupings called synods. Presbyterianism thus resembled a federation of local or regional religious organizations.

The role of the American Presbyterian Church was amplified by its unique imperial position as an alternative religious establishment: the Presbyterian

Church was the established Church of Scotland, its position secured by the Treaty of Union. Although the American church maintained no formal allegiance to its Scottish counterpart, ties between them were close. At times the American church claimed the protection of its overseas ally; for example, the Presbyterian Church of New York rested its charter in the General Assembly of the Scottish Church in order to circumvent opposition from New York's powerful Trinity Church to an incorporation of Dissenters.[18] Alliance with an established British church was no small asset for American Dissenters.

More than most other Dissenting denominations, Presbyterians promoted the goal of Protestant union. Almost from the moment the synod divided, Presbyterian leaders began to look for ways to reunite. That search was facilitated by the fact that on matters of essential doctrine, the division in that church was never so wide as it was in several other denominations. Both Old Side and New maintained a firm adherence to the basic Calvinist scheme; neither exhibited much evidence of a drift toward Arminianism. Nor did Presbyterians suffer from the divisions over the qualifications for membership that proved so divisive in New England and that cost Jonathan Edwards his pulpit. Even Gilbert Tennent's fractious *Danger of an Unconverted Ministry* advocated separating only from unregenerate *clergymen;* he never threatened separation from unregenerate laymen and laywomen. And Tennent soon repented even those remarks.

Presbyterians were not alone in the drive for union. As mainstream evangelicals backed off from the most confrontational aspects of revivalist religion, the impulse toward Christian unity came to the fore. Such an impulse was evident as early as 1745, as New England Congregationalists and their English and Scottish correspondents began to discuss plans for a transatlantic "Concert for Prayer," in which evangelical parishioners on both sides of the Atlantic would pray simultaneously for the revival of religion. The concert's very existence 'suggests the less aggressive posture of post-Awakening evangelicalism, which directed its efforts through supplication to God rather than through the provocation of worldly opponents. It reflected as well the desire among evangelicals to forge a united front of Christians to undertake the work of true religion.[19]

An Evangelical Educational Empire

For an event that began with such ambivalence toward secular learning, the Great Awakening, as well as the evangelical movement it fostered, had an unusually powerful impact on the development of higher education. The Colleges of New Jersey (Presbyterian), Rhode Island (Baptist), and New Hampshire, the last of which began as an Indian school, all owe their origins to the efforts of evangelicals in the aftermath of the Awakening to provide a trained and learned ministry for their sects. The revival's effects stretched even far-

ther: King's College in New York and the College of Philadelphia, both predominantly Anglican, were established by Old Lights largely as responses to
the challenge the evangelicals posed. And perhaps most important, evangelicals created a large network of lesser academies intended to provide a substantial evangelical education to young men from all regions and walks of life.

No group was more active in the creation of institutions of higher learning
than the Presbyterians. The College of New Jersey, founded in 1746 at Elizabethtown as a New Side institution, quickly became the most important college south of New England. Presbyterians were even more active in the creation of academies, beginning with the evangelical "Log College" in
Pennsylvania in 1727 and Francis Alison's Old Side academy at Newark in
Delaware. After 1740, Presbyterian ministers began to establish academies
wherever they settled, extending far into the backcountries of Maryland and
Pennsylvania (as far west as Carlisle) and south into the farthest reaches of
Virginia and North Carolina. They had established more than 20 academies
in the mainland colonies by 1760 and more than three times that number by
the end of the century, spreading the principles of piety and enlightenment
even into that remote countryside.[20]

One of the principal purposes of the colleges and academies was to educate
ministers; between 1748 and 1768 nearly half of the graduates of the College
of New Jersey became clergymen, more than 150 in all.[21] But that was not
that college's only purpose; it trained lawyers, physicians, merchants, and
gentlemen as well, thus providing a significant portion of the political leadership of colonies from New York to the Carolinas. Indeed, College of New Jersey graduates would become prominent statesmen during the Revolutionary
era, when the president, John Witherspoon, would sit in the Continental Congress and sign the Declaration of Independence. Nine graduates would attend
the Constitutional Convention in 1787, including James Madison. Presbyterian educational institutions were designed to inculcate piety and virtue
together in a generation of provincial community leaders. Educational outreach and the dissemination of the habits of piety and virtue became a significant part of the evangelical mission.

Aside from divinity courses, which were designed principally for candidates for the ministry, the curriculum at most provincial institutions of higher
learning was similar, merging the concerns of religion and Enlightenment.
Evangelicals and nonevangelicals taught from many of the same texts, especially adaptations of Francis Hutcheson's moral philosophy lectures. All
included extensive works as well in natural philosophy, history, and belles lettres. Thus the colleges provided their students with a much broader education
than one would have obtained in what were primarily clerical-training schools
a century before. Their primary models were the Scottish universities and
Britain's Dissenting academies, all of which made enlightened educations
available—unlike the Anglican colleges at Oxford and Cambridge—to members of the establishment and Dissenters alike.[22]

A good illustration of the diverse nature of that curriculum is the commencement activities at the College of New Jersey from the year 1760, the only commencement over which Samuel Davies presided. The proceedings mixed celebrations of religion, science, literature, and social progress. They included a lecture in praise of oratory, delivered by the future doctor Benjamin Rush, a member of the graduating class; another by Samuel Blair, son of the revivalist minister, on the Enlightenment hypothesis that the elegance of oratory consisted of making the words consonant to their sense; a Latin dispute on the connection between ethics and revelation; the singing of an Ode to Science composed by the president; and an address by another student on the flourishing state of public affairs in America.[23]

Evangelicals also extended their educational efforts outward toward non-evangelical and non-Christian groups, such as African-Americans and Indians. Whitefield's Georgia orphanage housed slaves as well as poor whites and sought to educate them in the principles of Christianity. In South Carolina, the Bryan brothers gathered slaves from the neighborhood to teach them Christianity, much to the alarm of neighboring planters. And everywhere groups of slaves and freed Negroes joined evangelical churches. But aside from those scattered efforts, evangelicals never worked as hard as Anglicans to educate slaves and bring them into the fold.[24]

Efforts to convert Indians were more visible. With financial help from the Society in Scotland for the Propagation of Christian Knowledge (S.S.P.C.K.), a number of evangelical preachers undertook extended missions to Indian groups in New England and the Middle Colonies. Probably the most famous of those preachers was the Yale-educated David Brainerd, who served for four years as a missionary to Indians in western Massachusetts and across the Middle Colonies from New York to Delaware until his death in 1747. Brainerd's journal, edited by Jonathan Edwards, was published as an example of the effect of evangelical piety on Christian behavior. In that work, Edwards portrayed the young evangelical as a prime example of evangelical benevolence. To Edwards, the opportunity to publish the journal had an additional benefit: it was an occasion to represent the workings of such an evangelical temper, hitherto depicted by Edwards only in the stories of women and girls, in the life of a grown man.[25]

Another ambitious missionary effort was the Indian school established by another Yale graduate, Eleazar Wheelock. Wheelock was among the leading radicals of the Awakening in his early days, before Davenport's excesses made him pull back from full support of his colleague. He devoted himself instead to establishing a broad correspondence with mainstream evangelicals on both sides of the Atlantic as well as to supervising a new evangelical school for Indians, which moved from Connecticut to New Hampshire and would form the seed of Dartmouth College. His first pupil at the school was Samson Occum, a Mohegan, who had been awakened by Davenport. Occum went on to become the first Indian ordained as a missionary in New England.[26]

Such efforts at evangelical outreach were not without limitations. In the great majority of cases, the principal goal was to educate and convert African-Americans and Indians in ways that would allow them to fit into their allotted roles in provincial society, not to improve their worldly positions. Whitefield was careful to inform Georgia slaveholders that Africans converted in his Georgia orphanage would remain slaves and would likely be better ones because of their religion. The evangelist supported the introduction of slavery in Georgia and at his orphanage, viewing the institution as a necessary support of his institution's economic viability. The Bryans' whole enterprise was threatened by their encouragement of slave independence, until they reversed course and accepted the compatibility of evangelical religion and slavery.

Natives and slaves did not always agree. The poet Phillis Wheatley, who was brought to America from Africa as a child in 1761 and became a pious Christian, dedicated a book of poems to the Countess of Huntingdon, an English woman revered for her support of evangelical causes, including evangelical antislavery. And in a famous published letter to the Indian preacher Samson Occum, Wheatley criticized those American slaveholders who proclaimed themselves defenders of colonial liberties. To Wheatley, such hypocrisy represented an "absurdity" of conduct among those "whose words and Actions are so diametrically opposite."[27]

Other Indians adapted evangelical forms in a manner that rendered their religion more directly suitable to overt resistance. After the middle of the century, a growing number of Indian nations on the western frontiers, increasingly threatened by the continuing advances of colonial settlement, began to develop a new synthesis of traditional Indian worldviews with Christian imagery and notions of religious revival to create a powerful ideology of resistance. All along the frontier, Indian prophets combined those traditions in support of ideas of Indian unity, employing myths and dreams with strong Christian overtones to assert authority as leaders in the rebuilding of their nations.[28]

The Uses of Learning

The evangelicals' focus on character went a long way toward reconciling them to the importance of secular learning. If evangelical moral philosophy shifted the emphasis from virtuous behavior to the sentiment behind it, so their evangelical philosophy looked beyond its formal status to its effect on useful learning in general. The key was to look beyond behavior itself to the disposition it suggested and to the values it promoted. It was in such a mind-set that Esther Burr, a profoundly pious woman, read extensively such previously circumscribed genres as the novel and the secualr poetry of the less than devout Mary Jones and even quoted them whenever they expressed useful moral sentiments.[29]

A striking illustration of a mainstream evangelical approach toward secular learning can be found in the journal kept by Samuel Davies, who succeeded Aaron Burr and Jonathan Edwards at the College of New Jersey. Davies had published poetry himself during his Virginia days, all of it on religious subjects. When the quality of his verses was derided by his Anglican opponents, the preacher made no attempt to defend their literary merit. Rather, he explained that the purpose of his poetry was simply to attach the affections to the sacred cause; the quality of the poetry was "subservient to the interests of religion and virtue," which he deemed far more important. Indeed, according to Davies, an excessively elegant style might even prevent the general reader from obtaining the benefits of his verse, however much it might impress those with a taste for literary refinement.[30]

In 1753, Davies, along with Gilbert Tennent, undertook a fund-raising trip to Great Britain on behalf of the College of New Jersey. While on shipboard, Davies busied himself with catching up on his reading, which included several novels. His taste was as moralistic as Esther Burr's. On the whole he was not impressed with what he saw; for example, he described Defoe's *Roxana* as "the Hystory of an abandoned Prostitute, pretendedly penitent." He also read the "Memoirs of a fortunate Maid," possibly a French piece translated by Eliza Haywood, which, he remarked, had "a better [tendency] than most that are so much in Vogue."[31]

There were two reasons Davies was able to read extensively during the voyage. One was that he had time on his hands; he could peruse those novels, about which he evidently had much curiosity, without detracting from his responsibilities to his congregation. The other was that he had an opportunity to do so in private, away from a public that might disapprove of a minister reading novels. In the north of England, Davies, out of curiosity, would even attend a play, at a time when the Presbyterian community was deeply divided over the morality of the theater. To Davies, the spirit in which he went to the play was more significant than the mere fact of his attendance. He chose to attend the play in that community, he wrote, because he would not be known there "and consequently could give no Offense."[32]

Despite continuing controversy over the theater, students at the College of New Jersey enacted plays during Aaron Burr's tenure; Esther Burr referred to one that even involved cross-dressing. She was hardly known for levity, but the episode left her "extreamly merry." The main point for her was that the play was put on "quite privately, and with no other desighn than to Lern the young sparks a good dilivery," and so she had no objection.[33]

In his recent study of Anglo-American discussions of the theater, Jean-Christophe Agnew has described eighteenth-century critiques of the theater as simple restatements of older Puritan arguments against theatricality. He cited in particular the tract written by John Witherspoon, another future president of the College of New Jersey, as part of a controversy that was covered extensively in William Smith's *American Magazine*.

Opposition to the theater had a long history in Protestant circles. English Puritans of the seventeenth century had loudly denounced the stage for its long-standing links to impiety and immorality and for its encouragement of falseness and dissimulation.[34] Yet there was an important change in emphasis in the eighteenth century that had been prefigured in the journals of Samuel Davies and Esther Burr. It was not the mere fact of plays but the tendencies they promoted to which eighteenth-century Presbyterians objected. Under proper circumstances, plays could promote piety, virtue, and learning, as those put on at the College of New Jersey were intended to do.

The principal objection of eighteenth-century Presbyterians was not to plays themselves but rather to the institution of the theater and to its organization along commercial principles. For such theaters to survive and attract a wide audience, they had to appeal to the lowest common denominator of popular sentiment. In short, they gratified the passions rather than promoting the principles of piety and virtue, the very opposite of the virtuous disposition they ought to instill. Commercial theater thus worked in a manner exactly opposite to the evangelical moral preaching Aaron Burr and Samuel Davies undertook, which insisted on avoiding temptation as the first step toward repentance and true virtue.[35]

This Protestant moral aesthetic contributed to the growing popularity of novels among a Protestant readership. Especially popular were Richardson's novels, in which the heroines upheld the principles of virtue, always motivated by piety of a decidedly nondenominational sort that was deeply inscribed in their characters. In his later novels, *Clarissa* and *The History of Sir Charles Grandison*, the heroines and heroes coupled their evangelical virtues with a strict but inner-felt adherence to Christian rules of honor, politeness, and taste. It was Pamela's inner disposition to virtue that led Esther Burr to refer to her as an "Angel imbodied."*

The Accommodation of Religion and Science

Evangelicals such as Davies also managed to accommodate their religion to the new science. Upon assuming the presidency of the College of New Jersey in 1759, he compiled a list of all of the books the college possessed and in his preface lamented in particular the shortage of adequate works in mathematics and natural philosophy; he composed his "Ode to Science" for the commencement the next year. Like many other eighteenth-century figures, Davies saw religion and science as not opposed but complementary. By displaying

---

*Richardson mixed an emphasis on character with a generalized version of the educational ideas of Locke, which Pamela discussed at great length in the second part of the novel. It may well have been through the reading of the second part of *Pamela* that Esther Burr first encountered those ideas directly stated.

the harmonies of the universe and the sublime work of the creator, science attached the wonder and the affections of humankind to religious truth. Such a position has often been associated with religious liberals; it was just as important among American evangelicals. Esther Burr evoked the general sentiment at Princeton. Upon visiting the new college's observatory and looking through its telescope, she wrote to Sally Prince of her desire that her friend could be there with them, to "see and wonder with us."[36]

Davies offered an illuminating example of the relationship between religion and science in a sermon he delivered on the subject of earthquakes, following the report of the disastrous quake at Lisbon in 1755. Earthquakes had long been a favorite sermon topic, as they provided ministers the opportunity to demonstrate in the most graphic manner an angry God's threats through his visible works. But the progress of the natural sciences had led to an alternative explanation: that the regular, though unpredictable occurrence of earthquakes, the product of natural geological forces, constituted not divine intervention in the ordinary laws of the natural world but rather their fulfillment.

Since early in the century, ministers had sought to take account of such scientific explanations without acceding to their naturalistic basis. In 1727, Thomas Prince had attempted to reconcile new understandings of the causes of earthquakes with an insistence on their spiritual significance. His main point was that although God might ordinarily utilize natural causes, that did not preclude his taking events into his own hands whenever he wished, overruling his own natural laws or utilizing the very secondary causes he had created to carry out his designs. Thus by whatever mechanism such quakes appeared, they were no less the product of the divine will and no less revealing as warnings to unrepentant peoples.[37]

Davies used all of those earlier arguments and went still further in accepting the findings of the new science. Although he was unwilling to deny God's ability to overrule the laws of nature—which would have been to deny the very essence of divine sovereignty—the preacher conceded that even in the case of earthquakes, He might have decided never to employ causes other than secondary ones. Moreover, earthquakes might well conform to, rather than deviate from, the ordinary course of affairs. What is noteworthy about Davies's view of the remarkable providence was that it now demonstrated providential power that did not overrule the ordinary course of nature but rather carried it out. Moreover, such a theory in no way undermined the notion of God's moral governance of the world. As Davies asked, might not an all-powerful creator have implanted in the earth "hidden springs" that would make tremors happen at exactly the time that he willed? Would not an all-knowing governor of the universe have foreseen exactly when nations would be ripe for threatenings and corrections and have planned for the appearance of such natural disasters? In short, did not the very existence of orderly secondary causes demonstrate unequivocally the absolute supervision of providence and the necessity of seeking salvation only by following the divine plan?[38]

John Winthrop IV, by John Singleton Copley. *Courtesy of the Harvard University Portrait Collection, gift of executors of the estate of John Winthrop, 1894.*

Such a perspective was not restricted to clergymen. In the same year, John Winthrop, descendant of the first governor of Massachusetts Bay of the same name and professor of mathematics and philosophy at Harvard College, published a lecture on earthquakes. After more than 20 pages explicating the workings of earthquakes by natural causes, the now-eminent scientist announced that he also had no doubt that "the operations of nature are conducted, with a view, *ultimately,* to *moral* purposes."[39] Winthrop responded testily to the suggestion by the Reverend Thomas Prince that the lecture had treated earthquakes merely from the perspective of natural philosophy, whereas Prince examined them as a student of divinity. The scientist responded that "the consideration of a DEITY" was "not peculiar to *Divinity,* but belongs also to *natural philosophy,*" for the main business of that subject was "to trace the chain of natural causes from one link to another, till we come to the FIRST CAUSE; who in Philosophy, is considered as presiding over, and continually actuating, this whole chain and every link of it."[40]

The Nature of True Virtue

Among the signs of evangelical involvement with the secular learning of the Enlightenment was an increasing concern with questions of moral virtue. In part such concern was simply a reaction, sometimes a defensive one, to the challenge of the Enlightenment, as we shall see. It reflected as well the maturing of evangelicalism itself. In the aftermath of the revival, evangelical converts, to whom conversion itself had previously constituted the principal concern, found themselves confronting the challenge of living as saints in this world. Thus they had to consider, in a way that revivalist preachers at the peak of the Awakening had not, the relationship between piety and the moral life.

The most famous such effort was penned by Jonathan Edwards. His *Nature of True Virtue*, written during the 1750s as the second of two "Dissertations" but not published until 1765, stands as the most sophisticated treatment of virtue from an evangelical perspective to emerge during his era. In that work, Edwards confronted Enlightenment philosophy directly. Having come to recognize the strength and appeal of the new moral philosophy, Edwards remained concerned with maintaining the Calvinistic principle that a purely natural moral sense is insufficient to promote a truly moral life. Yet as an educated eighteenth-century figure, he recognized that to do so he had to go beyond the simple statement of his faith: he had to make his case through logical demonstration of empirical facts. In other words, he had to defend Christianity through observation rather than from Scripture.[41]

The Nature of True Virtue, then, proceeded as a work of philosophy rather than of theology. Edwards identified a realm of "true virtue" that was rooted in piety, characterized by a love of all being, which was clearly distinguishable from its imperfect, partial, and worldly counterfeits, including the weak moral sense his philosophical counterparts lauded. Edwards equated the moral sense with the remnants of natural conscience in fallen humankind. Conscience had its uses, to be sure; it had been implanted by God to foster peace in civil society. But it was not part of true virtue, which proceeded only from regeneration and encompassed the love of all creation. True virtue, in Edwards's view, was composed of a love of *all* being—not just of oneself, or one's family or community or nation, such as one found in natural morality. A principle of love so complete, he contended, was attainable *only* through grace and religious conversion.

Edwards had a number of followers, especially among that segment of the New England clergy that adhered to what came to be called the New Divinity, led by such close associates of the Northampton preacher-philosopher as

Joseph Bellamy and Samuel Hopkins. The New Divinity men continued Edwards's effort to defend a "consistent Calvinism" against the attempts of Liberal preachers to modify its harsher tenets by compromising rigid doctrines of predestination and eternal damnation. Thus would Bellamy follow Edwards in interpreting the idea of the freedom of the will as consistent with predestination, attributing sinful behavior to a "free and voluntary bad temper."[42]

In their efforts to extend Calvinist consistency, the New Divinity men were often accused of engaging in overly abstract theology, removed from the needs of eighteenth-century men and women for a faith compatible with the tone of the age that would give them a basis for hope. When Hopkins, for example, described sin as "an Advantage to the Universe . . . yet this is no excuse for Sin," it is little wonder that he seemed to some to be engaging in little more than sophistry. Yet several of the New Divinity preachers were successful as emotional preachers nonetheless, continuing the revival tradition of their intellectual ancestor.[43]

Hopkins and Bellamy were both noted moral preachers as well, equating morality with holiness. Bellamy's writings insisted on the stringency of the moral law and on the necessity of upholding every aspect of it. Hopkins, among his other noted characteristics, acquired a reputation as a social reformer for his strident insistence on the contradiction between slaveholding and holiness.[44]

Edwards's approach to virtue was not the only one to emerge in the religious community, even among defenders of orthodoxy. Evangelical Presbyterians never fully accepted the Edwardsean position and in general were a good deal more comfortable with Enlightenment philosophy, a position rather closer to what their evangelical counterparts adopted in Britain. Although they agreed with Edwards that evangelical virtue could never be reduced to the mere performance of moral acts—the very essence of Arminianism, in their view—they were nonetheless able to construct an evangelical morality that emphasized the cultivation of the moral sense, organized around issues of character, using Enlightenment methods of sociability, reason, and reflection. Such revivalist preachers as Samuel Finley and Samuel Davies, both presidents of the College of New Jersey under whose guidance the college emerged as a center of religious but also Enlightened learning, shared that view, as did Aaron Burr, who preached on family reformation. It was even shared by Edwards's daughter.

Virtue, Conversation, and Friendship

During virtually the same years that the elder Edwards was writing his dissertation on true virtue, his daughter, Esther Edwards Burr, was keeping the journal that she sent, in packets, to her friend Sarah Prince. In its own way, the journal was itself a rumination on the moral life, albeit from a far more practical point of view than her father's work. Esther's production, despite its conversational tone, was also largely a product of the lamp, of reading and of reflection about the principles of virtue. Moreover, like her father, Esther Burr was concerned not simply with virtuous behavior but with a deeper realm of true virtue; indeed, she used the term herself, along with related concepts of true conversation and true friendship.[45]

One of the most striking aspects of Esther Burr's journal is the extent to which she employed the Enlightenment mechanisms of reading, reflection, and conversation in her pursuit of true virtue. In that aspect at least, the moral philosophy of Jonathan Edwards's daughter seems rather closer to that of the British Moralists than to that of her father, whose paramount concern was to separate a true virtue rooted in grace from the worldly imitations offered up by secular philosophy. Esther Burr's journal was very much an effort to refine her moral life through education and discussion in the pursuit of piety and virtue. Its existence provides a useful illustration of the fact that there were media other than the public prints that allowed for the creation of what might be called a semipublic sphere.

The term Esther Burr employed for such an effort was *conversation*. As she used the term, conversation was not just any discussion; it was restricted to those that were edifying. Thus she lamented her isolation in New Jersey, where she found herself surrounded principally by those that she referred to as "triflers and flirting misses." She had no one to converse with but her husband, "for Conversasion with any body elce I have about me, I dont call Conversasion. I dont know what to call it, but I believe *Chit-Chat* will do as well as any name, for indeed tis no easy matter to give a name to *Nothing*." True conversation, by contrast, was discussion, in the active pursuit of religion and improvement, among "charming friends . . . that one might unbosom their whole soul too." Religious conversation, Burr remarked in a phrase that she probably borrowed from the then recent and very popular work by the English Dissenter Philip Doddridge, was "one of the best helps to keep up relegion in the soul."[46]

The purpose of keeping up such a conversation with her friend was to harmonize and refine their sentiments. The process of adjusting their ideas was not unlike that described by Adam Smith in his 1759 work on *The Theory of Moral Sentiments*, among the most influential of the works of the British moralists, which explained the foundation of moral standards through the establishment of sympathy. In one section, Smith compared the refinement of sympathy to the process of tuning an orchestra, in which every player sought to refine his pitch by attending to the pitches of all of the other players around him and adjusting his tone accordingly.[47] In thus refining her morals through sociability, and in rooting moral standards in common opinion, Esther Burr's method bore little resemblance to that of her father's.

That the women used *Clarissa* as a model for their correspondence was thus significant; the novel was preeminently about friendship. One of the things that distinguishes *Clarissa* is that the heroine tells her story in letters not to her parents, as Pamela did, or to her sister, with whom her relations were extremely strained, but to her intimate friend Anna Howe, the only one to whom she could confide her true thoughts. Esther Burr shared both that heroine's situation—her relationship with her sister Lucy was clearly strained—and her sentiments, remarking in one of her earliest entries to Sarah Prince that she had "not one Sister I can write so freely to as to you the Sister of my heart." To Jonathan Edwards, human friendship represented only a pale imitation of that benevolence of feeling toward being in general. His daughter belonged to a generation that extended the meaning of friendship and made it integral to their personal and public selves. To Esther Burr, friendship, or rather what she distinguished as "true friendship," was one of the cornerstones of her personal faith.[48]

The journal was filled with remarks about friendship, indicating just how important it was in Esther's understanding of true virtue. Friendships were not of this world, Esther wrote, but "inkindled by a spark from Heaven." "I look on the ties of friendship as *sacred* . . . it ought to be [a] matter of Solemn Prayer to God (where there is a friendship contracted) that it may be preserved." Friendship was "the life of life." Sarah Prince quoted a passage out of Richardson's *History of Sir Charles Grandison* that stipulated that the character of a friend was the greatest that could be given, which Esther answered with a quotation to similar effect from the poetess Mary Jones. Later in the journal, Esther paid her friend one of her greatest compliments: there was, she told Sarah, "the very soul of a friend in all you write," the very phrasing of which suggests something of the inner quality of true friendship. Indeed, the only time the otherwise controlled Esther truly lost her temper during the period the journal covered was in response to the college tutor John Ewing's remark that he doubted that women were capable of anything "so cool and rational as friendship," after which she loosed her tongue for an hour of heated argument.[49]

Recent historians have demonstrated the considerable significance that such friendships assumed in the construction of female identity in the eighteenth and nineteenth centuries. They certainly played an important role in Esther Burr's emotional life, especially during the long periods when her husband was away on business and she was left at home to tend to household, children, and the ubiquitous company that arrived at the minister's house. Yet if friendship filled personal needs, what she called "true friendship" required more. It was also an important tool in the quest for self-improvement through the pursuit of piety and virtue. Thus when Esther found out that Sarah Prince had recovered from a long and serious illness, she remarked that, to her, it was as though God had given her a new friend, a second chance at friendship to see whether she would make a "better improvement" of it.[50]

One of the purposes of friendship was to stir up pious sentiments. There was, she wrote, nothing more "refreshing to the soul" than "the company and

society of a friend—One that has the spirit off, and relish for, true friendship."
She would find such a friend in New Jersey in Abigail Sergeant, a woman
whose temper was reserved at the outset but who later demonstrated her
"love to speak of relegion to those she is acquainted with." On one occasion,
when Esther was in low spirits, the two women "got into a room by our selves
a little while, and chated with some comfort."[51]

Yet there was more to friendship than the stirring of pious impulses.
Friends were also to watch over each other's actions and sentiments, to correct
each other's thoughts and feelings, and to note unintended errors on the path
to true virtue. A true friend, Esther and Sarah both insisted, accepted the
office of "monitor" of the other. "I think it one of the great essentials of friendship [that] the parties tell one another their faults," Esther recorded. "When
they will [say] it and take it kindly," she continued, that was "one of the best
evidences of true friendship." Tellingly, even on that matter she sought to
measure her own ideas against her friend's sentiments, appending a tentative
"I think" to the end of the last, otherwise definitive proclamation, and following it with the request that Sarah respond with her thoughts on friendship and
monitoring as well, with the idea that her own thoughts would be further
refined through such an exchange.[52]

Like Clarissa, Esther Burr had a much more distant relationship with her
father and her other close relations. She certainly revered her father and con-
sulted him faithfully about the spiritual state of her soul, but she differed from
him in personal style and in personal values. Thus when Aaron Burr had to
travel to Boston on College business, Esther described his visit to the Prince
household as she imagined it: her father would do most of the talking, Aaron
Burr would listen and laugh, and Sarah's father Thomas Prince would put in
the occasional word. The women would sit quietly until they got upstairs
alone, when they would have the opportunity to discuss their opinions among
themselves.[53]

Jonathan Edwards was not without affection for his daughter, but it was
affection of a particular kind. When she visited her family in Stockbridge,
Esther Burr was very glad to get counseling from her father on the state of her
soul, about which she remarked, "What a mercy that I have such a Father!
Such a guide!" But his guidance seemed to be limited to the formal state of
her soul; he did not attempt to enhance her piety through friendly conversation. Jonathan Edwards's letters to his daughter maintain a similar tone. Both
when Esther was severely ill, in 1753, and after her husband's untimely death
in 1757 the elder Edwards expressed concern. But his principal effort in both
letters was to point Esther away from her worldly troubles, to wean herself of
the world and resign herself to the will of God—just as a father who was also
a minister might be expected to do.[54] Something of the general tone of their
relationship can be garnered from Esther's listing of three ministers—Sarah's
father, Thomas Prince, of Boston, Caleb Smith of Newark, and her own husband—as the only suitable persons in the world to preach on the subjects of

charity and Christian love, because "they do realy *abound* in Charrity."[55] Her revered father was notably absent from the list.

That she refers to Aaron Burr as abounding in charity suggests that the gulf that separated Esther Burr from her father did not apply to all men, although it did to a good many, as we shall see. She experienced no such sense of distance from her husband. Throughout the journal, she consistently used affectionate terms to refer to Aaron Burr, such as "Dear Man" and her "best self," and remarked that he was the only one in her neighborhood with whom she could truly converse. She complained of loneliness on the frequent occasions when business took him away from home. When he lay seriously ill, Esther complained that she was unwilling to resign herself to the loss of all that was "near and dear" to her. Theirs was what has been called a "companionate" marriage, modeled on mutuality, emotion, and companionship rather than on worldly considerations of wealth, family, and status. As in the books Esther read, the ideal husband was also a friend.[56]

The couple shared more than just affection; they seem to have held quite similar sentiments about reading, correspondence, friendship, and conversation. Aaron Burr did converse with his wife, and with her friend as well. Esther regularly described her husband as anxious to receive Sarah Prince's journals. On one occasion, when Aaron Burr received the packet first, he opened it himself and began to read it without waiting for his wife, although it was addressed to her; Esther described him as "eager as well as I am" to read the letters. Aaron Burr encouraged both the women's correspondence and Sarah Prince's literary efforts in particular. While reading the published letters of Mary Jones, he pronounced Sarah's "ten times as well worth printing," and he wrote to Sarah directly to encourage her to continue her literary efforts, attempting to instill in her an interest in instructive conversation "in these degenerate Times." And when Aaron Burr traveled to Boston on College business in 1756, he kept a journal of exactly the sort that Esther and Sarah maintained and sent it to his wife in packets, which made her very proud.[57]

Not all men were as enlightened about women's opinions as was Esther's husband. One reason the women kept their correspondence private was that they feared it would spark controversy among some men who would regard it as outside of women's place, as her argument with the tutor John Ewing implied. When Esther wanted to tell Mrs. Browne about her correspondence with Sarah, she feared that "she would tell her MAN of it, and *he* knows so much better about matters than *she* that he would certainly make some Ill-natured remarks or other." She continued with the revealing remark, "[E]verybody hant [haven't] such a Man as I have about those things."[58]

Nonetheless, Esther Burr remained hopeful of a progressive unfolding of human knowledge and of an improved sentiment about women's conversation and about friendship. Of the intolerant Parson Brown she declared, "[T]hese *Hes* shall know nothing about our affairs *untill they are grown as wise as you and I are*." An even clearer indication of that belief was her observation that in years past, one had not encountered as many "just thoughts" on the subject of friendship than one had among "late authors." Her circle's very interest in keeping up with "late authors" suggests a view of the progress in knowledge and in friendship more in line with the views of Enlightenment moralists than with those of traditional Calvinism.[59]

Rather than simply waiting for sentiment to change, the women worked to extend their correspondence and friendship to suitable persons. Esther shared some or all of Sarah Prince's writings first with her husband and later with her Princeton neighbor the poetess Annis Boudinot, pious, virtuous, and a writer as well. Abigail Sergeant was let into the secret of their journals, as would Mrs. Browne have been were it not for her unenlightened husband. Sarah Prince apparently circulated a good many writings among her friends and extended their correspondence to include the group of Boston women referred to as "the sisterhood," or, more creatively, the "Freemason Club," a name that Esther Burr merrily adopted and that suggests the reflective and semipublic aspects of their undertaking.[60]

The reference to the Freemasons, a secret society of members dedicated to sociability, enlightenment, and improvement that was emerging during the eighteenth century, would have had several implications in the middle years of the eighteenth century. One was the association of masonry with elaborate ritual, to which the female freemasons could have matched their own ritual of daily writing. Another was the rule of secrecy, of keeping secrets from the uninitiated until such time as the world at large should be ready for them. Still another was the Freemasons' dedication to education, enlightenment, and the spread of virtue, equally goals of Sarah Prince and Esther Burr. The female freemasons, like their male counterparts, manifest a zeal for literacy, education, sociability, and moral improvement.[61]

The Tradesman's Enlightenment

The origins of Freemasonry was in the trades, the society of the masons. However much the Enlightenment was dominated by literati of genteel origins and styles, in its provincial form in particular it always retained a strong element of tradesmen's values. Tradesmen and artisans were working people; they valued industry and labor over the leisured lifestyle their social betters celebrated. Tradesmen often joined together in societies and organizations dedicated to promoting mutual interest; at the same time, tradesmen valued those attributes that could help working people advance: diligence, sobriety, assertiveness, and thrift. Thus tradesmen's values combined mutuality with self-improvement, an antipathy toward gentility with a marked emphasis on self-respect.

One of the reasons that evangelists such as Whitefield and Gilbert Tennent were able to establish such long-standing friendships with Benjamin Franklin was that they shared a significant portion of tradesmen's values. In Franklin's case that is obvious; he was raised as the son of an artisan and made his way in the world by following the printing trade. Although Whitefield and Tennent had dissimilar backgrounds, their core values were still closely connected to those of the trades.

One link between Franklin and those ministers was that they shared a marked moral commitment to the betterment of humanity. In none of them was that value immediately obvious. Whitefield and Tennent began their preaching careers emphasizing personal salvation over moral conduct and benevolence, whereas Franklin's pronouncements always seemed to stress the welfare of the self more than dedication to one's neighbors: "God helps them that help themselves" was one of his characteristic and better-known pronouncements. But for the printer as for his preaching friends, individual improvement was but a means with which to better the lot of humanity, whether in this world or the next.

It is often difficult for twentieth-century readers to take Benjamin Franklin's maxims wholly seriously. From 1733 to 1758, Franklin published an almanac under the pseudonym of "Poor Richard" that contained, among other things, a multitude of sayings and advice to help the reader turn diligence and thrift into riches and personal advantages; the last volume collected many of the maxims together under the title *The Way to Wealth*. In that compilation one finds such homespun ideas as "One today is worth two to-morrows," "Have you somewhat to do To-morrow, do it To-day," and "A word to the wise is enough." Other Poor Richard maxims include "Lost time is never found again," "Little strokes, fell great oaks," and "The art of getting riches consists very much in *thrift*."[62]

If Poor Richard's maxims strike many readers today as old-fashioned in the extreme, in the eighteenth-century they would have seemed less so. The values that that character projected were, on the whole, not so different from those that Franklin preached in his famous *Autobiography*, which is largely the story of a young man's rise to fame and fortune through study, application, and thrift. Franklin offered the story of his life as an example to many in what was, by then, the new nation of the United States. Implicit in his presentation were two conditions of his rise: his principal maxims of application and thrift worked *because* of the distinctive social conditions that provincial society America provided, and they were applicable in particular to young tradesmen.[63]

Several aspects of Franklin's ideas in fact were, if not altogether original, at least relatively new, albeit with precedents in the work of such earlier writers as Daniel Defoe. One was the complicated relationship between individual improvement and public benefit. Franklin has long been celebrated as an active proponent of individual values, and there can be little doubt of the validity of that assessment. Poor Richard's advice is directed almost entirely toward getting the individual to look after himself, to employ his time wisely, to spend cautiously, to guard his character and reputation, to avoid relying unnecessarily on the discretion of others. Franklin composed his *Autobiography* in part to disseminate the lessons of his life, first to his son and, later, to the citizenry of a new nation, to allow them to emulate his character and share in the success that followed.

Yet Franklin's goal was never to achieve economic success simply for its own sake, to acquire and save and accumulate endlessly. Once the young printer established a secure fortune in his printing business, he took on a managing partner for the print shop and retired from the active pursuit of business. Though well-to-do, Franklin never became truly wealthy. Instead, he devoted himself thereafter to scientific experiments and to public life, engaging in a multitude of projects designed to improve his city, his province, and later, his nation, from hospitals and library societies to political and diplomatic affairs. His moral pronouncements were in the same vein: he preached private success in part because the widespread achievement of private gain would result in the improvement of the public welfare. His privatism was largely motivated by his perception of its usefulness to the public.[64]

Although Franklin expressed considerable skepticism about following the tenets of any particular religion, he maintained an intense moralism throughout his life that shared many of the assumptions of the Dissenting Protestant tradition in which he was raised. In his *Autobiography*, Franklin attributes much of his character to several books that he read extensively in his youth. One was Cotton Mather's *Essays to do Good*, written in the later, evangelical phase of Mather's career, in which the minister attempted to harness piety in favor of good works. There he advocated that Christians be ever earnest in the pursuit of moral improvement, as well as in efforts to benefit humanity, a credo that Franklin always followed. At one point, Franklin adopted a plan of asking himself every day what good he had done that day, a plan modeled directly on Mather's ideas. In Philadelphia in 1720, Franklin was a charter member of the Junto, the assemblage of learned persons, mostly artisans, who met for discussion and "mutual improvement"; its structure was adapted directly from the societies that Mather began in Boston. The Junto, in turn, served as a model for a number of later societies dedicated to discussion and improvement.[65]

Another work that Franklin listed as particularly influential was Daniel Defoe's *Essay Upon Projects*. Defoe, like Franklin, was raised as a Dissenter and was educated in Charles Morton's famous Dissenting academy at Newington Green before that educator departed for New England. In the *Essay*, Defoe offered to the public a wide variety of plans or "projects" for both personal and public improvement, including road building to spur the inland trade, creating "friendly societies" for mutual protection and support, and constructing charity homes for the mentally retarded. The multitude of schemes Franklin offered throughout his long career fit rather closely the model that Defoe had established.[66]

Several other works by Defoe also either influenced Franklin directly or expressed values that Franklin came to share. *The Complete English Tradesman*, for example, is filled with instructions for young tradesmen not only about such matters as keeping accounts and conducting business but, most important, about "Diligence and application." The work also cautions against "extravagant and expensive living" and "marrying too soon," avoiding scandal and reproach, and "leaving business to servants."[67] All of those themes figured prominently in Poor Richard's aphorisms and in Franklin's *Autobiography*.

Most of the values that Franklin promoted in those works—diligence, industry, sobriety, and thrift—were closely related to traditional tradesman's values, which included as well independence, self-discipline, and self-worth. Artisans were early promoters of clubs and mutual-aid societies of all sorts; Franklin's Junto in Philadelphia was one, the political "Leather-Apron Club," which supported Pennsylvania's Governor Sir William Keith against the proprietors, was another. The leading cities of urban Britain established a multitude of mutual-aid societies as well, a trend that would slowly appear in the colonies. The goal of those aid societies was double edged: they were to provide relief for impoverished tradesmen, or their orphans and widows, but only those who were down on their luck through no fault of their own. Those whose poverty resulted from laziness or intemperance were excluded from benefits.[68]

The same sentiment informs Franklin's *Autobiography*. There he established a sharp contrast between himself and several of his earliest friends, such as John Collins, his Boston friend, a "bookish lad." In intellect and inquisitiveness, Collins was Franklin's equal, or so the autobiographer would have us believe. What he lacked was sobriety. The result, despite a promising start, was a career that quickly went into a downhill slide, his learning wasted. Franklin had little patience with such vices, and he dismissed the most intimate friend of his youth from the *Autobiography* in a single brief sentence.

In urban Britain, artisanal societies were both a leading source of religious Dissent and strong promoters of tradesmen's values. Evangelicals always found considerable support among artisans, especially weavers; so also did radical free thinkers, who questioned such basic Christian doctrines as the Trinity. If artisans and radicals represent opposite poles on the religious spectrum, both derived from the autonomous and independent character of tradesmen's societies, who ignored the deference to traditional authority demanded by the Anglican establishment and by traditional orthodoxy in favor of positions that shared an emphasis on personal conviction over a purely inherited faith.[69]

Franklin's religious skepticism derived as well from traditional tradesmen's culture. The young printer published his first statement of religious principles, entitled *A Dissertation on Liberty and Necessity, Pleasure and Pain*, while working as a journeyman printer in London at the age of 19, at a time when his principal associations were still with his fellow artisans. London's artisans maintained a disputatious culture, one in which a citizen was free to try out his ideas of all kinds against those of his fellows, as well as against those of traditional authorities. British tradesmen were renowned for their independent opinions in religion and politics; many would convey their ideas to America in the second half of the eighteenth century. But such free thinking was found earlier in the century in urban artisanal culture as well, in the world that surrounded the young Benjamin Franklin. It was also a world in which evangelical preachers such as Whitefield and Tennent found ample followings.[70]

In Franklin's *Autobiography* the narrator revealed how the young tradesman came to absorb that disputatious style. While working as a printer's apprentice in Boston, Franklin befriended Collins, with whom he engaged in regular discussion and argument both in conversation and in writing. The young Franklin perceived that he had the advantage over his opponent in the force of his arguments but perceived himself quite inferior in method and style. It was then that he first sat down with the *Spectator* and attempted to learn method and style from its renowned authors.

That was not the end of such disputes for the young Franklin. While working for his brother's paper he regularly lampooned leaders in both politics and religion, which made him less than popular among Boston's establishment. After running away to Philadelphia, Franklin settled in another group of associates at the print shop, including the printer Samuel Keimer, who was already famous for his heterodox opinions. Another was James Ralph, who after accompanying Franklin to London became a noted political polemicist there. Disputation formed a basic part of their discussion; indeed, Franklin claimed responsibility for having drawn Ralph away from orthodoxy and toward skepticism.[71]

The urban environs that produced such diverse religious opinions was somewhat more limited in the provincial than in the metropolitan world before 1760. Although historians have found that a variety of heterodox religious beliefs connected with such traditional realms as magic and astrology continued to flourish in parts of early America, and an evangelicalism bordering on enthusiasm emerged in parts of the backcountry, there is less evidence of clearly articulated forms of skepticism such as Deism or unbelief, which were found among the tradesmen of such communities as London and Glasgow. Instead, in both the cities and the countryside, the mainstream denominations and the many and varied forms of evangelical religion assumed an ever more visible presence.[72] And evangelicals increasingly projected the values of a tradesmen's culture, denouncing leisure and inactivity in favor of dedication to public projects, mutuality, and civic and personal improvement.

Thus would Samuel Davies also reflect the same values of the middling, tradesmen's culture that a number of his students expressed. When the literary quality of that minister's spiritual poetry came under attack from Anglican opponents, Davies did more than modestly disavow any claims to literary merit; he positively denied the intent. Instead, Davies argued for the advantages of using a plain and simple style that could reach general readers who could spread his evangelical message, even if it did not appeal to polite readers.[73]

In fact, the audience Davies addressed was increasingly both evangelical and enlightened. The provincial environment seemed to provide a context in which such traditional oppositions could be reconciled. In their widespread commitment to middling tastes and to a modest form of refinement, and in their striving for moral as well as economic improvement, provincials increasingly assumed the character of moral, virtuous, and self-reliant citizens. They displayed both the confidence and the competence to prescribe for themselves the basic ethical norms on which their communities relied.

six

Liberty, Province, and Empire

In February of 1746, Charles Chauncy mounted his pulpit in Boston to perform what was then a traditional New England rite: the delivery of a sermon of thanksgiving, this one for the defeat of a recent and dangerous rebellion. The uprising to which he alluded had been fought principally in Scotland and led by the Catholic prince Charles Edward Stuart, "Bonnie Prince Charlie," in the last of many attempts to restore to his father what had once been his grandfather's crown. New Englanders had not had much use for Stuart kings while they held the throne, and they certainly were not about to support them now: the Stuarts' Catholicism, their connections to the French court, and their past history of authoritarian rule all made them anathema to a British and Protestant populace. Thus Chauncy celebrated the recent defeat of the Jacobite armies, which had posed the specter of "*Popery* and *Slavery*" and threatened Britons in "the Enjoyment of their "*Rights* and *Liberties*, which distinguish them from the other Nations of the Earth."[1]

In his preaching on the subject of liberty, the Old Light Chauncy sounded much like the evangelical Samuel Davies of Princeton in Davies's sermon on the death of George II. Even Chauncy's most frequent antagonist, Jonathan Edwards, who was then composing the many works that challenged what he deemed the unsound theological positions of his rival, had no quarrel with the Bostonian's opinions of the Jacobite threat to Protestant liberties. Indeed, upon first hearing of the threat, Edwards expressed fear that the rebellion itself might represent a divine punishment to "the nations of Great Britain" for their sinful ways, although recent providential intervention in the New Englanders' attack on the French bastion at Louisbourg on Cape Breton made him hopeful that God remained on the side of Protestants and liberty.[2]

149

If a single catchword can represent most of what provincials valued within their world, that word would have to be *liberty*. To the extent that the Enlightenment signified the reconception of secular history in a progressive direction, liberty was the end toward which it moved. The term was nearly ubiquitous throughout the eighteenth-century British world, turning up in countless contexts in many realms of life. As with most terms that seem to capture collective aspirations at any given point in time, its meaning is hard to define with precision. It meant many things to many people. At the simplest level, liberty meant freedom from arbitrary restraint, the term *arbitrary* being the most critical one here. It certainly did not mean the absence of all regulation, which was not liberty in eighteenth-century understandings but anarchy or licentiousness; rational restraint was basic to civil society and to social well-being and, in short, to what eighteenth-century men and women referred to as social "happiness."

What distinguished arbitrary restraint was its absolute quality, the total subjection to another, or others, unrelated to any overriding social imperative. The term for that subjection was *slavery*, the very opposite of liberty. Slavery, in a political sense, signified the complete dependence on the will of another rather than simply the system of forced labor that we associate with the term. People living under arbitrary governments could bemoan their enslavement without implying that they lived under a system of bondage; slaveholders themselves could and did complain of their slavery, as we shall see.[3]

Liberty was part of many realms of life. In politics, liberty meant principally freedom from arbitrary rule and in particular from that of absolute monarchs, which was what Britons considered most of the world's rulers to be. In civil life, liberty signified the presence of specific legal protections, such as the right to hold property, for those who either had it or could aspire to it, and the established protections of the legal system for those entitled to it—in short, freedom from arbitrary punishment. In the religious culture of British Protestants, liberty meant the right to follow one's conscience in accordance with the word of God as revealed in Scripture, and freedom from arbitrary human authorities that tried to impose their wills above biblical commands; it was the creation of just such a human authority that rendered Catholicism an unfit religion in the minds of most Protestants and a threat to liberty of conscience. In cultural matters, liberty signified freedom of enquiry, without interference from church or state and without the tyrannical authority of superstition or ancient learning. Socially, liberty increasingly came to mean the right of citizens to pursue their fortunes without unnecessary hindrance from the authority of the state, or even from the tyranny of birth. Genteel origins might indeed provide privileges to those who possessed them but ought not to prevent the peaceful pursuit of prosperity and happiness among those of every station in life.

Some of the meanings of liberty varied from place to place and from group to group. Within the rural confines of Congregationalist New England, for example, liberty for many was often associated with the authority of local communities to conduct their own affairs without interference from the outside—even if those "outsiders" were merely claiming the liberty to worship in their own way. In Tidewater Virginia, liberty in its fullest sense was the property of the gentry, of male landowners, who claimed the right to govern, represent, and speak for their communities and their households— including wives, children, slaves, and servants—without restraint from the government of the colony or the empire. For mid-Atlantic farmers, liberty meant something like the ability to own or at least possess their farms, to be secure from rapacious landlords or onerous taxes from church or state. And nearly everywhere in the British colonies, liberty would come to be associated with a significant degree of provincial control over provincial affairs.[4]

There was little to distinguish the concept of liberty as it emerged in America from the mainstream of British thinking on political matters, unless it was the existence of a somewhat narrower range of meanings across the political spectrum; it was, after all, British liberty whose protection provincials claimed. Rather than departing from the core of British political ideas, provincials on the whole were rather close to the center, and there were few representations of the extremes of political thinking found in Britain itself. Not many Americans could be found on the extreme political right, which viewed liberty as deriving from aristocratic or at least gentle birth and protected by kings who held their authority by divine right. Although recent historians have found considerable support in many parts of Britain for the continuing claims of the Stuart dynasty to a legitimate right to the British throne, there were few avowed Jacobites in America.[5] The rebellion of 1715 attracted little conspicuous support in the colonies, that of 1745 almost none. Those movements derived the bulk of their support from Britain's farthest outlying regions—northern England, northern Scotland, and Celtic Ireland—not among the commercial towns and Protestant citizenries of provincial England and Lowland Scotland, the areas with which provincial Americans maintained their closest connections.

Neither were many Americans positioned on what might be considered the far left of the British political spectrum in the middle years of the eighteenth century—the emerging republican politics of radical groups in London and among the provincial Dissenters—at least not before 1760. To be sure, colonials voiced considerable support for London's John Wilkes in his ongoing battle against the British ministry. But Americans saw Wilkes principally as simply a defender of liberty against tyranny—"Wilkes and liberty" was the slogan associated with his supporters—rather than as a representative of any particular radical position. Moreover, the general weakness of royal authority in the colonies worked against the establishment of truly radical stances on political matters before the 1760s, as did the relative absence of urban centers of the sort that fostered them. Thus colonials viewed sympathy for Wilkes as entailing significant protest not against the system in general but only against abuses. To most provincial citizens, Wilkes could be defended on the basis of a British liberty that was firmly rooted in Protestantism, the common law, and the inherent safeguards of the British Constitution, all safely within the mainstream of British thinking.[6]

If one had asked a typical provincial British citizen of the eighteenth century the reasons for the blessing of liberty that he and his neighbors possessed, the questioner would likely have received one of several answers. One would have referred to religion, to British Protestantism and the freedom of enquiry it claimed to promote; civil and religious liberty were widely believed to be inextricably interconnected. A second would likely have been British virtue, the spirited defense of liberty that Britons had actively exhibited over the years against repeated attacks from the monarchy, especially by the Stuarts during the 1640s and the 1680s; such a spirit was at least partly attributed to Protestant independence as well.[7]

A third set of answers would have cited British institutions: the heritage of the English common law and the system of government established after the Revolution of 1688 and summarized by the phrase "the British Constitution." Unlike the Constitution of the United States, the British Constitution was not a written document. The phrase referred instead to the structure of government, the way the government conducted itself, and the powers that it held, deriving from traditional practice and from such revered documents as the Magna Charta and the Bill of Rights. At the heart of the Constitution was the tripartite system of government by a combination of crown, lords, and commons, working not through separation of powers but jointly in what was called "mixed government." That system met the twin goals of moderation and balance on the one hand—so resonant for partisans of the "moderate Enlightenment"—and of popular participation on the other.

Liberty, so conceived, was far from universal. If it seemed to most Britons to be the particular inheritance of Protestants, many doubted that it was safe to extend its blessings to others, who would likely commit to destroying the religion on which those liberties rested. Nor was liberty necessarily incompatible with the institution of slavery, despite what seems to us a contradiction in terms; liberty was the property of citizens and certainly did not belong to those whose interests ran counter to those of civil society. Even John Locke's famous triad of life, liberty, and property allowed for the institution of slavery in the case of captives in just wars, whose lives could otherwise have been forfeited. Liberty could be a prized possession without carrying implications that it had to belong to everyone.

In fact, liberty and bonded slavery seemed to be intimately connected everywhere in the colonial world. To the plantation owners in the southern provinces, the economic independence they derived from the profits of slave labor provided the very foundation of their liberties. And even the economic liberties that mid-Atlantic family farmers so highly valued—the opportunity to profit from the surplus produce of independent family farms—depended in large part on the ready market for that surplus that existed in the plantation economies to the south or in the West Indies, with their abundant supply of slave labor. Few provincials, with the exception of such attentive Quakers as John Woolman, thought much about that connection.[8]

As the persistence of slavery in the colonial world illustrates, the context in which provincial ideas of liberty developed differed from that which Britons experienced. The necessities of colonial society, and in particular the need for population, extended the reach of liberties from being the possession of a restricted class of property holders to a broader component of both propertied and nonpropertied white society. The political status of the American colonies also differed from that of Britain, and American provincials would come to root their liberties to an unusual degree in the particular legal forms of their colonial charters. More generally, the connotations of liberty that emerged there would be distinctive, as many provincials came to identify liberty in the broadest sense as both the natural state and as one of the principal advantages of provincial society.

Liberty, Virtue, and the Independent Reflector

Some of the meaning that liberty held for provincial citizens can be observed in the *Independent Reflector,* a series of polite essays offered to the New York citizenry by the New York lawyer William Livingston along with his associates William Smith Jr. and John Morin Scott. In style, the paper was something of a hybrid. In part it cultivated the polite style of the *Spectator* and of such literary journals as the *Gentleman's Magazine,* but its concerns were never "meerly literary," in Livingston's words. Rather, the paper's principal design, he announced in the first issue, was to vindicate the *"civil and religious* RIGHTS of my Fellow-Creatures" while exposing "publick *Vice* and *Corruption*." The *Reflector,* invoking a popular phrase, refused to be a "silent Spectator" where "the Rights of the Community are infringed, or violated"; it would devote itself instead to "displaying the amiable Charms of Liberty, with the detestable Nature of *Slavery* and *Oppression*."[9]

In its devotion to the cause of liberty, the *Independent Reflector* most closely resembled the essays by the English opposition writers of the early eighteenth century, John Trenchard and Thomas Gordon, especially those essays that appeared in the *London Journal* between 1720 and 1723 under the title *Cato's Letters,* although the name of their publication was drawn from Trenchard and Gordon's earlier *Independent Whig.* The reputation of the Roman patriot Cato as a defender of liberty was enhanced by Joseph Addison's popular play of that name, and both the play and the essays were widely read in the colonies. The essays were regularly reprinted or excerpted in the colonial press almost from their first appearance; one on the liberty of the press appeared in the *New England Courant* as early as 1722.[10]

THE

INDEPENDENT REFLECTOR:

O R,

Weekly Essays

O N

Sundry Important SUBJECTS.

More particularly adapted to the PROVINCE *of* NEW-YORK.

Ne quid falsi dicere audeat, ne quid veri non audeat.
CICERO.

N E W - Y O R K :

Printed (until tyrannically suppressed) in MDCCLIII.

Title page of William Livingston's *Independent Reflector. Courtesy Rare Books Division, The New York Public Library, Astor, Lenox and Tilden Foundation.*

The *Reflector*'s debt to the work of Trenchard and Gordon suggests an important aspect of the meaning of liberty in provincial America. Neither man was a great thinker, and their contributions have been overshadowed by those of such seminal writers as their predecessor John Locke, whose *Two Treatises on Government*, with its allocation to the government of the protection of life, liberty, and property, has long stood as a classic of political thought. Yet if such luminaries as Locke have left us a legacy to which historians of political theory must ever return, such popular writers as Trenchard and Gordon still have much to tell us about the meaning of political liberty to British citizens in the eighteenth century.[11]

Locke's works on politics have long been regarded as perhaps the classic statement of liberal theory, a theory of politics that emphasizes the rights of individuals and freedom from governmental interference with those rights. Trenchard and Gordon's work is based at least in part on a different tradition in political theory traceable to the work of the seventeenth-century writer James Harrington, author of *Oceana*, and, before him, to such humanist and classical writers as Machiavelli and even Aristotle. That tradition, called "civic humanism," viewed man as exercising his full liberty through civic participation; liberty here signified the freedom to participate in civic life—although not necessarily for everyone—more than it meant freedom from its authority. It valued public action over private interest and deemed the vigorous pursuit of the public welfare as essential to liberty's preservation. The term for that pursuit was *virtue*, and its presence among the citizenry was essential for preventing corruption, political decay, and the inevitable loss of liberty that would follow. It was thus a philosophy that valued public engagement over private tranquillity.[12]

As was the case with Cato's essays, the primary aim of the *Reflector* was to promote public virtue, or watchfulness, and especially to guard against abuses in public life. As Livingston wrote in the first *Reflector,* "Public Abuses are, in their own Nature, progressive; and tho' easily removed in their Origin, acquire Strength by their Duration, and at last become too potent to be subdued." Defenders of liberty had to remain always on their guard, because a failure to resist even "the least Invasion of civil or religious Liberty, is an encouragement to greater, and presages mightier Evils to come; while a seasonable Opposition might not only have vanquished the present, but discouraged all future Abuses of the like Nature."[13] Liberty was always under attack, a theme Cato enunciated in "Cautions against the natural Encroachments of Power," in which he contended that, "because Liberty chastises and shortens Power, therefore Power would extinguish Liberty; and consequently Liberty has too much cause to be exceeding jealous, and always upon her Defence."[14] And liberty, once lost, was very difficult to regain.

The guarding of liberty seemed especially important to eighteenth-century Britons because, from their perspective, it was not only fragile but rare. As Britons looked beyond their borders, they saw, or thought they saw, a world of absolutist monarchies, such as France and Spain were deemed to be. Beyond those lay a still-larger world full of what were generally referred to as "Oriental despotisms." Only in small, isolated pockets of Europe did liberty thrive, and except in Britain, it was largely restricted to such small and weak states as Switzerland or the Netherlands. Moreover, liberty was often under attack from abroad as well as at home, leading the *Reflector* to consider not simply domestic political abuses but also "the dangerous vicinity of the French to the British Plantations."[15]

Liberty in this sense also demanded that citizens place the public interest above their own, which was, in essence, the principal meaning of political virtue in the eighteenth century. That is a sense of the word *virtue* that has nearly been lost in our time, as we live under a system that maintains that the good of the whole is best attained when each individual promotes his or her own interest. Since the nineteenth century, the term *virtue* has been applied principally to the activities of individuals in private life, and especially to women; as we have seen, in the eighteenth century it was already basic to the vocabulary of such evangelical women as Esther Burr and to other Enlightened women. But in the eighteenth century the term also retained a very public meaning; virtue in that sense was essentially a masculine trait, employed in defense of an otherwise defenseless liberty whose connotations were, in that sense, feminine.[16]

The principal part of virtue was public spirit, the promotion of the community's interests above self-interest or even above the interest of one's family or neighbors. The pursuit of such "partial" interests was roundly condemned in this view, under the labels of *faction* or *party*. Neither was a term of approbation. The *Reflector*, for instance, included a whole paper on the subject of "Party-Divisions," which discussed how "zeal for the common Good" was "gradually extinguished by the predominating Fervor of a Faction."[17]

One reason that factious behavior was rendered so unsavory in the eighteenth century was its association with the passions. As the *Reflector* explained, "From the Moment that Men give themselves wholly up to a Party, they abandon their *Reason*, and are led Captive by their *Passions*." Their own cause "presents such bewitching Charms, as dazzle the Judgment," the other side "such imaginary Deformity, that no Opposition appears too violent."[18] People were drawn to factions for base reasons, such as the love of power or wealth. Such motives induced them to act against their better selves, against their reason, against the common good, as well as against principles of Christian charity. A well-ordered commonwealth thus resembled a well-ordered mind: the placing of the faculties in their appropriate order would lead to both individual and social happiness.

Yet if the *Reflector* generally denounced factious behavior, its antipathy to faction itself was not absolute. In other essays, the authors began to bring into their pages a different view of faction that was then emerging, one more often associated with liberal views than with civic ones, in which faction and the pursuit of individual interest could have positive as well as negative effects. At one point Livingston described the division of New York into "so great a Variety of Opinions and Professions" as an advantage, with "the Jealousy of all Parties combating each other," producing "a perfect Freedom for each particular Party."[19]

The *Reflector's* argument, it has been noted, anticipated that offered by James Madison in his famous *Federalist* essay #10 in 1787, which has been variously interpreted as exemplifying both liberal and civic ideals. There Madison also revealed his distaste for faction—indeed, Madison contended, one of the principal arguments for a new federal government was its ability to "break and control the violence of faction." Yet it was the violence of factions rather than factions themselves that Madison sought to break. Factions themselves had their advantages. The great number of factions that would emerge in the extensive territory that encompassed the new United States, Madison believed, and within the enlarged territorial districts from which representatives would be elected, would prevent any single interest from attaining too large a foothold in the government.

However clear the distinctions between the civic and liberal traditions may have seemed to historians of political thought, they were less carefully maintained by contemporaries. In fact, both Locke and Cato held honored places in the pantheon of Whig heroes that emerged in British and British-American discussion; also revered were the seventeenth-century radical and martyr Algernon Sydney, the eighteenth-century Tory critic Henry St. John, Viscount Bolingbroke, and the popular schoolmaster and essayist James Burgh, whose writings drew on all of those traditions. British political culture was a composite of many different views, linked only by the pervasive belief that all helped to advance liberty, the hallmark of an Enlightened age.[20]

That composite heritage allowed Britons and Americans both to celebrate monarchy at the same time that they lauded the accumulated restraints on monarchical power established in the Magna Charta and the Bill of Rights; kings as well as commons had a role to play in the history of liberty, serving as mutual checks on one another. The king and only the king, in theory, shared the interests of the whole nation and was not susceptible to those of any one group or faction. Kings were the protectors of the people, not only against invasion from abroad but also against corruption from within. This role of the king as protector led Americans, including Samuel Davies, to valorize George II on his death in 1760 and to await so eagerly the reign of George III. To celebrate monarchs as bastions of liberty was an important mechanism for promoting British and provincial identities.[21]

Thus Americans in the eighteenth century possessed a mixed political heritage, one that combined a civic fear of faction with a liberal attachment to interest, a reverence for kings with a devotion to popular government. What they shared was the conviction that theirs was in fact a nation of liberty in a world of tyrannies, whether they attributed that fact to the limitations on the

British monarchy, to its system of balanced power through mixed government, to ancient tradition, to the Common Law, or to the Protestant heritage. Thus would the *Reflector* claim for itself "the Privilege of a free Briton, to expose the Abuses of Government; and, when Occasion offers, to animadvert on the lawless Conduct of his Superiors." He would do so, indeed, with "the Spirit peculiar to an Englishman."[22]

The rhetoric of liberty played a prominent role in provincial politics. It was employed by what came to be called the "popular" party, led by Elisha Cooke, that rose up in Massachusetts under the new charter, which opposed the prerogatives of governors and officeholders and, at least in Boston, regularized such practices as the employment of explicit instructions by the town meeting to its elected representatives. It was part of the appeal of a series of repeated populist attacks on the Pennsylvania proprietorship David Lloyd undertook. In New York, claims of liberty had formed a component of ethnic politics even during the seventeenth century; in some instances, the claim of English liberties was used to suppress traditional Dutch political practices. In the next century, James Alexander and William Smith would oppose Governor Cosby through the instrument of John Peter Zenger's *New-York Weekly Journal*. In their first essay, they defended both the liberty of the press and the importance of guarding the liberties of the people from attack by entrenched powers.[23]

The politics of liberty was well suited to opposition styles, especially when joined to the emerging political press, which claimed the role of public watchman; indeed, William Livingston and his associates used the name "The Watch-Tower" for a series of essays that succeeded the *Reflector* in the *New-York Mercury*. *Cato's Letters*, published originally in the *London Journal*, proved so widely adaptable in the colonies expressly because of that union. Benjamin Franklin published an excerpt from Cato on the freedom of speech as "inseparable from Publick Liberty" in 1722 in response to his brother's imprisonment in Boston, as already noted. In New York, James Alexander and Lewis Morris, the aristocratic opponents of Governor Cosby, also employed Trenchard and Gordon's writings in their attack on executive prerogatives published in the *New York Weekly Journal*.[24]

Liberties Civil and Religious

The concern for liberty arose from more than just abstract ideas. From the middle of the 1740s, Britain and its colonies began two decades of active or impending war with France, Europe's leading Catholic power. Provincial Americans felt concern on several counts. Many lived under the very real threat of attack from French troops and their Indian allies, who launched extensive raids on the colonial frontiers, some of which were publicized in popular captivity narratives. They feared as well that if the colonies fell into

French hands, the result would be carnage and devastation, followed by the subjugation of provincials and the loss of their liberties, including the liberty to practice the Protestant religion that captives had sometimes suffered. Esther Burr described the quality of that fear in her journal:

> You cant conceive my dear friend what a tender Mother undergoes for her children at such a day as this, to think of bring[ing] up children to be *dashed against the stones by our barbarous enemies*—or which is worse, to be inslaved by them, and obliged to turn *Papist*.

Later, upon visiting her parents in the frontier town of Stockbridge, Esther found herself sleepless with fear.[25]

The *Independent Reflector* expressed some similar sentiments. Livingston agreed with Chauncy and Edwards that the Jacobite rebellion had posed a major threat to liberty. "Had our unrelenting Enemies succeeded in their detestable Designs," he wrote, "instead of enjoying our invaluable Liberties, we had long e'er now, beheld *Persecution* brandish her Sword. . . . In a Word, we had seen *Tyranny*, like a ravenous Harpy, devouring the Fruits of our Industry, and *Popery*, with her malignant Spirit, plunging us into the Depths of Misery."[26] It is little wonder that, under such circumstances, the causes of civil and religious liberty were almost invariably connected.

Livingston's characterization suggests an important aspect of British understandings of liberty, to which we have already alluded: they were inherently Protestant. Indeed, what distinguished Protestantism, according to Protestant interpretations, was the liberty it granted individuals to think for themselves in matters of religion and in other matters as well. No matter that such freedoms had often not been—and still were not—universally allowed in many Protestant states; liberty still seemed to be Protestantism's characteristic feature. By contrast, in Catholicism, or popery, as Protestants almost always called it, Popes and priests told individuals what to think and hid scriptural truth behind an unintelligible foreign tongue. The Pope was an arbitrary ruler as absolute in religious matters as the French monarch was in civil affairs. Together, the two constituted an unholy alliance of Catholic powers that threatened the liberties of Protestants everywhere through their expansionist designs. It was the threat they posed to Protestants' liberties, and not any persecuting design, Protestants argued, that rendered the toleration of Catholics unsafe in a Protestant state.

The fear of French victory was shared by American Protestants across the religious spectrum; another fear, that of encroachments from the Anglican Church, was more particular to Protestant Dissenters. Trenchard and Gordon's *Independent Whig* had been largely devoted to attacking the Church and its efforts to limit the rights of Dissenters, and the *Independent Reflector* continued that theme. Although the paper disavowed any intention of persecuting a denomination on the basis of doctrine or form of church government, the association of Anglicanism with imperial authority rendered its position both peculiar and problematic to provincials.

The paper's view of the proper role for religion in society was articulated most fully during the controversy over the establishment of King's College (now Columbia University) in New York City. At the outset, the *Reflector* enthusiastically endorsed the project, viewing the college as ideally suited "to improve [the] . . . Hearts and Understandings" of citizens and "to make them the more extensively serviceable to the Common-Wealth." The writers pulled back, however, when the Anglican Church offered to donate property to the college. In return, the Church expected that, as the city's dominant church in point of law and with a majority among the trustees, it would lead the college, which would become a liberal but Anglican institution, comparable to Congregationalist Harvard and Yale or the Presbyterian College of New Jersey. The college was to provide simultaneously for both the church's and the colony's educational needs.[27]

The authors of the *Reflector,* all Presbyterians, opposed the plan for a denominational college, or, as William Livingston called it, a "Party College," arguing instead that faculty and students should be allowed to attend "any Protestant Church at their Pleasure." The establishment of a purely Anglican institution would tend to turn the diverse colony into one in which office-holders and leaders would all be Churchmen and in which the worship of other religions would be tolerated not as a right but a privilege. Such restrictions would impair not only the colony's piety and prosperity but the institution's success; the advancement of learning, Livingston contended, was impossible where freedom of enquiry stood under any restraint.[28] If the Anglican Church took over the college, then "the Seat of Literature, the Abode of the Muses, and the Nurse of Science" would be "transform'd into a Cloister of Bigots, and Habitation of Superstition, a Nursery of ghostly Tyranny."[29]

It is tempting to look at the King's College controversy as nothing more than a denominational dispute, which was how Anglicans viewed the matter. Church spokesmen charged that the Presbyterian Livingston was really trying to suppress Episcopal competition with the Presbyterian institution in New Jersey. There is support for such a view; the *Reflector* did appeal to traditional Dissenter suspicions of Anglican power. Moreover, Livingston was reluctant to grant that church the same right to government support for colleges that he conceded to Dissenters in New Jersey and elsewhere, or, in the following decade, to allow the appointment of an Anglican bishop in America to ordain and supervise Anglican clergy.[30]

In fact the issue is considerably more complicated. For one thing, the *Reflector* was zealous in its advocacy of a college for New York, which no matter what its affiliation was bound to offer competition for the Presbyterian college at Princeton. Moreover, Livingston, with perfect sincerity, offered an enlightened argument in favor of religious liberty as beneficial to learning and to the prosperity of the colony. Yet the New Yorker had no objection to a College of New Jersey headed by Presbyterians, nor to the even more rigidly Congregationalist Yale, his alma mater. The "narrow principles" Livingston decried in the New York College were certainly no more narrow than Yale's. Moreover, the *Reflector* elsewhere took great pains to defend the rights of other Protestant denominations, such as the Moravians, whose theology was farther removed from the Presbyterians' than was that of most Anglicans.[31]

The problem derived instead from the fact that King's College was to be an Anglican institution that would represent a national church with a privileged position in the ecclesiastical order. Such a claim threatened the liberties that Dissenters had attained in the provincial world, where the principal Dissenting denominations were not simply tolerated but dominant, as was the case nearly everywhere in the kingdom and in the empire outside of England and the southern and West Indian colonies. The granting of any state privileges to an Anglican Church, if it did not necessarily threaten Dissenters' rights to worship as they chose, did challenge the secure position they had achieved in the province.

Religious liberty, as portrayed by the authors of the *Reflector*, meant denying civil authority every power over religion save that of preventing religions from interfering with one another. That was precisely the problem with the Anglican Church. From the middle of the century onward, a number of leading Anglicans in America had embarked on a concerted effort to secure the appointment of an Anglican bishop for the colonies. Although American Anglicans maintained that such a bishop would do no more than complete the structure of their church in the colonies and allow it to compete equally with other denominations, avoiding the difficulty of having to send their ministers to London for ordination, many provincials distrusted their design. Such a bishop, in their view, would inherently possess civil as well as religious authority, which could not be prevented in the British legal structure. Even an act of Parliament denying civil power to American bishops could not prevent a subsequent act from restoring such powers. From such a perspective, Protestant pluralism and Anglican establishment were incompatible.[32]

The *Reflector* distrusted all clerics who worked in league with civil authorities. In several essays, the authors displayed a touch of anticlericalism, calling any religious establishment, for example, an "engine of oppression." They maintained as well that whenever sovereigns in English history had attempted to enslave the people, they were almost always supported by churchmen proclaiming "*jus divinum*" [the divine right of kings] and "*hereditary succession.*"[33]

What the *Reflector* promoted was something else: a marketplace in religious ideas, like the economic marketplace that Adam Smith would write about shortly thereafter, in which Protestant sects could compete with one another without unfair influence from metropolitan authorities in church or state. As Livingston contended, it was the religious freedom that flourished in Pennsylvania that provided "the rising Prosperity of Pennsylvania" through a "vast Importation of religious Refugees." The *Reflector* opposed only free thinking, or unbelief, contending that New York ought to make no laws at all in regard to religion, "except such as compel them to attend Divine Service at some Church or other, every Sabbath, as they shall be able, lest so invaluable a Liberty be abused and *made a Cloak for Licentiousness.*"[34]

We shall have more to say about the significance of the metaphor of the marketplace in moral judgments shortly. First, we should notice that the threatening quality of Anglican supremacy was a particularly provincial phenomenon and that the dominance of religious Dissent was itself characteristic of British provincial society. In England, the vast majority of inhabitants still adhered to the Church; only in certain provincial towns and in London was Dissent substantial. On the other hand, Presbyterianism was the majority religion in Scotland and the north of Ireland, and it and other Dissenting persuasions dominated most of the colonies. And even in Virginia, which retained a dominant Anglican establishment, the local gentry resisted any efforts by the clergy to assert independent authority. Virginia Anglicanism was gentry-based, with local elites firmly retaining the upper hand.

Even in Virginia one could find expressions of anticlericalism directed against the Anglican Church, as occurred from the late 1750s onward in what came to be known as the "Parson's Cause." Unhappy as dependents of the parish vestry, Anglican clergymen in that decade began to use the courts to try to establish a degree of independence from the tight control of the local gentry as well as to profit and perhaps profiteer from the unusually high price of tobacco in a period of drought. In response, the Virginia Assembly in 1759 passed the "Twopenny Act," which guaranteed the clergy's income but precluded profiteering. When the Church appealed the case to London, Virginia gentlemen responded with harsh attacks. Among the most prominent opponents of the clergy were two of the most orthodox Anglican laymen in the colony, Landon Carter and Richard Bland, as well as a young politician named Patrick Henry.[35]

Whatever their limitations, provincial ideas of religious liberty in the eighteenth century certainly represented a greater degree of freedom than one would likely have found in the previous century. Unlike Puritan notions, for example, religious liberty in the eighteenth century signified something more than the simple freedom to follow the true religion, as their ancestors would have argued. To most provincials, freedom of conscience was guaranteed as long as the exercise thereof did not interfere with the peace of civil society or with others' freedom of conscience. The *private* practice of worship in any form was often disapproved of but was rarely punished. The limits on liberty were matters of this world only. False belief by itself was not dangerous; in the new marketplace of ideas that an Enlightened century was coming to envision, truth chased out falsehood. If the failure to grasp the truth was still regarded as likely to send one to hell in the eyes of most orthodox believers, most no longer thought that it was the job of civil authorities to see that nonbelievers got there any sooner.

Liberty, Provinciality, and Prosperity

What made the preservation of liberty seem so compelling to provincials in the eighteenth century was its apparent connection to nearly every other element of prosperity and social happiness. As the *Reflector* observed in a passage that was echoed countless times in the colonies, in absolute monarchies "the whole Country is overspread with a dismal Gloom. *Slavery* is stamp'd on the Looks of the Inhabitants; and *Penury* engraved on their Visages. . . . To prevent Complaints, the *PRESS* is prohibited. . . . The liberal Sciences languish: The politer Arts droop their Heads. . . . The Fields lie waste and uncultivate: Commerce is incumbured with supernumerary Duties: The Tyrant riots in the Spoils of his People; and drains their Purses, to replenish his insatiate Treasury."[36]

The situation under a system of liberty was altogether different. "The Subjects of a free State, have something open and generous in their Carriage; something of Grandeur and Sublimity in their Appearance, resulting from their Freedom and Independence. . . . They can think for themselves; publish their Sentiments, and animadvert on Religion and Government, secure and unmolested." Under such a system, "[a]griculture is encouraged, and proves the annual Source of immense Riches to the Kingdom: The Earth opens her fertile Bosom to the Ploughshare, and luxuriant Harvests diffuse Wealth and Plenty thro' the Land." The *Reflector* went on to ask whether the "rising Prosperity of Pennsylvania," the "Admiration of the Continent," was not the result of "the impartial Aspect of their Laws upon all Professions," which led to a "vast Importation of religious Refugees, to their Strength and their Riches."[37]

Liberty promoted not only prosperity but enlightenment, through the exercise of free inquiry. "The Restraint of civil Authority, in different Countries and Ages, upon the free Exercise of human Reason, has ever been attended with a Decay of all valuable Knowledge and Literature. It is as impossible for the Sciences to grow and flourish under the Frowns and Terrors of Oppression, as for a People to breath Liberty under the savage Administration of a Tyrant. The Advancement of Learning depends upon the free Exercise of Thought; it is therefore absurd to suppose, that it should thrive under a Government that makes it Treason even for a Man to think."[38]

Here again, Livingston and his colleagues drew from Trenchard and Gordon, who had pronounced liberty "the divine Source of all human Happiness." They continued, "to possess, in Security, the Effects of our Industry, is the most powerful and reasonable Incitement to be industrious. . . . where Property is precarious, labour will languish." Indeed, liberty would "increase Mankind, and the Happiness of Mankind. . . . Liberty naturally draws new People to it," and therefore "countries are generally peopled in Proportion as they are free."[39]

Such ideas were given additional force by what provincial Americans saw around them. During the first half of the eighteenth century, the British

colonies in North America found themselves in a period of dramatic demographic and economic growth. Between 1700 and 1750, the settler population
of the British colonies increased perhaps fourfold—to more than a million
people, including slaves—a rate of growth that was surprisingly close to that
imagined by provincials. American wealth and trade were also perceived to be
growing at a heady rate.[40]

Provincials were not unaware of the growth that surrounded them, which
they began to attribute to the relatively unconstrained nature of the colonial
economy, or, as they viewed it, the effects of economic liberty. As New York's
Archibald Kennedy observed, "liberty and encouragement" were the cornerstones of colonial prosperity.[41] From that perspective, within the context of
provincial society, prosperity, which traditional moral economists had portrayed as threatening to moral welfare, could be portrayed instead as its confirmation.[42]

From those observations, provincial commentators developed some particular perspectives on their economy. Perhaps the most famous was Benjamin
Franklin's 1751 essay on population, entitled "Observations Concerning the
Increase of Mankind, Peopling of Countries, &c."[43] Franklin hypothesized
that the availability of land and the prevalence of opportunity in the American
colonies was allowing for a dramatic growth of population, which he reckoned
was doubling every 25 years. Such growth was likely to continue, in Franklin's
view, as long as colonials did not fall prey to the dangers of overcrowding, the
loss of trade, or the importation of "foreign luxuries and needless manufactures."

Franklin's work was both original and influential, but it was not without
precedent. Some of his suggestions about population, for example, including
his famous estimate that colonial population was doubling every 25 years,
were anticipated by his friend and correspondent Archibald Kennedy in an
essay written the year before.[44] Perhaps more importantly, Franklin's concern
with population growth in particular was part of a much larger philosophical
inquiry into the causes and ramifications of population growth that was then
taking place in the British world. That discussion, largely the work of Scots
and Dissenters, fit with their general concerns about the likely condition of
Britain's outlying regions in the face of the continuing acquisition of wealth
and power by metropolitan interests. Among the most important contributions to that discussion was the famous population "debate" that took place
between David Hume and Robert Wallace in the Philosophical Society of
Edinburgh during the 1740s. It is likely that Franklin had access to their
debate before Wallace's tract was published in 1753; he became a member of
the Edinburgh society shortly thereafter.[45]

The interest in population growth provincials and Dissenters demonstrated
generally reflected the developing perception that in both population and
trade, provincial growth was outpacing that of England itself. That perception
was part of the inspiration for the new science of political economy, which is

often dated from the 1776 publication of Adam Smith's *Inquiry into the Nature and Causes of the Wealth of Nations*. In fact the *Wealth of Nations* developed out of a larger discussion of the principles of economics that formed an important part of Enlightenment science and of the Scottish Enlightenment in particular. It included contributions not only from academics and philosophers but from a wide variety of merchants and government officials at all levels. In Britain, its most important practitioners were Scots: Adam Smith, David Hume, Sir James Steuart, and a host of lesser figures, all concerned in their works with such basic questions as the effect on provinces and poorer trading partners of their ever-growing commercial relationships with wealthier and more power-ful neighbors, as in the case of provinces within the empire. In that sense, provincial political economy was substantially devoted to assessing the future commercial and political prospects of outlying regions.[46]

Despite the variety of contributions to the provincial discussion of com-merce, several common themes emerged. One was the substantial consensus in favor of the general principles of free trade. Free trade in that context meant something considerably less than the full operation of the free market, or *lais-sez-faire*, a position that even Adam Smith never fully endorsed. Rather, it sig-nified the liberty to buy and sell on the open market free from undue con-straint from entrenched interests. In particular it meant freedom from excessive metropolitan control such as that exerted over the American provinces by the Navigation Acts—unfairly, in the opinion of many—and especially from unfair competition from the chartered metropolitan trading companies, such as the British East India Company, which were linked to the corruptions and luxuries of the court. Free trade, so defined, was not incom-patible with the closing of imperial markets to foreign merchants, which served to maintain guaranteed markets for the raw materials that the colonies produced.[47]

Free trade in that sense was not necessarily deemed inconsistent with a form of structured trading, as long as it was designed to promote general eco-nomic interests and not to restrict unduly the particular commercial opportu-nities of any single part. It was antithetical to much of the British mercantile system, however, which under the Navigation Acts restricted numerous sec-tors of provincial commerce in favor of metropolitan trading interests. Thus Benjamin Franklin came to argue that the key to unifying the empire was to elevate the colonies to positions of equality with the metropolis in all their affairs—politically, through incorporation into an enlarged imperial parlia-ment to which the colonies would send members, and economically, through repeal of all trade regulations that discriminated against the colonies.[48]

Political economists began to portray the flow of commerce itself as a posi-tive good. In purely economic terms, increased trade came to seem the key to the creation of wealth. Such reasoning was part of the logic behind colonial efforts to create land banks, which were controversial in New England and elsewhere during the first half of the eighteenth century. Land banks were intended to use the wealth in land, which provincials possessed in abundance, to back paper money in a traditionally cash-poor economy. The Congregationalist minister John Wise, among the leading supporters of the land bank in Massachusetts, argued that such a bank would lead to a more rapid circulation of money and thus to increased population and development. Opposed to the bank were other merchants and leading citizens who decried its inflationary tendencies and the instability it would promote.[49]

At stake in the matter of land banks was the perennial issue of growth and opportunity versus stability and order. Well-established proponents of order opposed the land bank; provincial men on the make supported it. In that sense, the land bank controversy paralleled divisions in the region over the Regular Singing controversy, the Awakening, and other matters. But whichever side provincials took on the land bank issue, they shared the assumption that the circulation of money through trade would lead to an increase in money. Moreover, for many, the creation of prosperity—whether orderly or rampant—more than the quest for religion and virtue per se, was now the principal standard towards which the society ought to move. Indeed, prosperity would increasingly be portrayed as necessary to religion and virtue.[50]

The development of the science of political economy coincided with a significant shift in the rhetoric of social analysis, one in which morality and the market came to be almost inextricably intertwined. If earlier generations of theologians had commonly cited remarkable providences, or incidents that seemed to suggest the suspension of the common or natural order, as evidence of divine favor or disfavor, by the middle of the eighteenth century conformity to that order was increasingly equated with the providential plan. In that rhetorical shift, the metaphor of the market loomed large: the market, as it was being redefined by political economists, came to represent a grand mechanism for reconciling competing needs and goals in harmony with the natural order. Represented in that fashion, the market served to promote the balance and order so valued by adherents to the moderate Enlightenment; in fact, the market constituted an important tool in promoting harmony, peace, and civility. For similar reasons, prosperity and commercial expansion would come to serve as moral justifications for any social action, in effect demonstrating its conformity to nature and to the divine order.[51]

Such a shift had significant ramifications for the provincial world. If eighteenth-century analysts believed that one of the benefits of liberty was prosperity, so also did the evident prosperity of the provincial world implicitly endorse the nature of provincial society and the conditions of relative political and economic liberty in which it prospered. Thus would William Livingston cite Pennsylvania's prosperity as evidence of the rightness of that colony's policy of toleration and religious pluralism. So also would Benjamin Franklin use the colonies' growth and wealth as a confirmation of the virtues of a social order based on frugality and industry.[52]

In the provincial setting in particular, provincials came to assert, liberty, although far from universal, could expand beyond the privileged few to take in the bulk of a white settler population committed to the goal of economic development. Provincial liberty was the source of prosperity, of freedom of enquiry, of Enlightenment, and even of a pure form of religiosity. Thus in the provinces in particular, liberty, piety, prosperity, and Enlightenment all seemed to be strongly interconnected.

Liberty, Legislature, and Locality: The Rise of the Assembly

If provincial Americans almost uniformly praised the system of liberty in which they lived, few of them participated in that system at the imperial level. Most colonial business was transacted at court through hired colonial agents residing in the metropolis. For the overwhelming majority of even the voting population of the American colonies, politics was experienced no higher than at the provincial level.[53]

As late as the 1680s, the status of provincial politics, and even of the provincial governments, had been very much in doubt. In creating the Dominion of New England out of the northern colonies, the Stuart governments had revoked the original charters of several of those provinces; had the Glorious Revolution not intervened, they might have suppressed the rest. In the matter of their royal charters, few doubted that what the king gave, the king could also take away.

As late as the 1680s, colonials as subjects could be certain of few rights. In Massachusetts, those who protested the loss of the charter and resisted the newly organized Dominion of New England were told by one judge that they were mistaken is assuming that English liberties followed them "to the ends of the Earth." In fact, they had "no more Privileges left" than that they were not "bought and sold for slaves."[54] Colonials on the whole were likely to disagree. Already in 1687, the Congregational minister John Wise persuaded his town to insist on "their liberty as freeborne English subjects of his majesty" in opposing the arbitrary claims of the Dominion.[55]

If the Glorious Revolution stood for anything in the colonies, it was the right of Americans to be treated as something other than pure dependents, or provincial slaves. Liberty, property, and Protestantism were to be as secure in the colonies as elsewhere in the empire. But to say that they had rights was not the same as establishing precisely what those rights were or how far they extended. When, after that revolution, Increase Mather had sought a reissue of the Massachusetts charter, the king had demurred and granted instead a new, modified charter for the colony. Henceforth, Massachusetts was dependent on a royal governor. Equally important, the charter itself retained the status of a royal gift.

Over the next 60 years, charters gradually became much more secure. In part such security was simply the result of the passage of time; tradition and the constant exercise of authority were matters that held considerable weight in British constitutional theory.[56] In part it was an unanticipated consequence of changes in British politics after the Glorious Revolution: the augmented authority of Parliament and the lessening of the royal prerogative diminished the king's ability to alter the terms of charters at will.

Those same 60 years saw the various colonies adopt more uniform structures of government. Nearly all of the colonies moved toward a tripartite form that included a royal governor appointed by the Crown, a council working with the governor, and an elected lower house of assembly. Moreover, those elected assemblies almost everywhere dramatically increased their powers and posed a real challenge to the authority of often equally assertive royal governors, a phenomenon referred to as the "rise of the assemblies."[57]

The rise was more a matter of circumstance and practice than of positive law. It resulted in part from structural weaknesses in the office of the royal governors, who held positions that were, in theory, analogous to that of the king in British politics but without any of the mystique, and many of the actual powers, of that figure. Royal governors were hardly revered figures; even the most popular and powerful were commoners and career officials who received none of the respect or adulation accorded the monarch. Many were far from popular in any event.[58]

Royal governors also did not possess many of the powers of patronage and appointment that the king was able to use to influence legislators. Moreover, they lacked permanence and could be removed by the king at will, which often made their positions precarious. Those who bowed to the will of the assembly risked the monarch's displeasure, and even those who scrupulously followed royal policy rarely achieved job security in the process. Governors who alienated their assemblies by firm adherence to royal instruction often found themselves sacrificed by court officials seeking to mollify discontented colonials.[59]

However much provincials celebrated monarchy, they were far less complacent about the positions of the king's representatives in the colonies. Those officials lacked either a permanent interest in or a connection with the societies they administered. Most seemed to be there for their own benefit rather than for that of their societies; as one pamphleteer wrote, "[T]he chief End of many Governours coming to the Plantations" was "to get Estates for themselves."[60] They were therefore perfect subjects for the watchfulness of virtuous provincials.

The assemblies also rose in power because they were adaptable to the colonies' varying circumstances. In Virginia and elsewhere in the plantation south, the assembly was the principal forum for a planter elite serving as spokesmen for their society on the model of the virtuous, civic-minded landowner. In Congregational New England, the General Court represented not plantations but towns, who chose their representatives in town meetings to speak for the local community in the provincial government. In the heterogeneous mid-Atlantic, where the general conduct of politics seemed considerably more factious, the assembly often provided a focus for opposition factions such as that of Morris and Alexander to challenge the administration of Governor Cosby.

Although British political theory characterized the legislatures as the democratic branch of government, the rise of the assembly was not necessarily democratic in its implications. Because that body asserted its position as spokesmen for the colony against possible assaults from imperial officials, assemblymen often emphasized harmony and unity over contention. The result was often unchallenged elite control. Certainly those Virginia gentlemen who represented their colony so eloquently in the House of Burgesses were anything but spokesmen for the common person; on the contrary, virtually all belonged to a unified and interlocking group of families that comprised the colonial elite. Elsewhere, the assemblies were dominated by competing elite factions throughout the provincial period.[61]

Nor did the rise of the assembly signify a growing antipathy to monarchy. Provincials distrusted imperial officials far more than they did the kings who appointed them. Indeed, the attack on such officials was part of the ritual by which provincial citizens celebrated monarchy; it fit very neatly the fiction that although the king could do no wrong, his advisers and appointees could and did. Provincials implicitly contrasted patriotic and benevolent kings with the corrupt and profit-seeking men who served them.[62]

The rise of the assembly better reflected a stage in the phenomenon that the historian Edmund Morgan has called the "invention of the people," or, more specifically, the idea of the sovereignty of the people. Morgan contends that the idea of popular sovereignty came not from the people but from their leaders, who developed the concept of popular rule in order to exercise it themselves as representatives. Provincial leaders also promoted the authority of the lower or democratic houses of the legislature in order to assert their authority over provincial affairs against the interference of imperial officials, so that the rise of the assembly was synonymous with the consolidation of authority by a provincial elite.[63]

Thus the concept underlying the rise of the assemblies was never truly democratic. Even the most powerful assemblies constituted only one branch in a mixed political system. Within any mixed system, it is the officers of government, rather than the people they represent, who govern. In that sense, eighteenth-century ideas were not so far removed from those of the seventeenth-century Massachusetts minister John Cotton, who had asked the then-rhetorical question, "if the people be governors," then "who shall be governed?"[64]

On the surface, the rise of the assembly seemed compatible with the leading principles of British politics. The ascendancy of the lower houses of the colonial governments mirrored the rise of Parliament, and both apparently reflected the triumph of popular rule following the Glorious Revolution. But the analogy was again more a matter of practice than of law; it was never clear how secure the assemblies' authority was. Moreover, their rise created something of a paradox in the British system, since the charters from which their statutory authority derived had been granted not by Parliament but by the Crown. In that sense, the rise of the assemblies and of the royally chartered governments they represented and the ascendancy of Parliament were implicitly opposed. Of course, hardly anyone noticed the discrepancy before mid-century, and British policy during that period has been characterized by the term "salutary neglect." After 1760, however, the contest between Parliament and the assemblies would be a major factor in bringing on the Revolution.

By the middle years of the eighteenth century, two views of the colonial governments emerged in the British world. From the British point of view, the colonial governments represented local and inferior political units fully subordinate to a British Parliament under a British constitution that represented the source of British liberties everywhere. Yet exactly what the British constitution said about the colonial governments was less clear. Jack P. Greene has recently pointed out that tradition was at least as important as statutory law in that constitution, and for many years the colonial governments did not really behave as inferior units at all. Rather, the assemblies and the charters were the principal bastions of colonial liberty, which was experienced as something very much like home rule for the provinces. In that sense, political liberty to American provincials implied the general system of British liberties restricted by only a minimal exertion of metropolitan power.[65]

By that time, the power of the assemblies in fact, if not in theory, was almost universally acknowledged. Not everyone considered such power to be a good thing. Many royal governors and other imperial officers complained repeatedly about the assemblies' excessive powers, which seemed to them a direct violation of the principle of balance that comprised "the strength and beauty of the British Constitution," in the words of South Carolina's James Glen. Instead, "all the Weights that should trim and poise it [were] by different Laws thrown into the Scale of the People." The people hurt themselves by weakening the power of the Crown, in Glen's view, as "every deviation from the Constitution" represented a threat to stability, order, and virtue.[66]

Provincial Imperialists

Glen and a few of his fellow governors were one group that did challenge the growing initiatives of the assemblies, assisted by other imperial officials who found their administrative tasks in the colonies difficult to accomplish in the face of resistance from intractable lower houses. During the middle third of the eighteenth century, those officials began to send a steady stream of letters to

London complaining of the virtual independence of the assemblies and seeking redress from Britain. After 1748, when the Earl of Halifax became president of the Board of Trade, those complaints began to produce an extensive rethinking of the relationship between the provinces and the empire, reflected especially in the many and varied plans for restructuring the method of governing the colonies that were submitted to the board at about that time.[67]

It is tempting to think of all of those governors and other imperial officials simply as outsiders, representing a foreign interest in America, which was how the colonial assemblies often portrayed them. Such a portrayal is a bit misleading. A number of those most active in colonial affairs had long-term relationships with the colonies and lived in one or several of them for many years. James Abercromby, for instance, one of those most active in the movement to restructure the imperial relationship, resided in South Carolina from 1731 to 1744 and served for many years thereafter as colonial agent in London for North Carolina and Virginia. Although he was not born in the colonies, it would be inaccurate to portray him as simply an outsider. Other leading officials involved in the effort to restructure that relationship, such as New York's Archibald Kennedy, were permanent residents of America.

Many of those men had provincial origins themselves. Several of the most prominent governors who led the call for curbing the power of the assemblies were Scots, including James Glen of South Carolina and Robert Dinwiddie of Virginia. Others, such as Arthur Dobbs of North Carolina and Henry Ellis of Georgia, were Ulster men. Other imperial officials in America prominent in that effort included the Scots Henry McCulloh, John Rutherfurd, James Abercromby, Archibald Kennedy, and James Alexander, along with the Ulster native William Knox.

Those men have often been misunderstood. They have been castigated with names such as "Tory-Imperialist"; nearly all have been described as partisans of imperial interests who had no respect for colonial needs.[68] To the extent that they considered colonial government to be out of balance, with excessive and essentially unchecked powers residing in the local assemblies, such views are correct. Yet for many among them, their principal goal was less to extend metropolitan control over provincial affairs than to reconstruct imperial relations in a manner than would solidify imperial ties on the basis of extended commercial ties and mutual advantage. In that sense, their ideas were compatible with decidedly provincial views of the political economy of empire.

The reality of their situations was a good deal more complicated than might be supposed. Those men were well connected with many of the most prominent leaders of colonial society, some of whom would establish reputations as defenders of American liberties, including Benjamin Franklin and William Livingston. The plans they offered reflected their positions as members of provincial elites. As men of the Enlightenment, they shared some basic Enlightenment values, such as harmony and balance, liberty, and the moderating and civilizing influence of commercial ties.[69]

One of the most persistent of those officials was Henry McCulloh, who came to North Carolina in 1741 attached to a fellow Scot and associate, Governor Gabriel Johnstone, and speculated in land at the same time that he participated in politics and revenue collections. Around 1750, McCulloh began to write about imperial affairs. In a series of pamphlets and tracts appearing over the next several years, McCulloh advocated the establishment of a firm alliance with the northern Indians to repel the threat of French invasion and a reconstruction of provincial governments, including restraints on the assemblies, a firmer structure for intercolonial relations, and ominously, a stamp tax to pay the increased costs of administration. Yet McCulloh blamed the inefficiency of colonial government not on provincials but rather on lax and greedy officials, and the union he proposed for the colonies would have created a powerful provincial assembly of a sort that imperial officials in London would later reject. He suggested that any new measures be mild enough that colonials "should not have too great a temptation to resist." Even the stamp tax he proposed was designed to leave provincial matters in provincial hands; McCulloh suggested that revenues be directed into a dedicated fund that would be reserved for the colonies' exclusive use. He would oppose the stamp tax that the British Parliament finally passed in 1765.[70]

Another important figure was James Abercromby, sometime rival of McCulloh's, also a Scotsman and a longtime colonial agent and revenue official for several southern colonies. In 1752, Abercromby drafted a new plan for the regulation of the colonies, entitled "An Examination of the Acts of Parliament Relative to the Trade and the Government of our American Colonies." That proposal placed considerably more blame on the colonists than did McCulloh for the intractability of their governments, and Abercromby rejected most colonial claims to political rights within the empire. Nonetheless, he rejected wholesale changes in the powers colonials exercised, whether they held a right to them or not, unless they were absolutely necessary "to make them a part Depending on the Whole, for the good of the whole." He argued instead for aligning imperial relations with the growing "wealth and strength" of the colonies, a phrase he used three times.[71]

In the year 1754, amid threats of a new war with France originating from border conflicts along the western frontiers of British America, a congress of delegates, which included some of the most prominent leaders in the British colonies, met at Albany for the purpose of securing the Iroquois alliance and coordinating their defensive efforts. Together, the men sketched a plan for political union based upon a model suggested by Benjamin Franklin for aiding in their administration, diplomacy, and defense.

Such prominent provincial leaders as Benjamin Franklin, Archibald Kennedy, and James Alexander actively promoted the plan, but it stood little chance. It was ignored by Parliament, which was wary of vesting any new powers in what would be a purely provincial body. The plan proved equally unpopular in the colonial legislatures, where the new framework appeared a threat to the continuing autonomy of their provincial governments.[72] Franklin later contended that the plan had represented the best chance at establishing a permanent framework for colonial participation in the empire, but it was not to be. Its existence suggested considerable common ground among the most cosmopolitan of provincial and imperial elites. For those groups, liberty in the empire signified something like the opportunity for provincial citizens to prosper in a firm but balanced imperial union.

To a considerable degree, both the officials' call for imperial integration and the colonial resistance their plans engendered were traceable to a growing sense of provincial competence and confidence. That growth, which was as obvious to imperial officials as it was to colonials, led to fears that the colonies were on a road to breaking away from Britain; that was in part the implication of James Abercromby's repeated remarks on the colonies' growing "wealth and strength." Such suspicion also accounted for the tone of alarm that characterized the reports of such officials as James Glen that colonial legislatures were exercising virtual independence. The irony is that it was almost always British officials who envisioned the colonies breaking away; provincials uniformly discounted such predictions.[73]

Provincial Americans were no less aware of the developments on which such predictions were based. By mid-century, few Americans doubted that the colonial population and its trade were likely to grow faster than Britain's. Similarly, few doubted the reason: it was attributed to the relatively unconstrained colonial economy and to the air of liberty one found there, which impelled eager emigrants to seek out homes there. As New York's Archibald Kennedy observed, "liberty and encouragement" were the cornerstones of colonial prosperity.[74]

Two different visions of provincial liberty thus underlay those provincial reactions to the Albany Plan. Those who supported it shared a basic Enlightened vision of ordered liberty, of liberty guaranteed by harmony and moderation, by balanced government, and by the civilizing influences of expanded commercial ties. Its opponents evidenced a different vision of liberty, one rooted in local autonomy, with local leadership as the principal bulwark against grasping power and the potential for distant tyranny. Both versions were amply represented in provincial culture. Both were substantially rooted in provincial claims to the rights of citizenship and to the pursuit of provincial interests with the same legitimacy as those promoted from the metropolis.

A third set of ideas about liberty was also beginning to emerge in the provincial world in the eighteenth century, one that was increasingly populist in tone and might be called, for lack of a better term, a democratic form of liberty. That variety found few adherents among the provincial elite. Instead, its principal proponents were found among a diverse group that included some small farmers in the western sections of several colonies who resented eastern leadership, as in the case of the "Regulator" movements against the eastern monopolization of political power that appeared in the Carolinas; radical evangelicals who moved beyond the New Side wing of the established churches into Separate, Baptist, and other dissenting communions while attacking the claims to knowledge and authority of the settled clergy; urban tradesmen who viewed the claims of the right to leadership maintained by their social betters as nothing more than self-interest; and the merchant seamen of the leading port towns. It was evident, in varying measures, in the antiauthoritarian sentiment that was emerging in some—though not all—areas of the culture of the backcountry. Those varied groups shared no clear set of beliefs but some common sentiments. Those sentiments were diversely expressed, but in their different ways, each of those groups came to believe that the way to protect their liberties was to remove them from the hands of traditional leadership into more common hands. They shared with their fellow provincials the insistence on the principle of equity in political arrangements and—for some—a belief in locality as the remedy for oppression.[75]

Sentiments of that sort found their most overt political expression in the artisanal communities in the cities of New York, Philadelphia, and Boston and often resembled the emerging republican ideas that appeared among the tradesmen of such British cities as London and Glasgow. As was the case with radical religious ideas, they were somewhat less visible in the more restricted urban sector of provincial America than in its larger British equivalent. Moreover, many of the recorded expressions we have of antielite sentiment emanated from other elites, such as the populist appeals of David Lloyd and William Keith in Pennsylvania; Lloyd, in fact, was attacked by James Logan for his constant raising of the "rattle of rights and privileges" against the proprietary. But in seeking to undermine their opponents' power, those men appealed to artisans and other common sorts in a language of equality; William Keith's "Leather-Apron" club was one such example. The goal of those men was invariably not to unleash the populace but to use popular support to bolster their own power. Yet popular participation, once started, sometimes developed its own momentum.[76]

So it was with the political movement started by the religious awakening. Despite their occasional antiestablishment rhetoric, most evangelical leaders were not especially concerned with changing the political order; their concerns were religious, not political. Yet the separate churches and institutions that resulted, and the principles of equality and fellowship they embodied, helped spur political opposition as well. There was a clear connection, for example, between New Light radicalism and political opposition in frontier Connecticut and between the passionate call to action that appeared in the oratory of Patrick Henry and the evangelical preaching that emerged in the western Virginia counties in which he was raised. Nor is it simply coincidence that a politician such as Herman Husband, who appeared in such varied political agitations as the Carolina Regulation and later Pennsylvania's Whiskey Rebellion was raised in the culture of the Awakening in its most radical forms.[77]

In 1765, in response to the passage of the Stamp Act, those several varieties of liberty substantially came together in opposition to a tax that threatened the authority of the provincial legislatures, the principle of equity in the empire, and the local autonomy of rural farming communities. Even such imperial spokesmen as Henry McCulloh and Thomas Hutchinson expressed reservations about the act. Eventually provincials holding those differing positions divided over the relationship of empire and liberty. Whereas defenders of provincial authority generally supported American independence, those who took an imperial perspective ended up on both sides of the issue, often after considerable personal conflict. In the aftermath of the Revolution, Americans would divide yet again when confronted with the need to develop a workable central authority under a new and stronger constitution.[78]

seven

Epilogue: Provincial Americans

In 1759 and 1760, an English visitor named Andrew Burnaby, a minister of the Anglican Church, embarked on a tour of the "middle settlements" of North America. When he published his reflections on that tour more than a decade later, Burnaby recalled his surprise at everywhere encountering the idea that "empire is travelling westward," an idea that seemed to him as "strange as it is visionary." In America, he continued, "everyone is looking forward with eager and impatient expectation to that destined moment, when America is to give law to the rest of the world."[1]

Burnaby was not alone in his observations. Within the decade, even before Burnaby's recollections appeared in print, Hugh Simm, a young Scotsman from the town of Paisley, traveled to New Jersey in the company of his minister, John Witherspoon, who had just been appointed president of the college at Princeton. In a letter home to his brother, Simm also remarked that he was startled to hear that "the increasing power of America and her future empire" were "common subjects of conversation."[2] Over the next several years there would be numerous similar observations on both sides of the Atlantic.

In some respects, those predictions of a future American empire, with their seeming anticipation of American independence, seem far removed from Samuel Davies's celebration of British liberty following the death of George II in 1760, with which we began the story. In fact, it is only the subsequent separation of the American colonies from Britain in 1776 that make the two appear so different. Davies's contemplation of liberty in Britain was also a rumination on its effects on American society. In 1760 those effects, and the prospects for British America, seemed almost unlimited.

The origins of such predictions were varied. In part they derived from a provincial economy emphasizing the inevitability of economic growth under

176

conditions of provincial liberty. In part they can be traced to the Puritan idea of a providential mission to create an American "city upon a hill" for others to emulate, an image that would continue to reverberate throughout American history.[3] Those were not the only sources, however; the vision of liberty and the temporal power and prosperity that Davies and his contemporaries projected for America seem far removed from stringent Puritan conceptions of Godliness and orthodoxy. Nor were many who expressed such ideas, such as Samuel Davies himself or the mid-Atlantic populations that Burnaby and Simm encountered, raised in specifically New English rather than broader Reformed Protestant traditions. Indeed, in the years before American independence, most anticipations of an independent America came from British observers or from Americans born and raised in Britain. Provincial Americans, wanting to assure the mother country of their loyalty, took considerable pains to contradict them.[4]

Perhaps the most direct source of the vision of American empire that many were articulating was George Berkeley's famous poem "On the Prospect of Planting Arts and Learning in America," first published in 1752, which evoked what would become the very popular image of a westward course of empire. Berkeley, a bishop in the Irish Episcopal Church, was an important figure in British and American culture whose philosophical ideas about epistemology and moral philosophy influenced not only Americans but some of the most prominent Scots philosophers of the age, and many others. He wrote the poem while residing in Newport, Rhode Island, during the late 1720s and early 1730s, where he was attempting to plan an American college.

The often-cited poem reflects Berkeley's educational mission. In it, he predicted the appearance in the New World of "another golden Age, the Rise of Empire and of Arts." He finished with the following lines, repeated countless times after their initial appearance:

> Not such as *Europe* breeds in her decay;
>   Such as she bred when fresh and young,
> When heav'nly Flame did animate her Clay,
>   By future Poets shall be sung.
>
> Westward the Course of Empire takes its Way;
>   The four first Acts already past,
> A fifth shall close the Drama with the Day;
>   Time's noblest Offspring is the last.[5]

Berkeley's description of a westward course of empire helped provincial Americans articulate a vision of the western hemisphere not merely as a cultural backwater but as the future home of civilization. His words were echoed often; Benjamin Franklin, for instance, would write to a friend in Britain describing how "the Arts delight to travel Westward."[6]

After mid-century, predictions of a future American empire were picked up especially by Scottish writers, who had long attended to the ramifications of demographic and commercial growth and to the place of the peripheries within an expanding empire. To Scots, who had given up their distinct nationality in 1707, the image of an ascendant provincial America countering the previously unchallenged authority of the metropolis had a distinct appeal. Scots adopted with enthusiasm the prediction of a continual growth in provincial population and trade. To Berkeley's notion that America would be the future seat of arts and empire, Scottish writers added a twist: that America in the future would become not simply the seat of an empire but of the British empire and the British capital. Such predictions reflected the growing involvement of Scots with American culture and were soon employed to promote Scottish emigration as well as investment across the ocean.[7]

Perhaps the most famous Scottish pronouncement of a future American empire, although by no means the only one, was Adam Smith's solution to the imperial crisis of 1776, which he incorporated in his *Wealth of Nations*. Smith's plan was to grant the Americans representation in Parliament, with the understanding that as the trade and population of those provinces surpassed those of Britain, as they were sure to do, then not only political power, but even the capital itself, should move across the water to America.[8] The fact that the popular image of American empire could be accepted by so cautious a philosopher as Smith in an analytical work on political economy suggests just how pervasive the idea had become.

There are several points worth noticing about Smith's plan for the empire. The first is that Smith's solution treated the American colonies as a unit and assumed a common future. That hardly seems remarkable from the vantage point of the twentieth century, but it does suggest something of the distance that separated the developed provinces of the 1760s and 1770s from the remote and isolated colonies of a century before.

A second point about Smith's treatment of American affairs was that he considered the colonies to be not simply peripheral but integral to Britain itself. The measure of that importance for Smith, as for others in the eighteenth-century world, was commerce. To those writers, and to the popular audiences influenced by them, commerce served not only economic but integrating functions, uniting communities and establishing relationships across oceans and territorial boundaries. Increased American participation in the transatlantic world of commerce during the eighteenth century, like the growth of the press, was an important factor in encouraging Americans to imagine themselves as part of a transatlantic commercial community.[9]

A third point suggested by Smith's discussion of the imperial crisis is the extent to which he, like other observers, had come to view the rapid growth and development of America as the product of natural processes rather than providential intervention; the *Wealth of Nations* was part of a larger Enlightenment project to create a "science of man." To be sure, Providence still loomed large in many such works. To many interpreters, and possibly even to Smith, the harmonious functioning of the world of trade required providential oversight, and the principles of human nature that made it all work were those implanted by God in humankind. Yet even for the most devout observers, that represented a significantly different view of social development than was common a century earlier. However much God might supervise human affairs, nearly everyone now agreed that divine contravention of the laws of nature was not the rule but the exception.

One of the results of that way of thinking was that the particular characteristics of provincial society that emerged during the course of the eighteenth century came to seem to be the product not so much of a specific and very special set of historical circumstances surrounding the development of the American colonies, but of the natural course of things—like the sun crossing from east to west, in Berkeley's view. They were the product of demographic factors of the sort that Benjamin Franklin had outlined in his "Observations Concerning the Increase of Mankind." They resulted from natural economic forces. They were in accord with the general providential design. They could be predicted by the developing science of liberty. Indeed, the attributes of American society came to seem to be those to which any society would aspire under the "natural" condition of human liberty. Social patterns on the periphery, which previously had seemed to resemble a rude and backwards past from which European societies had only recently emerged, now came to seem humanity's inevitable future. Such ideas were reinforced by a tremendous surge in provincial self-confidence that developed after the Seven Years War and the Treaty of Paris of 1763, which ceded New France to Britain, opened vast new territories to further westward settlement, and promised to pacify the frontiers.

One apparently "natural" characteristic of provincial society was the seeming ubiquity of middling or tradesmen's values, those of mobility and opportunity, of industry and independence and frugality. Those were the values of *Poor Richard's Almanacks* and were later woven into Benjamin Franklin's *Autobiography*. For much of his life, as we have seen, Franklin himself had assumed a more genteel persona in his public life than that of Poor Richard the almanac-maker. So, also, had such writers as William Byrd and the authors of William Smith's *American Magazine*. But it was the Franklin of the *Autobiography* who would come to typify the American character, as the exemplar of what colonial citizens could achieve by working diligently to make their fortunes in the open environs of provincial society.

An even more striking development was the emergence of a new identification of just who Americans were. A century before there had been little difficulty in identifying the native inhabitants as Americans in lands that they occupied jointly with peoples called "English," or "New English" or "French" or "Dutch" or "Spanish." Thus had Mary Rowlandson, for example, referred to the "English" army of New England, then in pursuit of her Indian captors. In 1705, Robert Beverley had claimed the identity of an American writer by

referring to himself as an Indian.[10] The development of provincial identity
would leave provincial settlers firmly ensconced as the Americans.

A vivid illustration of that process was offered by the French-born author
and settler, J. Hector St. John de Crèvecoeur, in his famous *Letters from an
American Farmer,* in an essay entitled "What is an American?" To Crèvecoeur's
farmer, the answer seemed clear and unequivocal: the American was "either
an European, or the descendant of an European," all melted together into a
newly-developed race. Indians had virtually vanished from the conception:
Americans derived from "all nations," and Crèvecoeur listed them: "English,
Scotch, Irish, French, Dutch, Germans, and Swedes."[11]

The development of such a conception of Americans was gradual. As late
as the middle of the eighteenth century, Benjamin Franklin still worried about
the prospect of English-speaking colonists being overrun by the ever-increas-
ing migration of German speakers attached to a wholly different set of cultural traditions. Crèvecoeur resolved the problem with a pluralism that incorporated the whole of the settler population and was justified by the evident
prosperity of provincial society. To the American Farmer, it mattered not how
one worshipped, or even how one believed, so long as one was industrious and
productive. In so defining the American, of course, he omitted from his conception the original inhabitants of the land, along with any others not
involved in the settlement effort.[12]

The identities of the bulk of the settler population were British and provincial before they were exclusively American. Provincial conditions provided
Americans with the opportunity to prosper within an expanding empire of
liberty and trade, even as they were permitted to worship as they pleased.
Freedom from the domination of metropolitan interests provided provincials
with the political and moral authority to claim the rights and privileges of
imperial citizens and to view themselves as full-fledged contributors to the
security and prosperity of the empire. By 1760, with the end of the Seven
Years War, provincials were highly optimistic about the future of the
provinces within the empire.

Imperial policy after 1763, and especially the passage of the Stamp Act,
posed a considerable challenge to provincial concerns. The prospect of further
taxation and regulation threatened the prosperity that provincial conditions
allowed. That those taxes were to be imposed without American consent
threatened provincial autonomy and freedom from arbitrary control, while
denying provincials the rights and privileges of equal citizens. The assertion of
Parliamentary sovereignty and the limitation upon the responsibilities of the
colonial assemblies ran counter to American assumptions of provincial competence and challenged their self-image as full contributors to British security
and prosperity. Yet even after Americans were driven to revolt, they would
long continue to confront the problem of establishing a balance between the
benefits of an extended national territory and the privileges of assertive provincial communities.[13]

Chronology

1714   Succession of Protestant Hanoverians to British throne

1718   Publication of *Weekly Jamaican Courant*

1719   Publication of *Boston Gazette; American Weekly Mercury*

1720   Publication of *Cato's Letters*

1721   Publication of *New-England Courant*

1727   Publication of Cadwallader Colden's *History of the Five Indian Nations Depending on the Province of New-York;* New England earthquake

1731   Founding of the Library Company of Philadelphia

1732   Founding of Georgia

1733   First publication of *Poor Richard's Almanack*

1734   Beginning of Connecticut Valley Revival

1735   Trial of John Peter Zenger; establishment of the Log College

1739   George Whitefield begins his first American tour; Stono Rebellion in South Carolina

1740   Gilbert Tennent preaches on "The Danger of an Unconverted Ministry"

1742   Condemnation of James Davenport; first American publication of a novel, *Pamela*

1743   Founding of American Philosophical Society

1745   Last Jacobite rebellion led by Charles Edward Stuart; colonial army captures Louisbourg fortress

1746   Charter for the College of New Jersey

1747   Publication of William Douglass's *Summary, Historical and Political*

1749   Constitutions of the Public Academy in the City of Philadelphia

1751   Benjamin Franklin's "Observations Concerning the Increase of Mankind"

1754   Charter for the College of New York; Albany Plan of Union

1755   Earthquakes in New England and Lisbon; charter for the College of Philadelphia

1756   Beginning of Seven Years War with France; founding of the College of Rhode Island

1757   Publication of William Smith's *American Magazine*

1758   Reunion of the Presbyterian Church

1759   Publication of Adam Smith's *Theory of Moral Sentiments*

1760   Death of George II

Notes and References

Introduction

1. Samuel Davies, *A Sermon Delivered at Nassau-hall, January 14, 1761: On the death of His Late Majesty King George II* (New York, 1761).

2. Richard L. Bushman, *King and People in Provincial Massachusetts* (Chapel Hill: University of North Carolina Press, 1985), 17–23.

3. On the "Anglicization" of early America, see John M. Murrin, "The Legal Transformation: The Bench and Bar of Eighteenth-Century Massachusetts," in *Colonial America: Essays in Politics and Social Development*, ed. Stanley N. Katz (Boston: Little, Brown, 1971), 415–49, and "Anglicizing an American Colony: The Transformation of Provincial Massachusetts" (Ph.D. diss., Yale, 1966).

4. Perry Miller, *The New England Mind: From Colony to Province* (Cambridge, Mass.: Harvard University Press, 1953); David D. Hall, in "On Common Ground: The Coherence of American Puritan Studies," *William and Mary Quarterly* (hereafter, *WMQ*), 3d ser., 44 (1987): 193–229, discusses some of the directions Puritan studies have taken since Miller's day.

5. See, for example, David D. Hall, *Worlds of Wonder, Days of Judgment: Popular Religious Belief in Early New England* (Cambridge, Mass.: Harvard University Press, 1990), esp. chap. 1; Harry S. Stout, "Religion, Communications, and the Ideological Origins of the American Revolution," *WMQ*, 3d ser., 34 (1977): 519–41; and Richard D. Brown, *Knowledge Is Power: The Diffusion of Information in Early America* (New York: Oxford University Press, 1989).

6. See especially Margaret C. Jacob, *The Newtonians and the English Revolution, 1689–1720* (Ithaca, N.Y.: Cornell University Press, 1976), for the complicated story of the dissemination of that view.

7. The standard, though now dated, treatment of the American Enlightenment is Henry May, *The Enlightenment in America* (New York: Oxford University Press, 1976).

8. On the development of British identity, see Linda Colley, *Britons: The Forging of a Nation, 1707–1837* (New Haven: Yale University Press, 1992).

9. Davies, *Sermon Delivered at Nassau-hall*, 41.

Chapter One

1. (Cambridge, Mass.: Samuel Green, 1682). There are many modern editions of the narrative.

2. Cited in Ian K. Steele, *The English Atlantic, 1675–1740* (New York: Oxford University Press, 1986), 50. On the rude state of the Chesapeake, see especially Gloria L. Main, *Tobacco Colony: Life in Early Maryland, 1650–1720* (Princeton, N.J.: Princeton University Press, 1982), and James P. Horn, *Adapting to a New World: English Society in the Seventeenth-Century Chesapeake* (Chapel Hill: University of North Carolina Press, 1994).

3. Richard White, *The Middle Ground: Indians, Empires, and Republics in the Great Lakes Region, 1650–1815* (New York: Cambridge University Press, 1991).

4. Nicholas Canny, "English Migration into and across the Atlantic During the Seventeenth and Eighteenth Centuries," in *Europeans on the Move: Studies on European Migration, 1500–1800* (Oxford, England: Oxford University Press, 1994), 39–75; Richard S. Dunn, *Sugar and Slaves: The Rise of the Planter Class in the English West Indies, 1624–1713* (Chapel Hill: University of North Carolina Press, 1972); Peter Wood, *Black Majority: Negroes in Colonial South Carolina from 1670 through the Stono Rebellion* (Chapel Hill: University of North Carolina Press, 1974).

5. Edmund S. Morgan, *Visible Saints: The History of a Puritan Idea* (New York: New York University Press, 1963).

6. Harry Stout, *The New England Soul: Preaching and Religious Culture in Colonial New England* (New York: Oxford University Press, 1986); see also Theodore Dwight Bozeman, *To Live Ancient Lives: The Primitivist Dimension in Puritanism* (Chapel Hill: University of North Carolina Press, 1988).

7. Philip F. Gura, *A Glimpse of Sion's Glory: Puritan Radicalism in New England, 1620–1660* (Middletown, Conn.: Wesleyan University Press, 1984).

8. *The Wonder-Working Providence of Sions Saviour in New-England. By Captain Edward Johnson of Woburn, Massachusetts* (London, 1654).

9. Cotton Mather, *Magnalia Christi Americana, or, The Ecclesiastical History of New-England, from the First Planting in the year 1620 until the Year of our Lord, 1698* (London, 1702).

10. Perry Miller, *The New England Mind: The Seventeenth Century* (New York: Macmillan, 1939); Sacvan Bercovitch, *The American Jeremiad* (Madison: University of Wisconsin Press, 1978).

11. David D. Hall, *Worlds of Wonder, Days of Judgment: Popular Religious Belief in Early New England* (New York: Knopf, 1989).

12. Eric Maloney, "The Greater Migration: Puritans in Colonial Maryland" (Ph.D. diss., State University of New York at Stony Brook, 1996).

13. E. Brooks Holifield, *The Era of Persuasion: American Thought and Culture, 1521–1680* (Boston: Twayne, 1989), chap. 3.

14. Robert Beverley, *The History and Present State of Virginia*, ed. Louis B. Wright (1705; reprint, Chapel Hill: University of North Carolina Press, 1947).

15. *The Prose Works of William Byrd of Westover: Narratives of a Colonial Virginian*, ed. Louis B. Wright (Cambridge, Mass.: Harvard University Press, 1966).

16. Cotton Mather, *The Christian Philosopher: A Collection of the Best Discoveries in Nature, with Religious Improvements* (London, 1721).

17. The great classical work on the subject is Norbert Elias, *The Civilizing Process*, 3 vols. (1934; reprint, New York: Urizen Books, 1978).

18. White, *Middle Ground;* Francis Jennings, *The Ambiguous Iroquois Empire: The Covenant Chain Confederation of Indian Tribes with English Colonies from Its Beginnings to the Lancaster Treaty of 1744* (New York: Norton, 1983).

19. James Axtell, "The White Indians of Colonial America," *WMQ,* 3d ser., 32 (1975): 55–88.

20. On the emerging slave population, see especially Philip D. Morgan, "British Encounters with Africans and African-Americans, circa 1600–1780," in *Strangers within the Realm: Cultural Margins of the First British Empire,* ed. Bernard Bailyn and Philip D. Morgan (Chapel Hill: University of North Carolina Press, 1991), 157–219.

21. Bernard Bailyn, "Politics and Social Structure in Virginia," in *Seventeenth-Century America: Essays in Colonial History,* ed. James Morton Smith (Chapel Hill: University of North Carolina Press, 1950).

22. Barry Levy, *Quakers and the American Family: British Settlement in the Delaware Valley* (New York: Oxford University Press, 1988).

23. Frederick B. Tolles, *Quakers and the Atlantic Culture* (New York: Macmillan, 1960).

24. J. William Frost, *A Perfect Freedom: Religious Liberty in Pennsylvania* (Cambridge, Mass.: Harvard University Press, 1990).

25. Alan Tully, *Forming American Politics: Ideals, Interests, and Institutions in Colonial New York and Pennsylvania* (Baltimore: Johns Hopkins University Press, 1994), 16–27.

26. *A Narrative of a New And Unusual American Imprisonment of Two Presbyterian Ministers: and Prosecution of Mr. Francis Makemie One of them, for Preaching one Sermon at the City of New-York* (n.p., 1707), in *The Life and Writings of Francis Makemie,* ed. Boyd S. Schlenther (Philadelphia: Presbyterian Historical Society, 1971), 193–244.

27. Quoted in Schlenther, ed., *The Life and Writings of Francis Makemie,* 25.

28. See Ned C. Landsman, "The Provinces and the Empire: Scotland, the American Colonies, and the Development of Provincial Identity," in *An Imperial State at War: Britain from 1689 to 1815,* ed. Lawrence Stone (New York: Routledge, 1994), 258–87, for connections in all of these areas.

29. Mary Lou Lustig, *Robert Hunter, 1666–1734* (Syracuse, N.Y.: Syracuse University Press, 1983).

30. There is no adequate study of those doctors, but see especially C. Helen Brock, "Scotland and American Medicine," in William R. Brock and C. Helen Brock, *Scotus Americanus: A Survey of the Sources for Links between Scotland and America in the Eighteenth Century* (Edinburgh: Edinburgh University Press, 1982), 114–26, and Raymond Phineas Stearns, *Science in the British Colonies of North America* (Urbana: University of Illinois Press, 1970).

31. On the influx of newcomers to the region, see Bernard Bailyn, *The New England Merchants in the Seventeenth Century* (Cambridge, Mass.: Harvard University Press, 1955).

32. On the Latitudinarians, see chapter 3.

33. John Corrigan, *The Prism of Piety: The Catholick Congregational Clergy at the Beginning of the Enlightenment* (New York: Oxford University Press, 1991).

34. The basic documents can be found in *Documentary History of Yale University under the Original Charter of the Collegiate School of Connecticut, 1701–1745,* ed. Franklin Bowditch Dexter (New Haven: Yale University Press, 1916).

35. Paul Boyer and Stephen Nissenbaum, *Salem Possessed: The Social Origins of Witchcraft* (Cambridge, Mass.: Harvard University Press, 1974); Carol F. Karlsen, *The*

Devil in the Shape of a Woman: Witchcraft in Colonial New England (New York: Norton, 1987).

36. Ibid.; Christine Leigh Heyrman, "Specters of Subversion, Societies of Friends: Dissent and the Devil in Provincial Essex County, Massachusetts," in *Saints and Revolutionaries: Essays on Early American History,* ed. David D. Hall, John M. Murrin, and Thad W. Tate (New York: Norton, 1984), 38–74.

37. Keith Thomas, *Religion and the Decline of Magic* (New York: Scribner's, 1971); Robert Mandrou, *Magistrats et Sorciers en France au 17e Siècle* (Paris: Seuil, 1968).

38. Quoted in Michael G. Hall, *The Last American Puritan: The Life of Increase Mather, 1639–1723* (Middletown, Conn.: Wesleyan University Press, 1988), 286. On the career of Cotton Mather, see especially Kenneth J. Silverman, *The Life and Times of Cotton Mather* (New York: Harper and Row, 1984).

39. M. Hall, *Last American Puritan,* 167–74; D. Hall, *Worlds of Wonder,* 104–8.

40. Maxine Van De Wetering, "Moralizing in Puritan Natural Science: Mysteriousness in Earthquake Sermons," *Journal of the History of Ideas* 43 (1982): 417–38.

41. Bruce Tucker, "The Reinvention of New England, 1691–1770," *New England Quarterly* 59 (1986): 315–40; T. H. Breen, *The Character of the Good Ruler: A Study of Puritan Political Ideas in New England, 1630–1730* (New Haven: Yale University Press, 1970), 155 ff.

42. *The Secret Diary of William Byrd of Westover, 1709–1712,* ed. Louis B. Wright and Marion Tinling (Richmond, Va.: Dietz Press, 1941), 4, passim.

43. James Blair, *Our Saviour's Sermon on the Mount,* 4 vols., 2d ed. (London: 1740); see also Parke Rouse Jr., *James Blair of Virginia* (Chapel Hill: University of North Carolina Press, 1971). On Whitefield, see chapter 4.

44. "Rev. Thomas Bray: His Life and Selected Works Relating to Maryland," ed. Bernard Steiner, *Maryland Historical Society Publications* 37, n.d.; *Religious Philanthropy and Colonial Slavery: The American Correspondence of the Associates of Dr. Bray, 1717–1777,* ed. John C. Van Horne (Urbana: University of Illinois Press, 1985).

45. " 'Gospel Order Improved': The Keithian Schism and the Exercise of Quaker Ministerial Authority in Pennsylvania," *WMQ,* 3d ser., 31 (1974): 431–52; Levy, *Quakers and the American Family,* 157–72.

46. Garry Wills, *Inventing America: Jefferson's Declaration of Independence* (Garden City, N.Y.: Doubleday, 1978); Provost R. Foskett, "Some Scottish Episcopalians in the North American Colonies, 1675–1750," *Records of the Scottish Church History Society* 14 (1963): 135–50.

Chapter Two

1. A useful discussion is Richard D. Brown, *Knowledge Is Power: The Diffusion of Information in Early America* (New York: Oxford University Press, 1989).

2. Ian Steele, *The English Atlantic, 1675–1740: An Exploration of Communications and Community* (New York: Oxford University Press, 1986), chap. 8.

3. *American Bibliography,* comp. Charles Evans, 12 vols. (1903–1904; reprint, New York: Peter Smith, 1941–1942), vols. 1–2. A more up to date listing of American and British publications can be obtained on-line in the "Eighteenth-Century Short Title Catalogue."

4. "A Catalogue of the Books in the Library at Westover Belonging to William Byrd, Esqr.," in *The Writings of William Byrd of Westover in Virginia Esqr.,* ed. John Spencer Bassett (1901; reprint, New York: Burt Franklin, 1970), 413–43.

5. Norman S. Fiering, "The Transatlantic Republic of Letters: A Note on the Circulation of Learned Periodicals to Early Eighteenth-Century America," *WMQ*, 3d ser., 33 (1976): 642–60. The full title of the journal was *The Present State of the Republick of Letters*.

6. Jurgen Habermas, *The Structural Transformation of the Public Sphere* (Cambridge, Mass.: MIT Press, 1989).

7. Michael Warner, *Letters of the Republic: Publication and the Public Sphere in Eighteenth-Century America* (Cambridge, Mass.: Harvard University Press, 1990), is informative and provocative on all of these issues.

8. Benedict Anderson, *Imagined Communities: Reflections on the Origins and Spread of Nationalism* (London: Verso Editions, 1983); see also T. H. Breen, "An Empire of Goods: The Anglicization of Colonial America," *Journal of British Studies* 25 (1986): 467–99.

9. Steele, *The English Atlantic*, chap. 8.

10. Benjamin Franklin, *Benjamin Franklin's Autobiography*, ed. J. A. Leo Lemay and P. M. Zall (Knoxville: University of Tennessee Press, 1981), 16–17. Warner, *Letters of the Republic*, is especially useful here.

11. Raymond Phineas Stearns, *Science in the British Colonies of America* (Urbana: University of Illinois Press, 1970), 417–23.

12. Alexander, *A Brief Narrative of the Case and Trial of John Peter Zenger, Printer of the New York Weekly Journal*, ed. Stanley Nider Katz (1736; reprint, Cambridge, Mass.: Harvard University Press, 1963).

13. Davis, *A Colonial Southern Bookshelf* (Athens: University of Georgia Press, 1979); *The Secret Diary of William Byrd of Westover, 1709–1712*, ed. Louis B. Wright and Marion Tinling (Richmond, Va.: Dietz Press, 1941), 201, 202, passim; *The Journal of Philip Vickers Fithian*, ed. Hunter Dickinson Farish (Charlottesville: University of Virginia Press, 1957), 20.

14. Gerald Newman, *The Rise of English Nationalism: A Cultural History, 1740–1830* (New York: St. Martin's Press, 1987).

15. Benjamin Franklin, *Writings* (New York: Library of America, 1987), 5.

16. "History of the Dividing Line Run in the Year 1728," in *A Journey to the Land of Eden and Other Papers by William Byrd*, ed. Mark Van Doren (n.p.: Macy-Masius, 1928), 125–26.

17. Ibid., 63.

18. Richard L. Bushman, *The Refinement of America: Persons, Houses, Cities* (New York, Alfred A. Knopf, 1992).

19. Adam Smith, *The Theory of Moral Sentiments*, ed. D. D. Raphael and A. L. Macfie, vol. 1 of *Glasgow Edition of the Works of Adam Smith* (Oxford: Oxford University Press, 1976), esp. 15n.

20. David D. Hall, *Worlds of Wonder, Days of Judgment: Popular Religious Belief in Early New England* (New York: Alfred A. Knopf, 1989), chap. 1.

21. Robert D. Harlan, "David Hall's Bookshop and Its British Sources of Supply," in *Books in America's Past: Essays Honoring Rudolph H. Gjelsness*, ed. David Kaser (Charlottesville: University of Virginia Press, 1966), 1–24.

22. The evidence for much of this discussion will appear in forthcoming work by Richard Sher.

23. Thomas Bray, *An Essay Towards Promoting all Necessary and Useful Knowledge, Both Divine and Human, In all the Parts of His Majesty's Dominions, Both at Home and*

Abroad (London, 1697); Robert B. Winans, "The Growth of a Novel-Reading Public in Late Eighteenth-Century America," *Early American Literature* 9 (1975): 267–75; Winans, "Bibliography and the Cultural Historian: Notes on the Eighteenth-Century Novel," in *Printing and Society in Early America*, ed. William L. Joyce, et al. (Worcester, Mass.: American Antiquarian Society, 1983); Cathy N. Davidson, *Revolution and the Word: The Rise of the Novel in America* (New York: Oxford University Press, 1986), 27–29.

24. Chester T. Hallenback, "A Colonial Reading List: The Loan-Book of Hatboro Library, 1762–1774," *Pennsylvania Magazine of History and Biography* 56 (1932): 289–340.

25. Ian Watt, *The Rise of the Novel: Studies in Defoe, Richardson, and Fielding* (Berkeley: University of California Press, 1957).

26. This position is associated especially with such critics as Mikhail Bakhtin. For its implications in America, see Davidson, *Revolution and the Word*, 13–14.

27. *The Journal of Esther Edwards Burr, 1754–1757*, ed. Carol F. Karlsen and Laurie Crumpacker (New Haven: Yale University Press, 1984), 98–108 and passim.

28. Ibid.

29. *Letterbook of Eliza Lucas Pinckney, 1739–1762*, ed. Elise Pinckney (Chapel Hill: University of North Carolina Press, 1972), 47–48.

30. Richard Beale Davis, *A Colonial Southern Bookshelf*, 119–20.

31. Davidson, *Revolution and the Word*, chap. 4, provides a useful introduction to a complex and extensive literature on literacy. See also E. Jennifer Monaghan, "Literacy Instruction and Gender in Colonial New England," in *Reading in America: Literature and Social History*, ed. Cathy N. Davidson (Baltimore: Johns Hopkins University Press, 1989), chap. 2.

32. Kenneth A. Lockridge, *Literacy in Colonial New England: An Enquiry into the Social Context of Literacy in the Early Modern West* (New York: Norton, 1974); but see Monaghan, "Literacy Instruction and Gender in Colonial New England"; David D. Hall, "The Uses of Literacy," in *Worlds of Wonder, Days of Judgment*, chap. 1; and Linda Auwers, "Reading the Marks of the Past: Exploring Female Literacy in Colonial Windsor, Connecticut," *Historical Methods* 13 (1980): 204–14.

33. Ibid.

34. *The Journal of Esther Burr*, 103, passim.

35. Ibid., 183, 200.

36. Ibid., 257.

37. Ibid., 202.

38. Ellen Moers, *Literary Women* (Garden City, N.Y.: Doubleday, 1976), quoted in *The Journal of Esther Burr*, 22–23.

39. Hallenback, "Loan-Book of Hatboro Library."

40. Davis D. McElroy, *Scotland's Age of Improvement: A Survey of Eighteenth-Century Literary Clubs and Societies* (n.p., 1969); *Scotland in the Age of Improvement: Essays in Scottish History in the Eighteenth Century*, ed. N. T. Phillipson and Rosalind Mitchison (Edinburgh: Edinburgh University Press, 1970).

41. *The Journal of Esther Burr*, 102.

42. Ibid., 98, 107, 108.

43. Ibid., 98.

44. Hallenback, "Loan-Book of Hatboro Library."

45. Elizabeth Singer Rowe, *Friendship in Death: in Twenty Letters from the Dead to the Living* (London, 1733); *The Journal of Esther Burr*, 80.

46. See chapter 5.

47. Fiering, "Transatlantic Republic of Letters."

48. Hallenback, "Loan-Book of Hatboro Library."

49. Ronald L. Meek, *Social Science and the Ignoble Savage* (New York: Cambridge University Press, 1976).

50. Other depictions of the sense of imperial community can be found in Kathleen Wilson, "Empire of Virtue: The Imperial Project and Hanoverian Culture c. 1720–1785," in *An Imperial State at War: Britain from 1689 to 1815*, ed. Lawrence Stone (New York: Routledge, 1994), 128–64,; and in Breen, "Empire of Goods."

51. Smith, *The History of the Province of New-York: From the First Discovery to the Year 1732*, ed. Michael Kammen (1757; reprint, Cambridge, Mass.: Harvard University Press, 1972); Cadwallader Colden, *The History of the Five Indian Nations Depending on the Province of New-York in America*, 2 vols. (New York, 1727–1744); William Douglass, *Summary, Historical and Political, of the First Planting, Progressive Improvements, and Present State of the British Settlements in North-America*, 2 vols. (Boston, 1747–1752).

Chapter Three

1. *The Independent Reflector, or Weekly Essays on Sundry Important Subjects More Particularly Adapted to the Province of New-York*, ed. Milton M. Klein (Cambridge, Mass.: Harvard University Press, 1963).

2. Benjamin Franklin, *Benjamin Franklin's Autobiography*, ed. J. A. Leo Lemay and P. M. Zall (Knoxville: University of Tennessee Press, 1981).

3. *The Journal of Esther Edwards Burr*.

4. *The American Enlightenment: The Shaping of the American Experience and a Free Society*, ed. Adrienne Koch (New York: G. Braziller, 1965).

5. A useful and brief survey of recent treatments of the Enlightenment is Roy Porter, *The Enlightenment* (Atlantic Highlands, N.J.: Humanities Press, 1990). The classic treatment of the whole Enlightenment remains Peter Gay, *The Enlightenment: An Interpretation*, 2 vols. (New York, Alfred A. Knopf, 1966–1969).

6. For examples see Robert Darnton, *The Business of Enlightenment: A Publishing History of the "Encyclopedie," 1775–1800* (Cambridge, Mass.: Harvard University Press, 1979); Darnton, *The Literary Underground of the Old Regime* (Cambridge, Mass.: Harvard University Press, 1982); Margaret C. Jacob, *The Radical Enlightenment: Pantheists, Freemasons, and Republicans* (London: Allen and Unwin, 1981); David Jaffee, "The Village Enlightenment in New England, 1760–1820," *WMQ*, 3d ser., 57 (1990): 327–46; Ned C. Landsman, "Presbyterians and Provincial Society: The Evangelical Enlightenment in the West of Scotland, 1740–1775," in *Sociability and Society: The Social World of the Scottish Enlightenment*, ed. John Dwyer and Richard Sher, *Eighteenth-Century Life* 15 (1991): 194–209; *Women and the Enlightenment*, ed. M. Hunt, et al. (New York: Haworth Press, 1984).

7. Kant defined Enlightenment as "man's emergence from his self-imposed nonage," that is, from "the inability to use one's own understanding without another's guidance." The essay is conveniently excerpted in *The Enlightenment: A Comprehensive Anthology*, ed. Peter Gay (New York: Simon and Schuster, 1973), 384–89.

8. Carl Becker, *The Heavenly City of the Eighteenth-Century Philosophers* (New Haven: Yale University Press, 1932).

9. Henry May, *The Enlightenment in America* (New York: Oxford University Press, 1976).

10. A classical statement is A. Rupert Hall, *The Scientific Revolution, 1500–1800: The Formation of the Modern Scientific Attitude* (London: Longmans, Green, 1954); see also Herbert Butterfield, *Origins of Modern Science, 1560–1820* (New York: Macmillan, 1951). For newer, less celebratory approaches, see, for example, Steven Shapin, "The Social Uses of Science," in *The Ferment of Knowledge*, ed. G. S. Rousseau and Roy Porter (New York: Cambridge University Press, 1980), 93–139; Margaret C. Jacob, *The Newtonians and the English Revolution* (Ithaca, N.Y.: Cornell University Press, 1976); and *The Uses of Science in the Age of Newton*, ed. John G. Burke (Berkeley: University of California Press, 1983).

11. Porter, *Enlightenment*, 12–21; Mark Hessler, "Providence Lost: A Study of Epistemology and Religious Culture among New England Puritans, 1630–1730" (Ph.D. diss., State University of New York at Stony Brook, 1992).

12. On the implications of the encounter, see especially Stephen Greenblatt, *Marvelous Possessions: The Wonder of the New World* (Chicago: University of Chicago Press, 1991); Anthony Pagden, *European Encounters with the New World: From Renaissance to Romanticism* (New Haven: Yale University Press, 1993); and *America in European Consciousness, 1493–1750*, ed. Karen Ordahl Kupperman (Chapel Hill: University of North Carolina Press, 1994).

13. See Jacob, *The Newtonians and the English Revolution*.

14. Ronald L. Meek, *Social Science and the Ignoble Savage* (New York: Cambridge University Press, 1976); Roger L. Emerson, "Conjectural History and the Scottish Philosophers," *Historical Papers*, Canadian Historical Association, 1985.

15. Thomas J. Schlereth, *The Cosmopolitan Ideal in Enlightenment Thought: Its Form and Function in the Ideas of Franklin, Hume, and Voltaire, 1694–1790* (Notre Dame, Ind.: University of Notre Dame Press, 1977).

16. Ned C. Landsman, "The Provinces and the Empire: Scotland, the American Colonies, and the Development of British Provincial Identity," in *An Imperial State at War: Britain from 1689 to 1815*, ed. Lawrence Stone (New York: Routledge, 1994), 258–87.

17. May, *Enlightenment in America*.

18. A recent treatment is W. M. Spellman, *The Latitudinarians and the Church of England, 1660–1700* (Athens, Ga., 1993); see also Jacob, *Newtonians and the English Revolution*.

19. The phrase is Henry May's, from *Enlightenment in America*, part 1.

20. Norman Fiering, "The First American Enlightenment: Tillotson, Leverett, and Philosophical Anglicanism," *New England Quarterly* 54 (1981): 307–44.

21. Tillotson, "The Advantages of Religion to Particular Persons," in *The English Sermon: An Anthology*, ed. C. H. Sisson, Val Warner, and Michael Schmidt, vol. 2, 1650–1750 (Cheadle, England: Carcanet Press, 1976), 193–204.

22. A useful anthology is *Deism and Natural Religion: A Source Book*, ed. E. Graham Waring (New York: Frederick Ungar Publishing Co., 1967).

23. Jacob, *The Newtonians and the English Revolution*.

24. Parke Rouse Jr., *James Blair of Virginia* (Chapel Hill: University of North Carolina Press, 1971).

25. *The Secret Diary of William Byrd of Westover, 1709–1712*, ed. Louis B. Wright and Marion Tinling (Richmond, Va.: Dietz Press, 1941), 4, 6, 16, passim.

26. Fiering, "First American Enlightenment."

27. John Corrigan, *The Prism of Piety: The Catholick Congregational Clergy at the Beginning of the Enlightenment* (New York: Oxford University Press, 1991).

28. For the older Puritan view, see Norman S. Fiering, "Will and Intellect in the New England Mind," *WMQ*, 3d ser., 29 (1972): 515–58.

29. Quoted in Corrigan, *Prism of Piety*, 70.

30. Laura L. Becker, "Ministers and Laymen: The Singing Controversy in Puritan New England, 1720–1740," *New England Quarterly* 55 (1982): 79–96; Hessler, "Providence Lost," chap. 9.

31. Robert Findlay, *A Persuasive to the Enlargement of Psalmody* (Glasgow, 1763); Isaac Watts, *Hymns and Spiritual Songs. . . . With an Essay Towards the Improvement of Christian Psalmody* (London, 1707).

32. Teresa Toulouse, *The Art of Prophesying: New England Sermons and the Shaping of Belief* (Athens: University of Georgia Press, 1987), 58, 46–74, passim.

33. Maxine Van De Wetering, "Moralizing in Puritan Natural Science: Mysteriousness in Earthquake Sermons," *Journal of the History of Ideas* 43 (1982): 417–38; see also Thomas Prince, *Earthquakes the Works of God* (Boston, 1727).

34. Joseph Ellis, *The New England Mind in Transition: Samuel Johnson of Connecticut, 1696–1772* (New Haven: Yale University Press, 1973).

35. See especially Ezra Stiles, *A Discourse on Christian Union* (Boston, 1761).

36. See, for example, J. Hector St. John de Crèvecoeur, *Letters from an American Farmer and Sketches of Eighteenth-Century America*, ed. Albert E. Stone (New York: Penguin Books, 1981), esp. 124–25, passim; W. H. Barber, "Voltaire and Quakerism: Enlightenment and Inner Light," *Studies on Voltaire and the Eighteenth Century* 24 (1963): 81–91.

37. *The World of William Penn*, ed. Richard S. Dunn and Mary Maples Dunn (Philadelphia: University of Pennsylvania Press, 1986). For suggestive interpretations of the later development of Quakerism, see Richard T. Vann, *The Social Development of English Quakerism, 1655–1755* (Cambridge, Mass.: Harvard University Press, 1969), and Barry J. Levy, *Quakers and the American Family: British Settlement in the Delaware Valley* (New York: Oxford University Press, 1988).

38. Robert Barclay, *Apology for the True Christian Divinity of the People Called Quakers* (1676; reprint, London, 1780), 5.

39. Jon Butler, " 'Gospel Order Improved': The Keithian Schism and the Exercise of Quaker Ministerial Authority in Pennsylvania," *WMQ*, 3d ser., 31 (1974): 431–52.

40. Barclay, *Apology for the True Christian Divinity*, 4.

41. Frederick B. Tolles, *James Logan and the Culture of Provincial Pennsylvania* (Boston: Little, Brown, 1957).

42. Ibid., 208–10.

43. Ibid., "Quaker Virtuoso," chap. 12.

44. Ibid., 13.

45. Stephen Saunders Webb, *1676: The End of American Independence* (New York: Alfred A. Knopf, 1984), explores the relationship between expansive settlement and imperial diplomacy.

46. Sydney V. James, *A People among Peoples: Quaker Benevolence in Eighteenth-Century America* (Cambridge, Mass.: Harvard University Press, 1963); Jack D. Marietta, *The Reformation of American Quakerism, 1748–1783* (Philadelphia: University of Pennsylvania Press, 1984).

47. Jean R. Soderlund, *Quakers and Slavery: A Divided Spirit* (Princeton, N.J.: Princeton University Press, 1985), 47.

48. Ibid., passim.

49. Davis, *The Problem of Slavery in Western Culture* (Ithaca, N.Y.: Cornell University Press, 1966). See also Thomas Haskell, "Capitalism and the Origins of the Humanitarian Sensibility," *American Historical Review* 90 (1985): 339–61, 547–66.

50. Gary B. Nash and Jean R. Soderlund, *Freedom by Degrees: Emancipation in Pennsylvania and Its Aftermath* (New York: Oxford University Press, 1991).

51. David Brion Davis, *The Problem of Slavery in the Age of Revolution, 1770–1823* (Ithaca, N.Y.: Cornell University Press, 1975).

52. Levy, *Quakers and the American Family,* 207–30; Mary Maples Dunn, "Women of the Light," in *Women of America: A History,* ed. Carol Ruth Berkin and Mary Beth Norton (Boston: Houghton Mifflin, 1979), 115–33.

53. Elizabeth I. Nybakken, "New Light on the Old Side: Irish Influences in Colonial Presbyterianism," *Journal of American History* 68 (1981–1982): 813–32; Douglas Sloan, *The Scottish Enlightenment and the American College Ideal* (New York: Teacher's College, 1971), chap. 3.

54. Ibid. The distinction between Irish and Scottish New Lights, on the one hand, and American New Lights, on the other, has misled even attentive scholars.

55. William Robert Scott, *Francis Hutcheson: His Life, Teaching, and Position in the History of Philosophy* (Cambridge, England: Cambridge University Press, 1900); T. D. Campbell, "Francis Hutcheson: 'Father' of the Scottish Enlightenment," in *Origins and Nature of the Scottish Enlightenment,* ed. R. H. Campbell and Andrew S. Skinner (Edinburgh: John Donald, 1982), 167–85. The trail here also leads back to Gilbert Burnet; see *Letters Between the late Mr. Gilbert Burnet, and Mr. Hutchinson, Concerning the True Foundations of Virtue or Moral Goodness* (London, 1735).

56. Hutcheson, *Inquiry into the Original of our Ideas of Beauty and Virtue* (Dublin, 1725); *A Short Introduction to Moral Philosophy* (Glasgow, 1742).

57. Norman Fiering, *Moral Philosophy at Seventeenth-Century Harvard: A Discipline in Transition* (Chapel Hill: University of North Carolina Press, 1981) and *Jonathan Edwards's Moral Thought and Its British Context* (Chapel Hill: University of North Carolina Press, 1981), are highly suggestive on the relationship of moral sense philosophy to Reformed Protestantism.

58. Adam Smith, *The Theory of Moral Sentiments,* ed. D. D. Raphael and A. L. Macfie, vol. 1 of *Glasgow Edition of the Works of Adam Smith* (Oxford: Oxford University Press, 1976).

59. Sloan, *Scottish Enlightenment and the American College Ideal,* chap. 3; David Fate Norton, "Francis Hutcheson in America," *Studies on Voltaire and the Eighteenth Century* 154 (1976): 1547–68.

60. Paul Wood, "Science and the Aberdeen Enlightenment," in *Philosophy and Science in the Scottish Enlightenment,* ed. Peter Jones (Edinburgh: John Donald, 1988), 39–66; Peter Jones, "The Scottish Professoriate and the Polite Academy, 1720–1746," in *Wealth and Virtue: The Shaping of Political Economy in the Scottish Enlightenment,* ed. Istvan Hont and Michael Ignatieff (New York: Cambridge University Press, 1983), 89–119, and "Enlightened Aberdeen," section 2 in *Aberdeen and the Enlightenment,* ed. Jennifer J. Carter and Joan H. Pittock (Aberdeen: Aberdeen University Press, 1987).

61. Ibid.

62. Peter J. Diamond, "Witherspoon, William Smith, and the Scottish Philosophy in Revolutionary America," in *Scotland and America in the Age of the Enlightenment*, ed. Richard B. Sher and Jeffrey Smitten (Princeton, N.J.: Princeton University Press, 1990), 115–32.

63. Smith, *Some Reasons for Erecting a College in this Province, and Fixing the Same at the City of New-York* (New York, 1752); Smith, *A General Idea of the College of Mirania; With a Sketch of the Method of Teaching Science and Religion, in the Several Classes* (New York, 1753).

64. *American Magazine, or Monthly Chronicle for the British Colonies* (Philadelphia, 1757–1758).

65. David C. Humphrey, *From King's College to Columbia, 1746–1800* (New York: Columbia University Press, 1976), chap. 7, passim.

66. William Stith, *The Nature and Extent of Christ's Redemption. A Sermon Preached before the General Assembly of Virginia: At Williamsburg, November 11th, 1753* (Williamsburg, 1753); Samuel Davies, *Charity and Truth United or The Way of the Multitude Exposed in Six Letters to the Rev. Mr. William Stith, A. M. President of William and Mary College*, ed. Thomas Clinton Pears Jr. (Philadelphia: Presbyterian Historical Society, 1941).

67. Garry Wills, *Inventing America: Jefferson's Declaration of Independence* (Garden City, N.J.: Doubleday, 1978); Robert E. Schofield, *The Lunar Society of Birmingham* (Oxford: Oxford University Press, 1963).

68. Brooke Hindle, *The Pursuit of Science in Revolutionary America, 1735–1789* (Chapel Hill: University of North Carolina Press, 1956), chap. 1, passim; Raymond Phineas Stearns, *Science in the British Colonies of America* (Urbana: University of Illinois Press, 1970).

69. Ibid.

70. C. Helen Brock, "Scotland and American Medicine," in William R. Brock and C. Helen Brock, *Scotus Americanus: A Survey of the Sources for Links Between Scotland and America in the Eighteenth Century* (Edinburgh: Edinburgh University Press, 1982), chap. 6.

71. Stearns, *Science in the British Colonies of America*, 477 ff.

72. Stearns, *Science in the British Colonies of America*; Hindle, *Pursuit of Science in Revolutionary America*, chap. 2.

73. I. Bernard Cohen, *Benjamin Franklin's Science* (Cambridge, Mass.: Harvard University Press, 1990), chaps. 1–3.

74. James E. McClellan, *Science Reorganized: Scientific Societies in the Eighteenth Century* (New York: Columbia University Press, 1985).

75. Cohen, *Benjamin Franklin's Science*.

76. (New York, 1727–1744).

77. A similar theme appeared in Gary B. Nash, "The Image of the Indian in the Southern Colonial Mind," *WMQ*, 3d, ser., 29 (1972): 197–230; see also Meek, *Social Science and the Ignoble Savage*, and Roger L. Emerson, "American Indians, Frenchmen, and Scots Philosophers," *Studies in Eighteenth-Century Culture* 9 (1979): 211–36, on applications of the theory of the stages of civilization.

78. John Mitchell, "Essay upon the Causes of the Different Colours of People in Different Climates," *Philosophical Transactions* 43 (1744–1745): 102–50.

79. Winthrop Jordan, *White over Black: American Attitudes Towards the Negro, 1550–1812* (Chapel Hill: University of North Carolina Press, 1968).

80. Thomas Jefferson, *Notes on the State of Virginia,* ed. William Peden (Chapel Hill: University of North Carolina Press, 1954).

81. Ibid., 137–43.

82. Phillis Wheatley, *Poems on Various Subjects, Religious and Moral* (London, 1773).

Chapter Four

1. The estimates are from Whitefield's own journals. There is, of course, no way to verify his numbers in retrospect. Yet recent historians have tended to confirm the general picture that his journals provided. See especially Harry S. Stout, *The Divine Dramatist: George Whitefield and the Rise of Modern Evangelicalism* (Grand Rapids, Mich.: William B. Eerdmans, 1991), and Frank Lambert, *"Pedlar in Divinity": George Whitefield and the Transatlantic Revivals* (Princeton, N.J.: Princeton University Press, 1994).

2. Jon Butler, "Enthusiasm Described and Decried: The Great Awakening As Interpretive Fiction," *Journal of American History* 69 (1982–1983): 305–25, argues with considerable force that historians have exaggerated the universality of the Awakening and its influence on eighteenth-century America. Yet the idea that the revival represented a "great and general awakening" came from contemporaries rather than historians and suggests the dramatic perceptions it created at the time.

3. *The Great Awakening,* ed. C. C. Goen, vol. 4 of *The Works of Jonathan Edwards* (New Haven: Yale University Press, 1972), 27.

4. The versions of Edwards's narrative are conveniently collected in *The Great Awakening,* ed. C. C. Goen, 97–211.

5. James Tanis, *Dutch Calvinistic Pietism in the Middle Colonies: A Study in the Life and Theology of Theodorus Jacobus Frelinghuysen* (The Hague: Martinus Nijhoff, 1967).

6. "Documentary History of William Tennent, and the Log College," ed. Thomas C. Pears Jr. and Guy S. Klett, *Journal of Presbyterian History* 28 (1950): 37–64, 105–28, 167–204; Archibald Alexander, *Biographical Sketches of the Founder, and Principal Alumni of the Log College* (Princeton, N.J.: Princeton University Press, 1845).

7. William Tennent Jr., "An Account of the Revival of Religion at Freehold," in *The Christian History for the Year 1744,* ed. Thomas Prince (Boston, 1745), 298–310; Alexander, *Biographical Sketches;* Gilbert Tennent, preface to John Tennent, *The Nature of Regeneration Opened, and its Absolute Necessity, in Order to Salvation, Demonstrated* (Boston, 1735), ii–vi.

8. Milton J. Coalter Jr., *Gilbert Tennent, Son of Thunder: A Case Study of Continental Pietism's Impact on the First Great Awakening in the Middle Colonies* (New York: Greenwood Press, 1986), 71–75.

9. Michael J. Crawford, "The Spiritual Travels of Nathan Cole," *WMQ,* 3d ser., 33 (1976): 89–126.

10. Stout, *Divine Dramatist;* Lambert, *"Pedlar in Divinity."*

11. Fielding, *Joseph Andrew,* ed. R. F. Brissenden (1742; reprint, New York: Penguin Books, 1977), 92–93.

12. Stout, *Divine Dramatist,* 4–10, 39–43, passim.

13. Ibid., 110–12.

14. On Davenport, see especially Harry S. Stout and Peter Onuf, "James Davenport and the Great Awakening in New London," *Journal of American History* 70 (1983–1984): 556–78.

15. Butler, " 'Enthusiasm Described and Decried.' "

16. Edwards, "Sinners in the Hands of an Angry God," in *Jonathan Edwards: Representative Selections*, ed. Clarence H. Faust and Thomas H. Johnson (1935; reprint, New York: Hill and Wang, 1962), 155–72.

17. See also Patricia J. Tracy, *Jonathan Edwards, Pastor: Religion and Society in Eighteenth-Century Northampton* (New York: Hill and Wang, 1980), 132–35.

18. For example, *The Querist, or an Extract of Sundry Passages Taken out of Mr. Whitefield's Printed Sermons, Journals, and Letters* (Philadelphia, 1740).

19. Samuel Finley, *Christ Triumphing and Satan Raging* (London, 1741), 21–22.

20. Ibid., 28.

21. On itinerancy, see Timothy D. Hall, *Contested Boundaries: Itinerancy and the Reshaping of the Colonial American Religious World* (Durham, N.C.: Duke University Press, 1994).

22. Edwards, *A History of the Work of Redemption*, ed. John F. Wilson, vol. 9 of *The Works of Jonathan Edwards* (New Haven: Yale University Press, 1989); *Some Thoughts Concerning the Present Revival of Religion in New-England, and the Way in Which it Ought to be Acknowledged and Promoted* (Boston, 1742), in *The Great Awakening*, ed. Goen, 291–530.

23. Printed in *The Great Awakening: Documents Illustrating the Crisis and Its Consequences*, ed. Alan Heimert and Perry Miller (New York: Bobbs-Merrill, 1967), 71–99.

24. Stout and Onuf, "James Davenport and the Great Awakening."

25. *The Great Awakening and American Education: A Documentary History*, ed. Douglas Sloan (New York: Teacher's College, 1973); see chapter 5.

26. Alexander Garden, *Regeneration and the Testimony of the Spirit* (Charleston, S.C., 1740), in *The Great Awakening*, ed. Heimert and Miller, 47–61.

27. Ibid., 47, 61.

28. *Minutes of the Presbyterian Church in America, 1706–1788*, ed. Guy S. Klett (Philadelphia: Presbyterian Historical Society, 1976), 167 ff.

29. Gary B. Nash, *Urban Crucible: Social Change, Political Consciousness, and the Origins of the American Revolution* (Cambridge, Mass.: Harvard University Press, 1979); J. M. Bumsted, "Religion, Finance, and Democracy: The Town of Norton as a Case Study," *Journal of American History* 57 (1971): 817–31; Richard Bushman, *From Puritan to Yankee: Character and the Social Order in Connecticut, 1690–1765* (Cambridge, Mass.: Harvard University Press, 1967), chap. 12.

30. James Walsh, "The Great Awakening in the First Congregational Church of Woodbury, Connecticut," *WMQ*, 3d ser., 28 (1971): 543–62; Gerald F. Moran, "Religious Renewal, Puritan Tribalism, and the Family in Seventeenth-Century Milford, Connecticut," *WMQ*, 3d ser., 36 (1979): 236–54; Gerald F. Moran and Maris A. Vinovskis, "The Puritan Family and Religion: A Critical Reappraisal," *WMQ*, 3d ser., 39 (1982): 29–63; and Stephen R. Grossbart, "Seeking the Divine Favor: Conversion and Church Admission in Eastern Connecticut, 1711–1832," *WMQ*, 3d ser., 46 (1989): 696–740; Richard D. Shiels, "The Feminization of American Congregationalism, 1730–1835," *American Quarterly* 33 (1981): 46–62.

31. The mission activity of the Society in Scotland for the Promotion of Christian Knowledge is well documented throughout the *Christian Monthly History* (Edinburgh, 1743–1746), some of which is reprinted in *Historical Collections Relating to Remarkable Periods of the Success of the Gospel*, comp. John Gillies, 2 vols. (Kelso, 1845), vol. 2., 464–87.

32. See, for example, Keith Thomas, "Women in the Civil War Sects," *Past and Present* 13 (1958): 42–62; Phyllis Mack, *Visionary Women: Ecstatic Prophecy in Seventeenth-Century England* (Berkeley: University of California Press, 1992).

33. Charles Chauncy, *Seasonable Thoughts on the State of Religion in New-England* (Boston, 1743); Edwards, *Some Thoughts Concerning the Present Revival of Religion in New-England*, in *The Great Awakening*, ed. Goen, 289–530.

34. Chauncy, *The New Creature Described and Consider'd as the Sure Characteristick of a Man's Being in Christ* (Boston, 1741), printed in *Select Discourses from the American Preacher*, 4 vols. (Edinburgh, 1796), 2, 316–62.

35. Edwards, *The Distinguishing Marks of the Work of the Spirit of God* (Boston, 1741), in *The Great Awakening*, ed. Goen, 213–88.

36. Chauncy, *Enthusiasm Described and Caution'd Against* (Boston, 1742), in *The Great Awakening*, ed. Heimert and Miller, 229–56.

37. [Chauncy], *The Wonderful Narrative; or, a Faithful Account of the French Prophets, their Agitations, Extasies, and Inspirations* (Glasgow, 1742).

38. Chauncy, *Enthusiasm Described and Caution'd Against*, 248–54; *Seasonable Thoughts on the State of Religion in New-England*, 294 ff.

39. [Chauncy], *A Letter from a Gentleman in Boston to Mr. George Wishart, One of the Ministers of Edinburgh, Concerning the State of Religion in New-England* (Edinburgh, 1742), 9–13 ff.; *Seasonable Thoughts on the State of Religion in New-England*, 178–81.

40. Chauncy, *Enthusiasm Described and Caution'd Against*, 242–43.

41. Chauncy, *Seasonable Thoughts on the State of Religion in New-England*, 140–78.

42. Anne S. Pratt, "The Books Sent from England by Jeremiah Dummer to Yale College," in *Papers in Honor of Andrew Keogh, Librarian of Yale University* (New Haven: Yale University Press, 1938), 7–44.

43. Perry Miller, *Jonathan Edwards* (New York, 1949).

44. Edwards, *A Treatise Concerning Religious Affections* (Boston, 1746).

45. See especially Daniel Walker Howe, "The Political Psychology of *The Federalist*," *William and Mary Quarterly*, 3d ser. (1987): 485–509, and Howe, *Unitarian Conscience: Harvard Moral Philosophy, 1805–1861* (Cambridge, Mass.: Harvard University Press, 1970).

46. Amy Schrager Lang, " 'A Flood of Errors': Chauncy and Edwards in the Great Awakening," in *Jonathan Edwards and the American Experience*, ed. Nathan O. Hatch and Harry S. Stout (New York: Oxford University Press, 1988), 160–73; Alan Heimert, *Religion and the American Mind: From the Great Awakening to the Revolution* (Cambridge, Mass.: Harvard University Press, 1966).

47. Edwards, *A Faithful Narrative of the Surprising Work of God in the Conversion of Many Hundred Souls in Northampton* (London, 1736), in *The Great Awakening*, ed. Goen, 191–205; *Some Thoughts Concerning the Present Revival*, 331–41; *The Life of David Brainerd*, ed. Norman Pettit, vol. 7 in *The Works of Jonathan Edwards* (New Haven: Yale University Press, 1985).

48. Chauncy, *The Out-Pouring of the Holy Ghost* (Boston, 1742), in *Select Discourses from the American Preacher*, 2, 392–431 (the quotes are from pp. 401–2, 410); Chauncy, *The Gifts of the Spirit to Ministers considered in their Diversity* (Boston, 1741), in ibid., 362–91.

49. Chauncy, *New Creature Described*, in ibid., esp. 318; the use of the male gender in the phrase "inner man" was characteristic of both Old Side and New Side.

50. Charles H. Lippy, *Seasonable Revolutionary: The Mind of Charles Chauncy* (Chicago: Nelson-Hall, 1981); Edward M. Griffin, *Old Brick: Charles Chauncy of Boston, 1705–1787* (Minneapolis: University of Minnesota Press, 1980).

51. Lippy, *Seasonable Revolutionary*, 107–23.

52. See the discussion in ibid., 120–23.

53. *Glasgow Weekly History* (Glasgow, 1742); *Christian History for the Year 1743* and *Christian History for the Year 1744* (Boston, 1744–1745); *Christian Monthly History* (Edinburgh, 1743–1746).

54. John Erskine, *The Signs of the Times Consider'd: or, the High Probability, that the Present Appearances in New-England, and the West of Scotland, are a Prelude of the Glorious Things Promised to the Church in the Latter Ages* (Edinburgh, 1742); Jonathan Edwards to "a Correspondent in Scotland," 10 November 1745, in *Jonathan Edwards' Apocalyptic Writings*, ed. Stephen J. Stein, vol. 5 of *The Works of Jonathan Edwards* (New Haven: Yale University Press, 1977), 444–60; Edwards, *An Humble Attempt to Promote Explicit Agreement and Visible Union of God's People in Extraordinary Prayer for the Revival of Religion and the Advancement of Christ's Kingdom on Earth* (Boston, 1747); *Historical Collections Relating to Remarkable Periods of the Success of the Gospel*, comp. Gillies, vol. 2, 462–64.

55. [Chauncy,] *A Letter from a Gentleman in Boston, to Mr. George Wishart*.

56. Arthur Fawcett, *The Cambuslang Revival: The Scottish Evangelical Revival of the Eighteenth Century* (London, 1971); see also the narratives in *Historical Collections Relating to Remarkable Periods of the Success of the Gospel*, comp. Gillies, vol. 2, 433–62, passim.

57. Tracy, *Jonathan Edwards, Pastor*. On the controversy over communion in Northampton, see the editor's introduction to *Ecclesiastical Writings*, ed. David D. Hall, vol. 12 of *The Works of Jonathan Edwards* (New Haven: Yale University Press, 1994), 57–68.

58. Lippy, *Seasonable Revolutionary*.

59. C. C. Goen, *Revivalism and Separatism in New England, 1740–1800* (1962; reprint, Middletown, Conn.: Wesleyan University Press, 1987).

60. Robert E. Cray Jr., "More Light on a New Light: James Davenport's Religious Legacy, Eastern Long Island 1740–1840," *New York History* (1992): 5–27; Philip F. Gura, *A Glimpse of Sion's Glory: Puritan Radicalism in New England, 1620–1660* (Middletown, Conn.: Wesleyan University Press, 1984). See also *The Diary of Mary Cooper: Life on a Long Island Farm, 1768–1773*, ed. Field Horne (Oyster Bay, N.Y.: Oyster Bay Historical Society, 1981); and Peter S. Onuf, "New Light in New London: A Group Portrait of the Separatists," *WMQ*, 3d ser., 37 (1980): 627–43.

61. William G. McLoughlin, *Isaac Backus and the American Pietistic Tradition* (Boston: Little, Brown, 1967).

62. Goen, *Revivalism and Separatism*, 115–23.

63. Quoted in Goen, *Revivalism and Separatism*, 118.

64. Ibid., 151; see also Leigh Eric Schmidt, " 'A Second and Glorious Reformation': The New Light Extremism of Andrew Croswell," *WMQ*, 3d ser., 43 (1986): 214–44, and Stephen A. Marini, *Radical Sects of Revolutionary New England* (Cambridge, Mass.: Harvard University Press, 1982), chap. 4.

65. Goen, *Revivalism and Separatism*, 136–43; Barbara E. Lacey, "The World of Hannah Heaton: The Autobiography of an Eighteenth-Century Connecticut Farm Woman," *WMQ*, 3d ser., 45 (1988): 280–304. Similar cases appear in *Diary of Mary Cooper*.

66. Goen, *Revivalism and Separatism*, 114, 256, 302–27.

67. Ibid., 213–15; John L. Brooke, *The Heart of the Commonwealth: Society and Political Culture in Worcester County, Massachusetts, 1713–1861* (New York: Cambridge University Press, 1989), 83–92.

68. See, for example, Gilbert Tennent, *The Necessity of Holding Fast the Truth Represented in Three Sermons on Rev. iii. 3.* (Boston, 1743).

69. Harvey H. Jackson, "Hugh Bryan and the Evangelical Movement in Colonial South Carolina," *WMQ*, 3d ser., 43 (1986): 594–614, and Allan Gallay, "Jonathan Bryan's Plantation Empire: Land, Politics, and the Formation of a Ruling Class in Colonial Georgia," *WMQ*, 3d ser., 45 (1988): 253–79.

70. Samuel Davies, *The State of Religion Among the Protestant Dissenters in Virginia: in a Letter to the Reverend Mr. Joseph Bellamy of Bethlem, in New England* (Boston, 1751).

71. Rhys Isaac, *The Transformation of Virginia, 1740–1790* (Chapel Hill: University of North Carolina Press, 1984), chap. 8.

72. *The Carolina Backcountry on the Eve of the Revolution: The Journal and Other Writings of Charles Woodmason, Anglican Itinerant*, ed. Richard J. Hooker (Chapel Hill: University of North Carolina Press, 1953), 6–7.

73. Lemuel Briant, *The Absurdity and Blasphemy of Depreciating Moral Virtue* (Boston, 1749), in *The Great Awakening*, ed. Heimert and Miller, 546–47.

74. Chauncy, *The Benevolence of the Deity, Fairly and Impartially Considered* (Boston, 1784), quoted in Griffin, *Old Brick*, 112–13.

75. Conrad Wright, *The Beginnings of Unitarianism in America* (Boston: Starr King Press, 1955), and Daniel Howe, *The Unitarian Conscience: Harvard Moral Philosophy, 1805–1861* (Cambridge, Mass.: Harvard University Press, 1970).

76. Elizabeth I. Nybakken, "New Light on the Old Side: Irish Influences on Colonial Presbyterianism," *Journal of American History* 68 (1981–1982): 813–32; Richard B. Sher, *Church and University in the Scottish Enlightenment: The Moderate Literati of Edinburgh* (Princeton, N.J.: Princeton University Press, 1985).

77. Susan O'Brien, "A Transatlantic Community of Saints: The Great Awakening and the First Evangelical Network, 1735–1755," *American Historical Review* 91 (1986): 811–32.

78. Sir Henry Moncreiff Wellwood, *Account of the Life and Writings of John Erskine, D.D.* (Edinburgh, 1818).

79. Patricia U. Bonomi, *Under the Cope of Heaven: Religion, Society, and Politics in Colonial America* (New York: Oxford University Press, 1986), 155 ff.

80. *The Essential Rights and Liberties of Protestants. A Seasonable Plea for The Liberty of Conscience, and the Right of Private Judgment, In Matters of Religion, Without any Controul from Human Authority* (Boston, 1744), in *Political Sermons of the American Founding Era 1730–1805*, ed. Ellis Sandoz (Indianapolis: Liberty Press, 1991), 51–118.

81. Ibid., 93.

82. See especially Alan Heimert, *Religion and the American Mind: From the Great Awakening to the Revolution* (Cambridge, Mass.: Harvard University Press, 1966).

Chapter Five

1. Quoted in Harry S. Stout, *The Divine Dramatist: George Whitefield and the Rise of Modern Evangelicalism* (Grand Rapids, Mich.: William B. Eerdmans, 1991), 286–87, see also 220–33; Frank Lambert, "Subscribing for Profits and Piety: The Friendship of Benjamin Franklin and George Whitefield," *WMQ* 3d ser., 50 (1993): 529–54.

2. Frank Lambert, "Subscribing for Profits and Piety," and *"Pedlar in Divinity"*: *George Whitefield and the Transatlantic Revivals, 1737–1770* (Princeton, N.J.: Princeton University Press, 1994), 201–2; *American Bibliography*, comp. Charles Evans, 12 vols. (1903–1934; reprint, New York: Peter Smith, 1941–42), vols. 1–2.

3. James Davenport, *The Reverend Mr. James Davenport's Confessions and Retractions* (Boston, 1744).

4. Quoted in Edwin Scott Gaustad, *The Great Awakening in New England* (New York: Harper and Brothers, 1957), 37–41.

5. Gilbert Tennent, *The Necessity of Holding Fast the Truth Represented in Three Sermons on Rev. iii. 3.* (Boston, 1743).

6. Tennent, *The Necessity of Studying to Be Quiet, and Doing Our Own Business* (Philadelphia, n.d. [1744]), 10.

7. James Stoddart, *The Revival of Religion* (Glasgow, 1764), 10; see also Isaac Watts, *An Humble Attempt Towards the Revival of Religion Among Christians, and Particularly the Protestant Dissenters*, in *Works of the Reverend and Learned Isaac Watts, D.D.*, 6 vols. (London, 1810), vol. 3, 3–103; Philip Doddridge, *The Rise and Progress of Religion in the Soul* (London, 1745).

8. *The Journal of Esther Edwards Burr*, 246, 248.

9. Ibid., 249; see also the letters from Jonathan Edwards and Aaron Burr, published in *Historical Collections Relating to Remarkable Periods of the Success of the Gospel*, comp. John Gillies, 2 vols. (Kelso, 1845), vol. 2, 522–25, and William Tennent's letter of 27 February 1757, in Archibald Alexander, *Biographical Sketches of the Founder, and Principal Alumni of the Log College* (Princeton, 1845), 367–69.

For other British groups and their redefinitions of revival, see Watts, *An Humble Attempt Towards the Revival of Practical Religion*, and Stoddart, *Revival of Religion*; see also Mark Valeri, "The New Divinity and the American Revolution," *WMQ*, 3d ser., 46 (1989): 741–69. Even Gilbert Tennent came to modify his view of revivals and for the remainder of his career would repent his former rashness. Such modifications account for his sermons on *The Necessity of Studying to be Quiet, and Doing our own Business*, and *A Persuasive to the Right Use of the Passions in Religion* (Philadelphia, 1760), for example.

See also my "Presbyterians and Provincial Society: The Evangelical Enlightenment in the West of Scotland, 1740–1775," in *Sociability and Society: The Social World of the Scottish Enlightenment*, ed. John Dwyer and Richard Sher, *Eighteenth-Century Life* 15 (1991): 194–209.

10. *The Journal of Esther Edwards Burr*, 92.

11. John Davies, "The Rule of Equity," in *Sermons on Important Subjects*, ed. Albert Barnes, 3 vols. (New York, 1842), vol. 2, 62–75.

12. Samuel Blair, *The New Creature Delineated. In a Sermon, Delivered in Philadelphia, February 26, 1767* (Philadelphia, 1767), 22–23, 29–30; Blair, *Essays on the Nature, Uses and Subjects of the Sacrament of the New Testament. II. On Regeneration, wherein the Principle of spiritual Life thereby implanted; is particularly considered. . .* (New York, 1771).

13. Blair, *New Creature Delineated*, 29–30.

14. Blair, *A Persuasive to Repentance* (Philadelphia, 1743), 14–15.

15. Tennent, *The Danger of an Unconverted Ministry* (Philadelphia, 1740), in *The Great Awakening: Documents Illustrating the Crisis and Its Consequences*, ed. Alan Heimert and Perry Miller (New York: Bobbs-Merrill, 1967), 79; see also *The Necessity of Keeping the Soul. A Sermon Preach'd at Philadelphia, December the 23d, 1744* (Philadelphia, 1745), 14.

16. Edward Scott Gaustad, *Historical Atlas of Religion in America* (New York: Harper and Row, 1976).

17. Leonard J. Trinterud, *Forming an American Tradition: A Reexamination of Colonial Presbyterianism* (Philadelphia: Westminster Press, 1949), remains standard on the history of that church; also see Howard Miller, *The Revolutionary College: American Presbyterian Higher Education, 1707–1837* (New York: New York University Press, 1976).

18. William Smith Jr., *The History of the Province of New-York from the First Discovery to the Year 1732*, ed. Michael Kammen, 2 vols. (1757; reprint, Cambridge, Mass.: Harvard University Press, 1972), vol. 1, 205–7.

19. See also Ezra Stiles, *A Discourse on the Christian Union* (Boston, 1761).

20. Douglas Sloan, *The Scottish Enlightenment and the American College Ideal* (New York: Teacher's College, 1971); Howard Miller, "Evangelical Religion and Colonial Princeton," in *Schooling and Society*, ed. Lawrence Stone (Baltimore: Johns Hopkins University Press, 1976), 115–45, which uses the concept of an evangelical education empire.

21. Mark A. Noll, *Princeton and the Republic, 1768–1822: The Search for a Christian Enlightenment in the Era of Samuel Stanhope Smith* (Princeton: Princeton University Press, 1989), 18.

22. Francis L. Broderick, "Pulpit, Physics, and Politics," *WMQ*, 3d ser., 6 (1949): 42–68; Norman Fiering, *Moral Philosophy at Seventeenth Century Harvard: A Discipline in Transition* (Chapel Hill: University of North Carolina Press, 1981); Sloan, *Scottish Enlightenment*.

23. John Maclean, *History of the College of New Jersey, 1746–1854*, 2 vols. (1877; reprint, New York: Arno Press, 1969), vol. 1, 216–17.

24. Jon Butler, *Awash in a Sea of Faith: Christianizing the American People* (Cambridge, Mass.: Harvard University Press, 1990), chap. 5.

25. Jonathan Edwards, *The Life of David Brainerd*, ed. Norman Pettit, in *The Works of Jonathan Edwards*, vol. 7 (New Haven: Yale University Press, 1985); *Christian Monthly History* (Edinburgh, 1743–1746), passim.

26. James Axtell, "Dr. Wheelock's Little Red School," in *The European and the Indian: Essays in the Ethnohistory of Colonial North America* (New York: Oxford University Press, 1981), 87–109. There is no adequate study of Wheelock. Also see Michael Elliot, " 'This Indian Bait': Samson Occum and the Voice of Liminality," *Early American Literature* 29 (1994): 233–53.

27. Quoted in Betsy Erkilla, "Phillis Wheatley and the Black American Revolution," in *A Mixed Race: Ethnicity in Early America*, ed. Frank Shuffleton (New York: Oxford University Press, 1993), 225–40.

28. Anthony F. C. Wallace, *The Death and Rebirth of the Seneca* (New York: Alfred A. Knopf, 1969); Gregory Dowd, *A Spirited Resistance: The North American Indian Struggle for Unity, 1745–1815* (Baltimore: Johns Hopkins University Press, 1991).

29. *The Journal of Esther Edwards Burr*, 62, 94.

30. Davies, *Miscellaneous Poems Chiefly on Divine Subjects* (Williamsburg, 1752), preface.

31. *The Reverend Samuel Davies Abroad: The Diary of a Journey to England and Scotland, 1753–1755*, ed. George William Pilcher (Urbana: University of Illinois Press, 1967), 38–39.

32. Ibid., 106. On the theater controversy within British Presbyterianism during the 1750s, see especially Richard B. Sher, *Church and University in the Scottish Enlighten-*

ment: The Moderate Literati of Edinburgh (Princeton: Princeton University Press, 1985), 74–92.

33. *The Journal of Esther Edwards Burr,* 83.

34. Jean-Christophe Agnew, *Worlds Apart: The Market and the Theater in Anglo-American Thought, 1550–1750* (New York: Cambridge University Press, 1986).

35. The most important eighteenth-century attack on the theater, *A Serious Enquiry into the Nature and Effects of the Stage. Being an Attempt to Show, that Contributing to the Support of a Public Theatre, is Inconsistent with the Character of a Christian* (Glasgow, 1757), came from a later president of the College of New Jersey, John Witherspoon. The controversy was covered in Philadelphia in William Smith's *The American Magazine, or Monthly Chronicle for the British Colonies* (Philadelphia, 1757–1758), passim.

36. *The Journal of Esther Edwards Burr,* 125.

37. Sally Prince, *Earthquakes the Works of God* (Boston, 1727); Maxine Van De Wetering, "Moralizing in Puritan Natural Science: Mysteriousness in Earthquake Sermons," *Journal of the History of Ideas* 43 (1982): 417–38.

38. Davies, "The Religious Improvement of the Late Earthquakes," in *Sermons on Important Subjects,* vol. 3, 176–93.

39. Winthrop, *A Lecture on Earthquakes; read in the Chapel of Harvard-College in Cambridge, N. E. November 26th 1755* (Boston, 1755), 29, in *The Scientific Work of John Winthrop,* ed. Michael N. Shute (New York: Arno Press, 1980); Charles Chauncy, *Earthquakes a Token of the Righteous Anger of God* (Boston, 1755).

40. *A Letter to the Publishers of the Boston Gazette,* 23 February 1756, in Shute, *Scientific Work of John Winthrop.*

41. Edwards, *The Nature of True Virtue,* in *Two Dissertations, I. Concerning the End for which God created the World. II. The Nature of True Virtue* (Boston, 1765), in *Ethical Writings,* ed. Paul Ramsey, vol. 8 of *The Works of Jonathan Edwards* (New Haven: Yale University Press, 1989), 539–627.

42. Bellamy, *True Religion Delineated, or Experimental Religion, as Distinguished from Formality on the one Hand, and Enthusiasm on the Other* (1750), in *Works of the Reverend Joseph Bellamy, Late of Bethlem, Connecticut,* 3 vols. (New York, 1811), vol. 1, 41–462, 153.

43. William Breitenbach, "The Consistent Calvinism of the New Divinity Movement," *WMQ,* 3d ser., 41 (1984): 241–64; Mark A Valerie, *Joseph Bellamy;* Samuel Hopkins, *Sin, Through Divine Intervention, an Advantage to the Universe; and Yet this is no Excuse for Sin* (Boston, 1759).

44. Bellamy, *True Religion Delineated,* 112 ff.; Hopkins, *A Dialogue Concerning the Slavery of the Africans* (Norwich, Conn., 1776).

45. *The Journal of Esther Edwards Burr,* 182; see also 50–51, 79, passim.

46. Ibid., 79, 93, 112; Philip Doddridge, *The Rise and Progress of Religion in the Soul; Illustrated in a Course of Serious and Practical Addresses* (London, 1745).

47. Smith, *The Theory of Moral Sentiments,* ed. D. D. Raphael and A. L. Macfie, vol. 1 of *Glasgow Edition of the Works of Adam Smith* (Oxford: Oxford University Press, 1976), 22.

48. *The Journal of Esther Edwards Burr,* 53.

49. Ibid., 50–51, 62–63, 92, 185, 257. Sarah Prince, in her private book of meditations, also considered friendship to be one of the principal measures of her personal faith; see *Dying Exercises of Mrs Deborah Prince, and Devout Meditations of Mrs Sarah Gill, Daughters of the Late Reverend Mr Thomas Prince, Minister of the South Church, Boston* (Edinburgh, 1785). Also see the discussion in Mary Beth Norton, *Liberty's Daughters: The*

Revolutionary Experience of American Women, 1750–1800 (Boston: Little, Brown, 1980), 106–8.

50. An important and pioneering essay is Carroll Smith Rosenberg's "The Female World of Love and Ritual: Relations between Women in Nineteenth-Century America," *Signs* 1 (1975): 1–29.

51. *The Journal of Esther Edwards Burr,* 142, 155, 185.

52. Ibid., 59.

53. Ibid., 54–55.

54. Ibid., 224, 285–87, 297–99.

55. Ibid., 82.

56. Ibid., 58, 79, 146, 202. Lawrence Stone, *The Family, Sex, and Marriage in England, 1500–1800* (New York: Harper and Row, 1977), chap. 8. The importance of friendship between wife and husband was basic to all of Richardson's novels, but especially to *The History of Sir Charles Grandison*.

57. *The Journal of Esther Edwards Burr,* 67, 153, 202, 279–81.

58. Ibid., 183, 200.

59. Ibid., 63, 183.

60. Ibid., 163, 183, 196.

61. A recent treatment of early masonic lodges as cells of Enlightenment is Margaret C. Jacob, *Living the Enlightenment: Freemasonry and Politics in Eighteenth-Century Europe* (New York: Oxford University Press, 1991). Steven C. Bullock, "The Revolutionary Transformation of American Freemasonry, 1752–1792," *WMQ,* 3d ser., 47 (1990): 347–69, emphasizes the rise of ancient masonry in mid-century America as a challenge by artisanal groups to the privileged claims of elite modern masons; the female freemason club in a sense represented a similar challenge.

62. Benjamin Franklin, *Poor Richard: The Almanacks for the Years 1733–1758* (Garden City, N.Y.: International Collectors Library, n.d.).

63. Benjamin Franklin, *Benjamin Franklin's Autobiography,* ed. J. A. Leo Lemay and P. M. Zall (Knoxville: University of Tennessee Press, 1981).

64. See Gordon S. Wood, *The Radicalism of the American Revolution* (New York: Alfred A. Knopf, 1992), 197–200, passim.

65. *Benjamin Franklin's Autobiography,* 9, 47–49, 67 ff.

66. Daniel Defoe, *An Essay upon Projects* (London, 1697).

67. Defoe, *The Complete English Tradesman* (London, 1726).

68. E. P. Thompson, *The Making of the English Working Class* (New York: Vintage, 1963), chap. 9; Robert Malcolmson, "Workers' Combinations in Eighteenth-Century England," in *The Origins of Anglo-American Radicalism,* ed. Margaret C. Jacob and James R. Jacob (1984; reprint, Atlantic Highlands, N.J.: Humanities Press, 1991), 169–81; Ned C. Landsman, "Evangelists and Their Hearers: Popular Interpretation of Revivalist Preaching in Eighteenth-Century Scotland," *Journal of British Studies* 28 (1989): 120–49; Eric Foner, *Tom Paine and Revolutionary America* (New York: Oxford University Press, 1977), chap. 2.

69. Thompson, *Making of the English Working Class;* Norman Murray, *The Scottish Hand Loom Weavers, 1790–1850: A Social History* (Edinburgh: John Donald, 1978), 165–73; Landsman, "Evangelists and Their Hearers."

70. Gary B. Nash, *Urban Crucible: Social Change, Political Consciousness, and the Origins of the American Revolution* (Cambridge, Mass.: Harvard University Press, 1979); Frank Lambert, "Subscribing for Profits and Piety."

71. *Benjamin Franklin's Autobiography,* 9–12, 25–27, 33–36.

72. Butler, *Awash in a Sea of Faith,* chap. 3, "Magic and the Occult"; Patricia U. Bonomi, *Under the Cope of Heaven: Religion, Society, and Politics in Colonial America* (New York: Oxford University Press, 1986), esp. chap 1, "The Religious Prospect."

73. Davies, *Miscellaneous Poems,* preface; see also the preface to Joseph Bellamy, *True Religion Delineated.*

Chapter Six

1. Chauncy, *The Counsel of Two Confederate Kings to Set the Son of Tabeal on the Throne, Represented As Evil* (Boston, 1746), 43.

2. Jonathan Edwards to "a Correspondent in Scotland," 10 November 1745, in *Jonathan Edwards' Apocalyptic Writings* (New Haven: Yale University Press, 1977), 444–60.

3. On the related but changing meanings of liberty and slavery, see the works of David B. Davis, especially *The Problem of Slavery in Western Culture* (Ithaca, N.Y.: Cornell University Press, 1966).

4. Excellent discussion of the varied meanings of liberty can be found in Michael Kammen, *Spheres of Liberty: Changing Perceptions of Liberty in American Culture* (Madison: University of Wisconsin Press, 1986), and David Hackett Fischer, *Albion's Seed: Four British Folkways in America* (New York: Oxford University Press, 1989).

5. J. C. D. Clark, *English Society, 1688–1832* (New York: Cambridge University Press, 1985), and Paul Kleber Monod, *Jacobitism and the English People, 1688–1788* (New York: Cambridge University Press, 1989).

6. Pauline Maier, "John Wilkes and American Disillusionment with Britain," *WMQ,* 3d ser., 20 (1963): 373–95; George Rude, *Wilkes and Liberty* (New York: Oxford University Press, 1962).

7. For a general discussion of the ideology of liberty in eighteenth-century Britain, see H. T. Dickinson, *Liberty and Property: Political Ideology in Eighteenth-Century Britain* (London: Holmes and Meier, 1977).

8. The best treatment of the connection between slave labor and concepts of American liberty is Edmund S. Morgan, *American Slavery, American Freedom: The Ordeal of Colonial Virginia* (New York: Norton, 1975).

9. *The Independent Reflector, or Weekly Essays on Sundry Important Subjects More Particularly Adapted to the Province of New-York,* ed. Milton M. Klein (Cambridge, Mass.: Harvard University Press, 1963), 55–60.

10. Many of Trenchard and Gordon's essays have been republished in *The English Libertarian Heritage,* ed. David L. Jacobson (1965; reprint, San Francisco: Fox and Wilkes, 1994).

11. The role of Trenchard and Gordon has been highlighted in such works as Caroline Robbins, *The Eighteenth-Century Commonwealthman: Studies in the Transmission, Development and Circumstance of English Liberal Thought from the Restoration of Charles II Until the War with the Thirteen Colonies* (Cambridge, Mass.: Harvard University Press, 1959); Bernard Bailyn, *The Ideological Origins of the American Revolution* (Cambridge, Mass.: Harvard University Press, 1967); and J. G. A. Pocock, *The Machiavellian Moment: Florentine Political Thought and the Atlantic Republican Tradition* (Princeton, N.J.: Princeton University Press, 1975), among many others.

12. Pocock, *Machiavellian Moment.*

13. *Independent Reflector,* 58.

14. *English Libertarian Heritage,* 86.

15. *Independent Reflector,* 444.

16. Ruth H. Bloch, "The Gendered Meanings of Virtue in Revolutionary America," *Signs: Journal of Women in Culture and Society* 13 (1987): 37–58.

17. *Independent Reflector,* 143–50.

18. Ibid., 143. See also Daniel W. Howe, "The Political Psychology of *The Federalist,*" *WMQ,* 3d ser., 44 (1987): 485–509.

19. *Independent Reflector,* 195.

20. See especially Isaac Kramnick, *Bolingbroke and His Circle: The Politics of Nostalgia in the Age of Walpole* (Cambridge, Mass.: Harvard University Press, 1968), and "James Burgh and 'Opposition' Ideology in England and America," in *Republicanism and Bourgeois Radicalism: Political Ideology in Late Eighteenth-Century England and America* (Ithaca, N.Y.: Cornell University Press, 1990), 200–69.

The term *Whig* arose originally in seventeenth-century Scotland referring to the opponents of the Episcopal regime of the Stuarts. By the eighteenth century, Whiggery had come to stand for all supporters of the privileges of Parliament and opponents of the royal prerogative. They ranged from court Whigs identified with the powerful ruling regime under the government headed by the longtime "Prime Minister" Sir Robert Walpole to their critics, the opposition or "radical" Whigs, such as Trenchard and Gordon.

21. Richard L. Bushman, *King and People in Provincial Massachusetts* (Chapel Hill: University of North Carolina Press, 1985), 14–17.

22. *Independent Reflector,* 74–75.

23. Gary B. Nash, *The Urban Crucible: Social Change, Political Consciousness, and the Origins of the American Revolution* (Cambridge, Mass.: Harvard University Press, 1979), 140 ff.; Patricia U. Bonomi, *A Factious People: Politics and Society in Colonial New York* (New York: Columbia University Press, 1971); John M. Murrin, "English Rights as Ethnic Aggression: The English Conquest, the Charter of Liberties of 1683, and Leisler's Rebellion in New York," in *Authority and Resistance in Early New York,* ed. William Pencak and Conrad Edick Wright (New York: New-York Historical Society, 1988), 56–94.

24. See especially Michael Warner, *The Letters of the Republic: Publication and the Public Sphere in Eighteenth-Century America* (Cambridge, Mass.: Harvard University Press, 1990), 49 ff.; [Trenchard and Gordon], "Of Freedom of Speech: That the Same Is Inseparable from Publick Liberty," in *English Libertarian Heritage,* 38–44.

25. *The Journal of Esther Edwards Burr,* 142, 220–25.

26. *Independent Reflector,* 77–78.

27. The *Reflector*'s comments on the college proposal appear in numbers 17–22, pp. 171–214.

28. Ibid., 180, 315.

29. Ibid., 214.

30. Carl Bridenbaugh, *Mitre and Sceptre: Transatlantic Faiths, Ideas, Personalities, and Politics, 1689–1775* (New York: Oxford University Press, 1962).

31. Ibid., 89–95.

32. When the struggle over the Anglican Episcopate heated up in the following decade, Livingston himself contributed one of the major pamphlets in opposition, *A Letter to the Right Reverend Father in God, John, Lord Bishop of Llandaff* (New York, 1768).

33. *Independent Reflector,* 91, 319.

34. Ibid., 183, 201.

35. Rhys Isaac, "Religion and Authority: Problems of the Anglican Establishment in Virginia in the Era of the Great Awakening and the Parsons' Cause," *WMQ*, 3d ser., 30 (1973), 3–36.

36. *Independent Reflector,* 78–79.

37. Ibid., 183.

38. Ibid., 315.

39. *English Libertarian Heritage,* 133–34.

40. John J. McCusker and Russell R. Menard, *The Economy of British America, 1607–1789* (Chapel Hill: University of North Carolina Press, 1985), chap. 10. Provincial population estimates are discussed below.

41. Archibald Kennedy, *Observations on the Importance of the Northern Colonies under Proper Regulations* (New York, 1750), 12.

42. J. E. Crowley, *This Sheba, Self: The Conceptualization of Economic Life in Eighteenth-Century America* (Baltimore: Johns Hopkins University Press, 1974); J. G. A. Pocock, "Virtue and Commerce in the Eighteenth Century," *Journal of Interdisciplinary History* 3 (1972): 119–34; see also his *Virtue, Commerce, and History: Essays on Political Thought and History, Chiefly in the Eighteenth Century* (New York: Cambridge University Press, 1985).

43. *The Papers of Benjamin Franklin,* ed. Leonard W. Labaree, Whitfield J. Bell Jr., et al. (New Haven: Yale University Press, 1959– . . .), vol. 4, 227–34. See Drew McCoy, "Benjamin Franklin's Vision of a Republican Political Economy for America," *WMQ*, 3d ser., 35 (1978): 605–28.

44. Kennedy, *Observations on the Importance of the Northern Colonies,* 3–4.

45. Robert Wallace, *A Dissertation on the Numbers of Mankind in Ancient and Modern Times* (1753; reprint, New York: A. M. Kelley, 1969); David Hume, "Of the Populousness of Ancient Nations," in *David Hume: Writings on Economics,* ed. Eugene Rotwein (Madison: University of Wisconsin Press, 1970), 108–83; and Janet Ann Riesman, "Origins of American Political Economy," (Ph.D. diss., Brown University, 1983), chap. 2. On the Philosophical Society of Edinburgh, see the first two articles in a trio of papers by Roger L. Emerson in *British Journal for the History of Science* 12 (1979): 154–91; 14 (1981): 133–76.

46. Istvan Hont, "The 'Rich Country-Poor Country' Debate in Scottish Classical Political Economy," in *Wealth and Virtue: The Shaping of Political Economy in the Scottish Enlightenment,* ed. Istvan Hont and Michael Ignatieff (New York: Cambridge University Press, 1983), 271–315.

47. Examples of the latter include Benjamin Franklin, *The Interest of Great Britain Considered. With Regard to Her Colonies, and the Acquisitions of Canada and Guadaloupe* (London, 1760), in *Papers of Benjamin Franklin,* vol. 9, 53–8; David Loch, *Essay on the Trade, Commerce, and Manufactures of Scotland* (Edinburgh, 1775).

48. Loch, *Essay on the Trade of Scotland;* Franklin, *Interest of Great Britain Considered.*

49. Riesman, "Origins of American Political Economy," chap. 4; John L. Brooke, *The Heart of the Commonwealth: Society and Political Culture in Worcester County, Massachusetts, 1713–1861* (New York: Cambridge University Press, 1989), 55–65; Richard L. Bushman, *From Puritan to Yankee: Character and the Social Order in Connecticut, 1690–1765* (Cambridge, Mass.: Harvard University Press, 1967), 115–34.

50. The parallel between the land bank and revival discussions has been noted in a number of places, especially Brooke, *The Heart of the Commonwealth,* chaps. 2–3. Also

see Rosalind Remer, "Old Lights and New Money: A Note on Religion, Economics, and the Social Order in 1740 Boston," *WMQ*, 3d ser., 47 (1990): 566–73; Mark Hessler, "Providence Lost: A Study of Epistemology and Religious Culture among New England Puritans, 1630–1730," (Ph.D. diss., State University of New York at Stony Brook, 1992); and Crowley, *This Sheba, Self.*

51. Nicholas Phillipson, "Adam Smith as Civic Moralist," in *Wealth and Virtue*, ed. Hont and Ignatieff, 179–202; Jean-Christophe Agnew, *Worlds Apart: The Market and the Theater in Anglo-American Thought, 1550–1750* (New York: Cambridge University Press, 1986).

52. *Independent Reflector*, 183; McCoy, "Benjamin Franklin's Vision of a Republican Political Economy."

53. Alison Gilbert Olson, *Making the Empire Work: London and American Interest Groups, 1690–1790* (Cambridge, Mass.: Harvard University Press, 1992).

54. Quoted in T. H. Breen, *The Character of the Good Ruler: A Study of Puritan Political Ideas in New England, 1630–1730* (New Haven: Yale University Press, 1970), 145.

55. Ibid., 144.

56. Jack P. Greene, *Peripheries and Center: Constitutional Development in the Extended Polities of the British Empire and the United States, 1607–1788* (Athens: University of Georgia Press, 1986).

57. Jack P. Greene, *The Quest for Power: The Lower Houses of Assembly in the Southern Royal Colonies, 1689–1776* (Chapel Hill: University of North Carolina Press, 1963).

58. Richard Bushman, *King and People in Provincial Massachusetts* (Chapel Hill: University of North Carolina Press, 1985).

59. Bernard Bailyn, *The Origins of American Politics* (New York: Alfred A. Knopf, 1967).

60. *An Essay upon the Government of the English Plantations on the Continent of America* (1701), quoted in Bushman, *King and People*, 99.

61. Charles S. Sydnor, *Gentleman Freeholders: Political Practices in Washington's Virginia* (Chapel Hill: University of North Carolina Press, 1952), is the classic survey.

62. Bushman, *King and People*, 91–99.

63. Edmund S. Morgan, *Inventing the People: The Rise of Popular Sovereignty in England and America* (New York: Norton, 1988).

64. "Copy of a Letter from Mr. Cotton to Lord Say and Seal," quoted in E. Brooks Holifield, *The Era of Persuasion: American Thought and Culture, 1521–1680* (Boston: Twayne Publishers, 1989), 140.

65. Greene, *Peripheries and Center.*

66. James Glen to Board of Trade, 10 October 1748, in *Great Britain and the American Colonies, 1606–1763*, ed. Jack P. Greene (Columbia: University of South Carolina Press, 1970), 261–67.

67. See especially Jack P. Greene, " 'A Posture of Hostility': A Reconsideration of Some Aspects of the Origins of the American Revolution," *American Antiquarian Society Proceedings* 87 (1977): 27–68.

68. Max Savelle, *Seeds of Liberty: The Genesis of the American Mind* (New York: Alfred A. Knopf, 1948), 292–305.

69. Ned C. Landsman, "The Legacy of the British Union for the North American Colonies: Provincial Elites and the Problem of Imperial Union," in *A Union for Empire: Political Thought and the British Union of 1707*, ed. John Robertson (Cambridge: Cambridge University Press, 1995), 297–317.

70. Henry McCulloh, *A Miscellaneous Essay Concerning the Courses Pursued by Great Britain in the Affairs of the Colonies* (London, 1755), esp. 85–86.

71. *Magna Charta For America: James Abercromby's An Examination of the Acts of Parliament Relative to the Trade and the Government of our American Colonies* (1752), ed. Jack P. Greene, Charles F. Mullett, and Edward C. Papenfuse Jr. (Philadelphia: American Philosophical Society, 1986), 158, 162, passim.

72. Alison Gilbert Olson, "The British Government and Colonial Union: 1754," *WMQ*, 3d ser., 17 (1960): 22–34.

73. J. M. Bumsted, " 'Things in the Womb of Time': Ideas of American Independence, 1633 to 1763," *WMQ*, 3d ser., 31 (1974): 533–564; John Murrin, "A Roof without Walls: The Dilemma of American National Identity," in *Beyond Confederation: Origins of the Constitution and American National Identity*, ed. Richard Beeman, Stephen Botein, and Edward C. Carter II (Chapel Hill: University of North Carolina Press, 1987), 333–48.

74. Kennedy, *Observations on the Importance of the Northern Colonies*, 12.

75. Nash, *Urban Crucible*; Marcus Rediker, *Between the Devil and the Deep Blue Sea: Merchant Seamen, Pirates, and the Anglo-American Maritime World, 1700–1750* (New York: Cambridge University Press, 1987); David S. Lovejoy, *Religious Enthusiasm in the New World: Heresy to Revolution* (Cambridge, Mass.: Harvard University Press, 1985); Rhys Isaac, "Evangelical Revolt: The Nature of the Baptists' Challenge to the Traditional Order in Virginia, 1765–1775," *WMQ* 31 (1974): 345–68; Marvin L Michael Kay, "The North Carolina Regulation, 1766–1776: A Class Conflict," in *The American Revolution: Explorations in the History of American Radicalism*, ed. Alfred F. Young (Dekalb, Ill.: University of Northern Illinois Press, 1976), 71–123. For a markedly exaggerated but still informative analysis of backcountry culture, see Fischer, *Albion's Seed*. For a more balanced summary based on an extensive and growing literature, see Gregory H. Nobles, "Breaking into the Backcountry: New Approaches to the Early American Frontier," *WMQ*, 3d ser., 46 (1989): 641–70.

76. Gary B. Nash, *Quakers and Politics: Pennsylvania, 1681–1726* (Princeton: Princeton University Press, 1968); Nash, *Urban Crucible*, 93–101, 148–66.

77. Patricia Bonomi, *Under the Cope of Heaven*; Rhys Isaac, "Preachers and Patriots: Popular Culture and the Revolution in Virginia," in *The American Revolution: Explorations in the History of American Radicalism*, 125–56; Herman Husband, *Some Remarks on Religion, with the Author's Experience in Pursuit Thereof* (Philadelphia, 1761), excerpted in *The Great Awakening: Documents Illustrating the Crisis and Its Consequences*, ed. Alan Heimert and Perry Miller (New York: Bobbs-Merrill, 1967), 636–54.

78. Thomas P. Slaughter, "The Tax Man Cometh: Ideological Opposition to Internal Taxes, 1760–1790," *WMQ*, 3d ser., 41 (1984): 566–91; Landsman, "Legacy of the British Union."

Chapter Seven

1. Andrew Burnaby, *Travels through the Middle Settlements in North-America* (2d ed.: London, 1775), 110.

2. Hugh Simm to Andrew Simm, 2 December 1768, Correspondence of Hugh Simm, Princeton University Library.

3. See especially Perry Miller, "Errand into the Wilderness," *WMQ*, 3d ser., 10 (1953), 3–32, and Sacvan Bercovitch, *The American Jeremiad* (Madison: University of

Wisconsin Press, 1978). Miller's essay, if read carefully, claims far less for the Puritan legacy than have some of his intellectual disciples.

4. Murrin, "A Roof without Walls," 333–48. See also J. M. Bumsted, " 'Things in the Womb of Time," 533–64.

5. Quoted in Edwin S. Gaustad, *George Berkeley in America* (New Haven: Yale University Press, 1979), 75–76.

6. Kenneth Silverman, *A Cultural History of the American Revolution* (New York: Columbia University Press, 1987), 10–11.

7. On the promotion of emigration, see especially Bernard Bailyn, *Voyagers to the West: A Passage in the Peopling of America on the Eve of the Revolution* (New York: Alfred A. Knopf, 1986), chap. 2, passim, and Ned C. Landsman, "The Provinces and the Empire: Scotland, the American Colonies and the Development of British Provincial Identity," in *An Imperial State at War: Britain from 1689 to 1815*, ed. Lawrence Stone (London: Routledge, 1994), 258–87.

8. Smith, *An Inquiry into the Nature and the Causes of the Wealth of Nations*, ed. R. H. Campbell and A. S. Skinner, vol. 2 of *Glasgow Edition of the Works of Adam Smith* (Oxford: Oxford University Press, 1976), book 4, chap. 7. See also Archibald Grant to an unknown correspondent, 7 March 1764, Grant of Monymusk Manuscript, Scottish Record Office; William Thom, *Seasonable Advice to the Landholders and Farmers in Scotland* (1770), printed in *Works of the Reverend William Thom* (Glasgow, 1799), 159–229, among others.

9. T. H. Breen, "An Empire of Goods: The Anglicization of Colonial America," *Journal of British Studies* 25 (1986): 467–99. On Smith and integration, see Nicholas Phillipson, "Adam Smith as Civic Moralist," in *Wealth and Virtue: The Shaping of Political Economy in the Scottish Enlightenment*, ed. Istvan Hont and Michael Ignatieff (New York: Cambridge University Press, 1983), 179–202.

10. *The Sovereignty & Goodness of God, together, with the Faithfulness of His Promises Desplayed; Being a Narrative of the Captivity and Restauration of Mrs. Mary Rowlandson,* (Cambridge, Mass., 1682); Beverley, *The History and Present State of Virginia*, ed. Louis B. Wright (1705; reprint, Chapel Hill: University of North Carolina Press, 1947), 9.

11. J. Hector St. John de Crèvecoeur, *Letters from an American Farmer and Sketches of Eighteenth-Century America*, ed. Albert E. Stone (New York: Penguin Books, 1981), 68–70.

12. Ibid., 74–75; Franklin, "Observations Concerning the Increase of Mankind, Peopling of Countries, &c.," *The Papers of Benjamin Franklin*, vol. 4, ed. Leonard W. Labaree, Whitfield J. Bell Jr., et al., (New Haven: Yale University Press, 1959– . . .) 227–34.

13. See especially Jack P. Greene, *Peripheries and Center: Constitutional Development in the Extended Polities of the British Empire and the United States 1607–1788* (Athens: University of Georgia Press, 1986).

Bibliographic Essay

Comprehensive studies of the intellectual life of eighteenth-century America have not been attempted often. Perhaps the first was that of Samuel Miller, a Presbyterian clergymen, entitled *A Brief Retrospect of the Eighteenth Century*, 2 vols. (New York, 1803), still one of the more useful surveys of the American Enlightenment. Subsequent efforts include those of a nineteenth-century literary historian, Moses Coit Tyler, *A History of American Literature during the Colonial Time, 1607–1765*, 2 vols. (New York, 1878), Vernon L. Parrington's *Main Currents in American Thought*, (New York: Harcourt, Brace, and Co., 1927–1930), Max Savelle's *Seeds of Liberty: The Genesis of the American Mind* (New York: Alfred A. Knopf, 1948)—the most comprehensive twentieth-century survey—and Louis B. Wright's contribution to the New American Nation Series, *The Cultural Life of the American Colonies 1607–1763* (New York: Harper & Row, 1957).

For intellectual changes in the period, nothing surpasses in explanatory power Perry Miller's classic *New England Mind: From Colony to Province* (Cambridge, Mass.: Harvard University Press, 1953). Although Miller confined his story to New England, others, and occasionally Miller himself, have extended his framework to cover all of early America. The most ambitious such efforts are those of Alan Heimert, *Religion and the American Mind: From the Great Awakening to the Revolution* (Cambridge, Mass.: Harvard University Press, 1966), and Sacvan Bercovitch, *The American Jeremiad* (Madison: University of Wisconsin Press, 1978). Although the argument here differs considerably from those, the power of their interpretive model is greatly admirable.

On New England itself, no one has looked more carefully at intellectual changes over the course of the eighteenth century than Harry S. Stout, *The New England Soul* (New York: Oxford University Press, 1986), based on the

209

reading of vast quantities of both published and manuscript sermons. Stephen Foster, *The Long Argument* (Chapel Hill: University of North Carolina Press, 1991) places the development of Puritanism within a longer, as well as wider, transatlantic context. Other useful interpretations have been more narrowly based: Richard L. Bushman, *From Puritan to Yankee* (Cambridge, Mass.: Harvard University Press, 1967), details cultural change in the province of Connecticut; John L. Brooke, *The Heart of the Commonwealth* (New York: Cambridge University Press), derives a provocative thesis from the history of a single county; Christine Leigh Heyrman, *Commerce and Culture* (New York: W. W. Norton & Company, 1984), finds equally suggestive material in the history of two communities. Michael Zuckerman, *Peaceable Kingdoms* (New York: Alfred A. Knopf, 1970) effectively treats the character of a large group of Massachusetts communities.

Other studies have examined individuals or groups of ministers; among those, the most suggestive are a pair of biographies of the Mathers: Michael G. Hall, *The Last American Puritan* (Middletown: Wesleyan University Press, 1988), which chronicles the life of Increase Mather, and Kenneth Silverman, *The Life and Times of Cotton Mather* (New York: Columbia University Press, 1985), on his son. John Corrigan, *The Prism of Piety* (New York: Oxford University Press, 1991), is informative on Benjamin Colman and the whole of the "Catholick" Congregational clergy; Patricia J. Tracy, *Jonathan Edwards, Pastor* (New York: Hill and Wang, 1979), sets that important minister within his local context.

The master of southern intellectual history remains Richard Beale Davis, whose many works include *Intellectual Life in the Colonial South 1585–1763*, 3 vols. (Knoxville: University of Tennessee Press, 1978). Two suggestive treatments of Virginia culture in the eighteenth century are Rhys Isaac's provocative and well-illustrated *The Transformation of Virginia 1740–1790* (Chapel Hill: University of North Carolina Press, 1982), an attempt at historical ethnography, and Timothy H. Breen, *Tobacco Culture* (Princeton: Princeton University Press, 1985). The culture of their southern neighbors is less well covered, but see especially Joyce Chaplin, *An Anxious Pursuit* (Chapel Hill: University of North Carolina Press, 1993), and Rachel Klein, *Unification of a Slave State* (Chapel Hill: University of North Carolina Press, 1990).

There is nothing comparable to the work of Miller or Davis for the Middle Colonies. There are excellent treatments of selected topics, including Fredrick B. Tolles, *Meeting House and Counting House* (Chapel Hill: University of North Carolina Press, 1948), Barry Levy, *Quakers and the American Family* (New York: Oxford University Press, 1988), and Jean Soderlund, *Quakers and Slavery* (Princeton: Princeton University Press, 1985), on Quakers, and Richard W. Pointer, *Protestant Pluralism and the New York Experience* (Bloomington: Indiana University Press, 1988), and Joyce D. Goodfriend, *Before the Melting Pot* (Princeton: Princeton University Press, 1992), among the many works on New York. Carl and Jessica Bridenbaugh's *Rebels and Gentlemen* (New York:

Oxford University Press, 1942) remains the leading portrait of Enlightened Philadelphia; Thomas Bender, *The New York Intellect* (Baltimore: Johns Hopkins University Press, 1987), has interesting suggestions about the Enlightenment in that city. George William Pilcher, *Samuel Davies* (Knoxville: University of Tennessee Press, 1971), and Milton J. Coalter Jr., *Gilbert Tennent, Son of Thunder* (New York: Greenwood Press, 1986), are clerical biographies.

A topic that has attracted considerable recent interest is the history of printing and of the book. Especially challenging is Michael Warner's *The Letters of the Republic* (Cambridge, Mass.: Harvard University Press, 1990), which employs literary theory and the philosophical ideas of Jürgen Habermas. Other useful works include Charles E. Clark, *The Public Prints* (New York: Oxford University Press, 1994), and Isaiah Thomas's classic *History of Printing in America* (1810; reprint, New York: Weathervane Books, 1970). Cathy N. Davidson, *Revolution and the Word* (New York: Oxford University Press, 1986), surveys the rise of the novel in America; see also her edited collection *Reading in America* (Baltimore: Johns Hopkins University Press, 1989). David S. Shields, *Oracles of Empire* (Chicago: University of Chicago Press, 1990), considers provincial poets and the world of commerce; Jean-Christophe Agnew's *Worlds Apart* surveys the theater, the market, and much more. Richard D. Brown, *Knowledge Is Power* (New York: Oxford University Press, 1989), and Ian K. Steele, *The English Atlantic* (New York: Oxford University Press, 1986), both examine transatlantic communications from divergent points of view.

The best general work on the American Enlightenment is Henry May, *The Enlightenment in America* (New York, 1976); also the Spring 1976 issue of the *American Quarterly*, with several fine articles on that subject. One is by Donald H. Meyer, who also contributed *The Democratic Enlightenment* (New York: G. P. Putnam's Sons, 1976). Also included in the *American Quarterly* issue is Linda Kerber's path-breaking "The Republican Mother: Women and the Enlightenment—An American Perspective."

On philosophy, see Norman Fiering's *Jonathan Edwards's Moral Thought and Its British Context* (Chapel Hill: University of North Carolina Press, 1981), successor to the same author's *Moral Philosophy at Seventeenth-Century Harvard* (Chapel Hill: University of North Carolina Press, 1981), which, despite its title, has much to say about the eighteenth century; also Elizabeth Flower and Murray G. Murphey, *A History of Philosophy in America*, vol. 1 (New York: Capricorn Books, 1977). On science, Raymond Phineas Stearns, *Science in the British Colonies of America* (Urbana: University of Illinois Press, 1970), and Brooke Hindle, *The Pursuit of Science in Revolutionary America 1735–1789* (Chapel Hill: University of North Carolina Press, 1956), are useful surveys. I. Bernard Cohen, *Benjamin Franklin's Science* (Cambridge, Mass.: Harvard University Press, 1990), and Michael N. Shute, ed., *The Scientific Work of John Winthrop* (New York: Arno Press, 1980), describe the work of two important scientific figures.

There has been much good work on provincial revivalism; see especially two books on George Whitefield: Harry S. Stout, *The Divine Dramatist* (Grand

Rapids, Mich.: William B. Eerdmans Publishing Company, 1991), and Frank Lambert, *Pedlar in Divinity* (Princeton, N.J.: Princeton University Press, 1994). On evangelical culture in New England, Alan Heimert, *Religion and the American Mind*, cited previously, is effective, although it overstates the relationship between evangelicals and liberal politics; more reliable is C. C. Goen's *Revivalism and Separatism in New England* (1962; reprint, Middletown, Conn.: Wesleyan University Press, 1987). Goen's *The Great Awakening*, vol. 4 of the *Works of Jonathan Edwards* (New Haven: Yale University Press), reprints the principal evangelical works of that figure. Rhys Isaac's *Transformation of Virginia*, cited previously, is most effective on evangelical culture in Virginia; Leigh Eric Schmidt, *Holy Fairs* (Princeton, N.J.: Princeton University Press, 1989), is good on the Middle Colonies. Patricia U. Bonomi, *Under the Cope of Heaven* (New York: Oxford University Press, 1986), explores the relationship between evangelicalism and politics throughout the colonies, and Jon Butler's *Awash in a Sea of Faith* (Cambridge, Mass.: Harvard University Press, 1990) questions the overall significance of revivalism in a bold and provocative synthesis of religious life.

The revival's opponents have been less well covered. There are two modest but informative biographies of Charles Chauncy: Charles H. Lipp, *Seasonable Revolutionary* (Chicago: Nelson Hall, 1981), and Edward M. Griffin, *Old Brick* (Minneapolis: University of Minnesota Press, 1980). A useful if inconsistent discussion of Old Side Presbyterians is Elizabeth Nybakken, "New Light on the Old Side: Irish Influences on Colonial Presbyterianism," *Journal of American History* 68 (1982): 813–32. Works on Anglicans are spotty, but see Parker J. Rouse, *James Blair of Virginia* (Chapel Hill: University of North Carolina Press, 1971), and Carl Bridenbaugh's *Mitre and Sceptre* (New York: Oxford University Press, 1962).

The revival and the Enlightenment were both transatlantic events; Michael Kraus, *The Atlantic Civilization* (1949; reprint, Ithaca, N.Y.: Cornell University Press, 1966) was a pioneering effort. In both movements, provincials established close ties with principal figures of the Enlightenment or of the Awakening in Scotland; see especially Richard Sher and Jeffrey Smitten, eds., *Scotland and America in the Age of the Enlightenment* (Princeton, N.J.: Princeton University Press, 1990). For a general summary, see William R. Brock, *Scotus Americanus* (Edinburgh: Edinburgh University Press, 1982), supplemented by Douglas Sloan, *The Scottish Enlightenment and the American College Ideal* (New York: Teachers College, 1971); Daniel W. Howe, "European Sources of Political Ideas in Jeffersonian America," *Reviews in American History* 10 (1982):, 28–44; Ned C. Landsman, "The Provinces and the Empire," in Lawrence Stone, ed., *An Imperial State at War* (London: Routledge, 1994), 258–87.

The political culture of the British colonies is well covered. See especially Bernard Bailyn, *The Origins of American Politics* (New York: Alfred A. Knopf, 1968); Jack P. Greene, *Peripheries and Center* (Athens, Georgia: University of Georgia Press, 1986); Gordon S. Wood, *The Radicalism of the American Revolu-*

tion (New York: Alfred A. Knopf, 1992); and Alan Tully, *Forming American Politics* (Baltimore, Johns Hopkins University Press, 1994), which highlights the mid-Atlantic experience. John M. Murrin, "Political Development," in Jack P. Greene and J. R. Pole, eds., *Colonial British America* (Baltimore: Johns Hopkins University Press, 1984), provides a useful and provocative survey.

Women's culture has only recently begun to receive the attention it deserves. See especially Laurel Thatcher Ulrich, *Good Wives* (New York: Alfred A. Knopf, 1982), on women in rural New England, and Joan M. Jensen, *Loosening the Bonds* (New Haven: Yale University Press, 1986), on their mid-Atlantic counterparts; on reading, see Davidson, *Revolution and the Word*, cited previously. The role of women in witch trials, and the context in which they occurred, are insightfully discussed in Carol F. Karlsen, *The Devil in the Shape of a Woman* (New York: W. W. Norton & Co., 1987). General works include Linda Kerber, *Women of the Republic* (Chapel Hill: University of North Carolina Press, 1980), and Mary Beth Norton, *Liberty's Daughters* (Boston: Little, Brown, and Co., 1980).

Much recent work explores the various ethnic cultures of early America. On the Dutch, see especially Donna Merwick, *Possessing Albany* (New York: Cambridge University Press, 1990). A. G. Roeber, *Palatines, Liberty, and Property* (Baltimore: Johns Hopkins University Press, 1993), explores German culture, and Ned C. Landsman, *Scotland and Its First American Colony 1683–1765* (Princeton, N.J.: Princeton University Press, 1985), discusses Scots. Good books on other groups, notably the Protestant Irish, are harder to find, but see James G. Leyburn, *The Scotch-Irish* (Chapel Hill: University of North Carolina Press, 1962). Less well served has been African-American culture in the colonial period, but see Peter H. Wood, *Black Majority* (New York: Alfred A. Knopf, 1974), Mechal Sobel, *The World They Made Together* (Princeton, N.J.: Princeton University Press, 1987), and Philip D. Morgan, "British Encounters with Africans and African-Americans, circa 1660–1780," in *Strangers within the Realm*, ed. Bernard Bailyn and Philip D. Morgan (Chapel Hill: University of North Carolina Press, 1991), 157–219. Two standout works on slavery and race have now become classics: Winthrop D. Jordan, *White over Black* (Chapel Hill: University of North Carolina Press, 1968), and David Brion Davis, *The Problem of Slavery in Western Culture* (Ithaca, N.Y.: Cornell University Press, 1966).

The culture of American Indian groups in this period has received a number of fascinating recent treatments. James Merrell, *The Indians' New World* (Chapel Hill: University of North Carolina Press, 1989), Daniel K. Richter, *The Ordeal of the Longhouse* (Chapel Hill: University of North Carolina Press, 1992), and Richard White, *The Middle Ground* (New York: Cambridge University Press, 1991), are among the more important examples. Cultural conversion and captivity have also been treated by James Axtell, *The Invasion Within* (New York: Oxford University Press, 1985), Alden T. Vaughan and Edward W. Clark, eds., *Puritans among the Indians* (Cambridge, Mass.: Harvard University Press, 1981)—a collection of captivity narratives—and John Demos, *The Unredeemed Captive* (New York: Alfred A. Knopf, 1994).

The cultures of French and Spanish America have also experienced a resurgence within the literature. David J. Weber, *The Spanish Frontier in North America* (New Haven: Yale University Press, 1992), W. J. Eccles, *Essays on New France* (New York: Oxford University Press, 1987), Inga Clendinnen, *Ambivalent Conquests* (New York: Cambridge University Press, 1987), James Lockhart, *The Nahuas After the Conquest* (Stanford, Cal.: Stanford University Press, 1992), and Irene Silverblatt, *Moon, Sun, and Witches* (Princeton, N.J.: Princeton University Press, 1987), are just a few among many interesting works.

A number of authors have attempted general surveys of early American culture. Among these are Jack P. Greene, *Pursuits of Happiness* (Chapel Hill: University of North Carolina Press, 1988), and the same author's *Intellectual Construction of America* (Chapel Hill: University of North Carolina Press, 1993). Jay Fliegelman, *Prodigals and Pilgrims* (New York: Cambridge University Press, 1982), is an interesting treatment by a literary scholar that focuses on metaphors of the family. Nicholas Canny and Anthony Pagden, eds., *Colonial Identity in the Atlantic World, 1500–1800* (Princeton, N.J.: Princeton University Press, 1987), places the British colonies within a larger Atlantic context. Less satisfactory is David Hackett Fischer, *Albion's Seed* (New York: Oxford University Press, 1989), which asserts a provocative thesis about the cultural roots of America's regional "folkways" from the eighteenth century far beyond what either reason or the evidence allows.

Index

215

The Author

Ned C. Landsman is professor of history at the State University of New York at Stony Brook. A graduate of Columbia College and the University of Pennsylvania, he has written on a variety of topics in early American history and the history of early modern Scotland. In *Scotland and Its First American Colony 1680–1765* (1985), he placed the history of an early Scottish settlement in East New Jersey and its development into an important center of Scottish influence within the mid-Atlantic region against the background of social and cultural developments in Scotland during those same years. He has written numerous articles on Scottish migration and on Presbyterian religion on both sides of the Atlantic. He has held fellowships from the American Council of Learned Societies, the American Philosophical Society, and the National Endowment for the Humanities. He and his wife, Alison, live in Huntington, New York. They have a daughter, Emily.